00 3053

50

TIGHT MONEY TIMING

TIGHT MONEY TIMING

The Impact of Interest Rates and the Federal Reserve on the Stock Market

Wilfred R. George

PRAEGER

PRAEGER SPECIAL STUDIES • PRAEGER SCIENTIFIC

Library of Congress Cataloging in Publication Data

George, Wilfred R.
    Tight money timing.

    Bibliography: p.
    Includes index.
    1. Stock price forecasting.   2. Monetary
policy—United States.   3. Interest and
usury—United States.   4. Board of Governors
of the Federal Reserve System (U.S.)
I. Title.
HG4637.G46   332.64′273   81-12131
ISBN 0-03-059272-0   AACR2

Published in 1982 by Praeger Publishers
CBS Educational and Professional Publishing
a Division of CBS Inc.
521 Fifth Avenue, New York, New York 10175 U.S.A.

© 1982 by Praeger Publishers

23456789   145   987654321

Printed in the United States of America

FOREWORD

Many years ago at weekly meetings attended by various departments of what was then Bache & Company (now Bache Halsey Stuart Shields, Inc.) I would report on activities of the Federal Reserve in the money markets. The prime focus of attention concerned changes in reserves held by the member banks, now identified as part of the monetary base. As the weeks went by, the glaze covering everyone's eyes would thicken as I once again rose to speak and record the changes and interpret their meaning.

In short, the Federal Reserve was there but not really a center of attention, and I am sure many people wondered why we kept on addressing developments in this area. The world has taken several turns since then and the Federal Reserve has increasingly become more significant as a factor of influence to the eclectic world of investment.

While I do not fully agree with the full dimension of Bill George's assessment of the relationship of stock market fluctuations and changes in interest rate and monetary policy, I certainly am in accord that monetary policy is very meaningful. My sense of hesitation essentially derives from the fact that monetary policy does not function in a vacuum and it, too, is influenced by other factors.

I believe Bill George's work is of great interest and value in drawing attention to the level of the impact of monetary policy and enhancing a sense of awareness of its significance. Without a doubt, monetary policy is a major factor of influence on investment outlook and Bill George's treatment is scholarly and perceptive.

Monte J. Gordon
Vice President &
Director of Research
The Dreyfus Corporation

PREFACE

The Federal Reserve System (commonly known as the "Fed") is the central bank of the United States and the single most powerful influence over the U.S. stock market. It has the power to make money "tight" or "easy."

Tight money is what happens when the Fed forces interest rates up, and makes it very difficult to borrow money. Under very tight money conditions, the stock market is likely to collapse. Easy money is what happens when the Fed drives interest rates down, and makes money easy to borrow. Easy money *almost always* brings about a strong bull market.

The Fed has left its "fingerprints" on every stock market boom and bust since its inception in 1913. These fingerprints provide clues that *you* can observe and monitor. They tell you when money stops being tight and starts getting easier. They encourage you to buy stocks before the emerging bull market becomes obvious. And later, when money starts getting tight, they warn you to brace for a possible major decline: To sell your stocks and move into money market investments until after the tight money cycle has run its course.

Tight and easy money signals are the basis of changes in stock market trends, and the best fundamental tools available for forecasting the stock market.

Fortune tends to smile on investors who follow tight and easy money signals. For example, although the stock market indexes haven't made much progress since 1965, there have been four very profitable buying opportunities (in which the markets subsequently rose from 30 to 64 percent), and four selling opportunities (in which the markets subsequently declined from 13 to 48 percent). During the 15 years since then, the cost of money has risen or fallen, and money itself has been either more or less available and has been steadily losing its buying power. And all this because the Fed has been tightening money (to curtail inflation or the growth in money supply) or easing money (to encourage business growth and reduce unemployment). These imbalances tend to persist— and as long as they do, there will be large stock market swings.

Today, inflation is as certain as death and taxes. Because of inflation, the 1980 dollar is completely different from the 1967 dollar; in terms of buying power, the latter is worth two and a half times the former. Anyone who has saved 1967 dollars will get for them only what today's dollar will buy.

For the investor, however, inflation can be an ally. Like Siamese twins, inflation rates and interest rates can't be separated. As politicians and their spending programs encourage inflation by creating too much paper money and too many IOUs, the Fed will continue to create tight and easy money conditions. In the process, the Fed will create dynamic opportunities for investors. By knowing how to take advantage of such opportunities, you can make money grow in the stock market faster than inflation can take it away from you.

Are tight and easy money signals a new phenomenon? Definitely not. For 67 years, the stock market has reacted to changes in interest rates and Federal Reserve monetary policy. Significantly enough, *one or more tight money signals have preceded every major bear market* since 1913, including those of 1916–17, 1920–21, 1929–32, 1937–38, 1961–62, 1966, 1968–70, and 1973–74. (For more graphic illustrations, see Appendix D.)

Similarly, *easy money signals have preceded every major bull market* since 1915, including those of 1915–16, 1921–22, 1924–29, 1932–33, 1935–37, 1942–46, 1949–52, 1953–56, 1957–59, 1960–61, 1962–65, 1966–68, 1970–72, 1974–76, and 1980. (See Appendix E.)

In the bull market of 1915, four easy money signals were in evidence beforehand. Sixty years later, the surging bull market of 1975 was preceded by five easy money signals. Clearly, nothing has changed: Tight and easy money signals are just as effective now as ever.

If you rely on the signals themselves, rather than on the opinions of newspapers, you stand to be well rewarded. For example, the *Wall Street Journal* reported on April 14, 1980 that the Fed "could begin easing its credit brakes by early summer." However, according to easy money signals, the Fed had *already* made money easier—the bull market had already started! Investors who recognized these easy money signals would have been fully invested, but investors who relied on newspaper reports would have missed most of that bull market, which later rose over 26 percent!

Considering the effects of the Fed-initiated monetary changes on the stock market, as an investor it's worth your while to make use of the practical knowledge offered by this book. You will learn, for example, how to:

- Recognize tight and easy money signals;
- Draw the appropriate conclusions; and
- Take the appropriate action to maximize profits (how to buy in the early stages of a rising market; how to sell in the early stages of a market top).

For a comprehensive understanding, start at the beginning of this book and read all the way through. Or you can skip the background and go directly to the heart of the Tight Money Timing method by reading Chapter 1 ("Tight Money Timing"), Chapter 3 ("Monitoring TMT Signals"), and Chapter 8 ("Observations and Conclusions").

It took four years to complete the research necessary for this book, and the end result was like turning on a light in a very dark room. After 20 years of investing in the stock market, I learned two very important things:

- The Fed is the prime mover of the market; and
- The Fed's actions, motives, and heartbeats (so to speak) can be followed in a systematic manner.

Every investor knows that it's important to pick the right stocks—but even more important to invest just before a bull market. The same stocks that double and triple in a surging bull market are often the worst stocks to own in a collapsing bear market. Accurate forecasting is crucial, and Tight Money Timing offers a unique, sound approach to forecasting the stock market. I sincerely hope that you will profit from my system as much as I have, and that it will give you the peace of mind it has given me.

Wilfred R. George

ACKNOWLEDGMENTS

It took me four years to complete the research necessary for this book, and as with all such Herculean tasks the efforts of many people helped make the final product possible. I cannot thank by name every single person who contributed to my project, but I would at least like to thank those whose input was most invaluable.

To begin, let me thank Carlos T. DeArrigunaga and Walter A. Landauer.

For the time and information freely given in discussions with me, I wish to thank William Q. Steinmetz, Warren Greene, Monte Gordon, Vic Vadakan, Jack Ross, James B. Morse, Rodney McKnew, John P. Caulfield, Sue E. Wong, Henry Ritchie, Joe Wahead, Richard Hoey, and the Federal Reserve economists who, because of the sensitive nature of the topic, asked to remain anonymous.

For the interviews they generously gave, my thanks to Sherman J. Maisel and William M. Burke.

For their lectures, thanks to Michael W. Keran and Arthur A. Merrill.

For their general assistance, my gratitude to H. L. Collins, Jr. and H. E. Menker.

For reading the many versions of the manuscript, I thank Richard A. Hanan and Henry O. Pruden. For critiquing the same, thanks to Robert J. Genetski and the members of the Technical Securities Analysts of San Francisco and its founder, Paul Ferwerda.

For editorial assistance, thanks to Irene Elmer and Naomi Steinfeld.

For cartography, thanks to Adrienne E. Morgan.

Finally, my thanks to Otto Butz for his encouragement, and to the countless others who gave advice, information, and support to this project. To all, may the information within this book bring prosperity.

CONTENTS

LIST OF TABLES

LIST OF FIGURES

INTRODUCTION

BACKGROUND

Congress established the Federal Reserve System (the "Fed") in 1913. Having a healthy respect for the power of money, it ruled that no agency of the government, no segment of the population, and no section of the country should have full control of the Fed. The United States had entered a new era—there would be no more booms and no more busts. Or so Congress thought. Unfortunately, however, the cycle of booms and busts continued—right up to the biggest bust of all, the Great Depression of the 1930s.

Because the Fed had failed to diagnose the economic problems of that period, the cures it proposed were ineffective. At first, economists and government policymakers saw the Great Depression as just another depression, and thought that it could be corrected by increasing the control of the supply of money.[1] Later they rejected this theory, deciding that this particular depression was less the result of monetary instability than of insufficient investment opportunities. This new interpretation called for more drastic measures than the simple use of monetary policy (that is, altering the supply of money and interest rates); it called instead for the use of fiscal policy and the socialization of investment. One economist who took this position was John M. Keynes, the English economist.[2]

During World War II, economists feared that the economy would stagnate and that unemployment would rise when wartime government spending ended. As it turned out, however, this fear was unfounded. The economic problem of the 1940s and 1950s was neither economic stagnation nor an inability to generate spending, but the combination of inflation and excessive economic fluctuation. Moreover, it was becoming clear that monetary policy and the conditions under which investments and credit were created in financial markets were causing unexpected economic problems. A new solution was needed, and this need led to new controversies over the role of monetary policy.

The financial community has long recognized the extreme importance of monetary policy. The controversy over this subject has focused on two points: (1) the impact of that monetary policy on inflation, employment, investment, consumption, and government spending; and (2) the way these factors are timed to create economic stability. Financial markets have been used to implement policy, and the fluctuations of these markets have been the inevitable by-product of changes in monetary policy and market forces. Theorists generally have ignored the precise impact of monetary policy on the stock market. Yet millions of citizens and institutions invest in the stock market every day.

In fact, stringent monetary policy has a devastating effect on the stock market. Consider the period 1970–75. In late 1972 and early 1973, the Fed instituted an extremely tight monetary policy, and the stock market declined substantially thereafter. Between 1970 and 1975, the number of U.S. shareholders dropped from 30 million to 25 million—a bad sign for an economic system based on free enterprise. Most of these investors took heavy losses, *because they didn't know when to buy or when to sell*. Apparently, the investors who left the market felt that they had lost too much on their investments and that the risk of loss was too great to be offset by any possible future profit, either in dividends or in capital gains.[3]

Stock prices fell most sharply in the speculative area, which is the source of capital for new enterprise. By the end of 1974, venture capital was virtually nonexistent,[4] and fewer new jobs was the result. Investors in all categories lost heavily. As you can see, stringent monetary policy can have drastic, far-reaching effects.

This book will show you which aspects of monetary policy are related to the fluctuations of the stock market and will illustrate how certain monetary policies create tight money conditions and easy money conditions. Finally, it reveals the profound and predictable impact of these tight and easy money conditions on the stock market.

If you read over a few old stock market forecasts, you will soon become skeptical of anyone's ability to accurately forecast the market's behavior. For one thing, different forecasters make different assumptions. For example, in September 1976, some economists were forecasting an inflation rate of 3 percent annually for the next two years. Others were forecasting an inflation rate of 10 percent. Forecasts of the prime rate ranged from 6 to 15 percent; those of the unemployment rate, from 3 to over 10 percent.

However, such forecasts are no help to investors. What *is* helpful is knowing that an accurate forecast of the stock market depends on a close look at the Fed's actions—and this book provides this knowledge. In addition, it shows that monetary policies are the prime cause of many severe bear markets and long-term bull markets. Therefore, investors who learn how to recognize changes in monetary policy will improve their forecasts and their investment results.

Look at Figure I-1. It shows that *when U.S. Treasury bill rates fell below taxable U.S. government bond rates, the subsequent long-term rise of the composite stock index indicated a good time to buy stocks.*

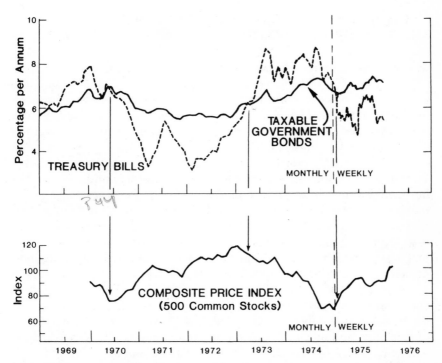

FIGURE I-1. Treasury bill and government bond rates versus S&P 500 stock index. [*SOURCE:* Reproduced from U.S. Congress, Joint Economic Committee, *Economic Indicators, June 1976,* prepared by the Council of Economic Advisers. Washington, D.C.: Government Printing Office, 1976, pp. 30, 31.]

Conversely, when Treasury bill rates rose above taxable government bond rates, the subsequent long-term drop in the composite stock index indicated a good time to sell. Treasury bill rates dropped below taxable government bond rates in July 1970, and again in January 1975. Both of these drops occurred at stock market low points. In April 1973, when the market was close to a high point, Treasury bill rates rose above taxable government bond rates.

When I first discovered this phenomenon, I applied it all the way back to 1919. I found that it worked best during periods of high interest rates. This suggested that there is a positive relationship among the factors of monetary policy that create tight or easy money. I consequently discovered that there is indeed such a relationship, and that it has a predictable and consistent impact on the stock market.

"TIGHT MONEY" IS TAKEN SERIOUSLY IN THE SECURITIES INDUSTRY

The research that I did on tight money is covered in detail in Chapter 2, and summarized briefly below. My sources (listed in the bibliography) include interviews and correspondence with portfolio managers, research directors, and other financial experts, as well as the books and securities periodicals that deal with interest rates, availability of money, and their effect on the stock market.

The securities industry takes the term "tight money" seriously. Warren Greene, Vice-President of American Investors Fund, told me that he "would rather be out of the market when the Fed tries to choke off money."[5] Monte Gordon, Director of Research for Dreyfus Corporation, said that "the stock market has become more sensitive to interest rates, less sensitive to money supply."[6] Edson Gould, stock market analyst and financial writer for *Findings and Forecasts*, agreed that monetary indicators always precede changes in the stock market.[7]

And yet "tight money" is a vague term. When Paul Volcker, now chairman of the Federal Reserve System, was asked "How will you tell whether money is tight or easy?" he replied, "You have to look at a variety of indicators and inevitably compromise among them."[8] I also asked Dr. Arthur F. Burns, former chairman of the Federal Reserve Board, for his definitions of tight and easy money.[9] Burn's special assistant, Normand Bernard, answered:

> There is no single financial variable whose movement always captures the changes that occur in a complex set of financial markets. Similarly, stock market reactions to changes in money and capital markets vary over time, so that there is no specific point at which stock prices become vulnerable to tight money.[10]

In short, those who are in the best position to know are not always anxious to define tight money. Notice that Bernard's answer tends to underplay the importance of the Fed's actions, which do, in fact, bring about market reactions. Various Fed employees have assured me that the Fed is very sensitive to the topic of tight money.[11]

Stock market analysts have established rules for timing their decisions. Some of these rules are based on the relationships between interest rates and the stock market. For example, Merrill Lynch, the largest securities firm in the United States, believes that the direction of the trend in short-term interest rates is critical to market timing.[12] Michael W. Keran, Vice-President and Director of Research at the Federal Reserve Bank of San Francisco, presents a model for forecasting stock prices that is based on expected earnings and expected interest rates.[13]

The "three-step-and-stumble" rule was formulated by Arthur Weisen-berger & Company. According to this rule, when the Fed makes three successive moves to tighten money (for example, by raising margin requirements, reserve requirements, and/or discount rates), the market is likely to fall sharply.[14] This rule has a good track record; however, it failed to signal at least two bear markets (in 1937 and 1962). And it only applies to market tops.

Another financial analyst, Arthur A. Merrill, relates the market's behavior to discount rates and margin and bank reserve requirements. He describes these factors as "pressures" that can encourage the market to continue up or down.[15] Merrill maintains that changes in the discount rates affect stock prices for as much as three months.[16]

A. Hamilton Bolton, former editor of the *Bank Credit Analyst* and author of *Money and Investment Profits* considers the bank debit-to-loan ratio to be the single most useful index of economic data for interpreting the stock market. The next most useful indexes are net loanable funds and bank deposits and excess reserves.[17] Irwin L. Kellner, Economist and Vice-President of Manufacturers Hanover Trust, used Federal Reserve credit policy to forecast share price trends.[18]

Finally, there's the Federal Reserve Board's flow of funds analysis. This report gives an excellent statistical picture of the financial economy of the United States. Unfortunately, the data it contains are three to six months old by the time they are published.[19]

Does the growth of money supply affect the behavior of the stock market? This is a controversial issue. Robert D. Auerbach, for one, questions the statistical techniques and methodology used by other experts in their money-growth studies. These experts seek to prove a strong relationship between money-supply changes and future stock prices.[20] Auerbach holds that changes in stock prices are related to both current and future changes in money supply, but not to past changes.[21]

In sum, a wide variety of experts in the area of finance and investments agree that actions on the part of the Fed, interest rates,[22] and money availability do affect the stock market's behavior. But although they agree that this is generally true, they don't know the extent of its importance. This book offers several hypotheses that test in detail the specific instruments of the Fed. These hypotheses are designed to measure the impact on the stock market of changes in monetary policy.

WHAT THIS BOOK IS ABOUT

This book isolates the monetary policy factors that result in tight and easy money conditions, and demonstrates their effect on stock market performance. Investors need better guidelines for forecasting stock market trends and timing transactions. *Tight Money Timing* sheds new light on this old problem. The book is organized in terms of:

- Defining tight and easy money for the purpose of testing the hypotheses described below;
- Proposing and examining two hypotheses: (1) that tight money conditions created by changes in Fed policy are one consistent, major cause of a declining stock market; and (2) that easy money conditions created by changes in Fed policy are one consistent, major cause of a rising stock market;
- Exploring the historical impact of Fed policy instruments, and how these instruments affect financial market conditions, particularly the behavior of the stock market;
- Developing an investment approach—Tight Money Timing (TMT)—based on the findings described above;
- Defining the context in which TMT should be used; and
- Explaining how to implement TMT and where to get the necessary information.

The Introduction summarizes the classic definitions of tight and easy money. Chapter 1 restates these definitions in the form of two general hypotheses and then examines the hypotheses in terms of eight specific TMT signals. Chapter 2 analyzes each TMT signal and takes a look at what other experts have to say.

Chapter 3 proposes a method of following TMT signals. This method uses both worksheets and workcharts to plot TMT signals over the 67 year period from 1914 to 1981 (the period during which TMT signals have affected market behavior). Chapter 4 describes the effect of TMT signals on the corporate bond market.

Chapter 5 deals with the Federal Reserve System: what it is, how it works, and why it creates tight or easy money policies. Chapter 6 provides case histories of two periods: 1972–75, when money became extremely tight and then easy; and 1929–32, when nothing the Fed did seemed to work. Chapter 7 describes the international and domestic effects of tight money. And Chapter 8 summarizes the ideas presented in this book.

WHAT IS TIGHT MONEY? WHAT IS EASY MONEY?

The term "tight money" is used to describe a policy of monetary restraint. This restraint is often imposed by the Federal Reserve System. The supply or rate of growth of credit is reduced, and interest rates (particularly short-term rates) rise. Tight money tends to relieve inflationary pressures caused by excess demand in the market.

Money may be tightened in various ways. The Fed can carry out open-market sales of government securities, increase the required-reserve ratios of U.S. commercial banks, or increase discount rates. All these are active ways of tightening money.

The Fed can also take passive action to tighten money. For example, it can refrain from increasing reserves in the face of an increasing demand for credit. Without excess funds in the system, banks are forced to borrow from the Fed, reduce their loans, or dispose of securities. They will then try to satisfy loan requests from good deposit customers of long standing. Thereafter they will restrict their loans by reducing the maturity of term loans, or by applying higher credit requirements and lending smaller sums.

The net free-reserve positions of the Fed member banks are reported every week in the *Wall Street Journal* (Fig. I-2). These positions are one indication of current monetary policy. In the past, free reserves of less than $150 million indicated a policy of monetary restraint. Negative free, or net borrowed, reserves indicated a policy of tight money.[23]

Severe tight money conditions can bring about a financial panic. This happens when banks, individuals, and corporations try to become more liquid. They want to hold as much money as possible, to ensure that they will have enough cash and to guarantee that they will remain solvent. In such a situation, securities are sold, interest rates rise, security prices fall, loans are called, and net assets are diminished.

"Easy money," on the other hand, can be defined as a substantial quantity of available credit. The Fed can create easy money conditions in one of two ways: (1) by lowering reserve requirements; or (2) by increasing the money supply to increase the deposit inflows and the free reserves of commercial banks.[24] This makes it possible for banks to increase their lending. However, banks may not do so immediately, especially if they believe that they have already lent too much in relation to their existing capital resources.

Congresspersons and economists tend to believe that money is easy if interest rates are relatively low, no matter how slowly the money supply may be growing.[25] If business in general is slow, there is little demand for loans with which to expand. This takes the pressure off the capital markets and creates a period of easy money. Business people will use surplus money for expansion only if they believe it is worth the marginal cost. For example, in the early 1930s, the business outlook was bleak. This attitude held down the demand for credit, the willingness of banks to lend, and the willingness of business to invest. Excess reserves piled up in the banking system and remained idle.

MEMBER BANK RESERVE CHANGES
Changes in weekly averages of member bank reserves and related items during the week and year ended January 7, 1981 were as follows (in millions of dollars) – b

	Jan. 7, 1981	Chg fm wk end Dec. 31, 1980	Jan. 9 1980
Reserve bank credit:			
U.S. Gov't securities:			
Bought outright	119,139	+2,041	+ 350
Held under repurch agreemt	2,310	+1,800	+ 2,310
Federal agency issues:			
Bought outright	8,739	....	+ 523
Held under repurch agreemt	311	+ 213	+ 311
Acceptances – bought outright			
Held under repurch agreemt	268	+ 77	+ 268
Borrowings from Fed	1,117	– 510	+ 387
Seasonal borrowings	112	– 4	+ 50
Float	5,991	–3,058	– 1,619
Other Federal Reserve Assets	8,390	– 154	+ 2,762
Total Reserve Bank credit	146,266	+ 409	+ 5,293
Gold stock	11,161	....	+ 40
SDR certificates	2,518	– 607	+ 718
Treasury currency outstanding	13,427	+ 1	+ 471
Total	173,372	– 198	+ 6,523
Currency in circulation	136,111	– 801	+11,270
Treasury cash holdings	449	+ 4	+ 17
Treasury dpts with F.R. Bnks	2,979	– 307	+ 167
Foreign deposits with F.R. Bnks	373	– 2	+ 1
Other deposits with F.R. Bnks	653	+ 237	+ 221
Other F.R. liabilities & capital	4,903	+ 46	+ 162
Total	145,467	– 825	+11,836
Reserves			
With F.R. Banks	27,905	+ 628	– 5,314
Total inc. cash	41,225	– 171	– 3,446
Required reserves	40,374	– 184	– 4,169
Excess reserves	851	+ 355	+ 723
Free reserves	–154	+ 861	

b-The figures reflect adjustment for new Federal Reserve rules that impose reserve requirements on most deposit-taking institutions, including non-member commercial banks, mutual savings banks and savings and loan associations.

MONETARY AND RESERVE AGGREGATES
(daily average in billions)

	One week ended:	
	Dec. 31	Dec. 24
Money supply (M1-A) sa	381.4	383.7
Money supply (M1-B) sa	406.8	409.3
	Jan. 7	Dec. 31
Monetary base	160.37	160.38
Total Reserves	40.27	40.06
Nonborrowed Reserves	39.15	38.44
Required Reserves	39.41	39.57
	Four weeks ended:	
	Dec. 31	Dec. 3
Money supply (M1-A) sa	384.5	389.2
Money supply (M1-B) sa	410.1	414.4
sa-Seasonally adjusted.		

KEY INTEREST RATES
(weekly average)

	Jan. 7	Dec. 31
Federal funds	20.06	18.45
Treasury bill (90 day)	14.06	14.26
Commercial paper (dealer, 90 day)	15.63	16.60
Cerffs of Deposit (resale, 90 day)	16.34	17.21
Eurodollars (90 days)	17.06	17.79

FIGURE I-2.   Free reserves.   SOURCE: [Reproduced from "Interest Rates Are Seen Resuming Decline as Money Supply Drops Sharply Again," *Wall Street Journal*, January 12, 1981, p. 26.]

Where does surplus money go in periods of easy money? It tends to find its way into securities. It moves into the bond markets, driving bond prices up and yields down. Money also flows into the stock market, which also drives prices up and yields down.

SUCCESSFUL INVESTING

Successful investing sounds simple enough—just buy stocks when money becomes easy and sell them when it becomes tight, right? But how do you know *when* money has started to become tight or easy? Tight Money Timing will help you solve this problem.

This book, then, has three purposes: (1) to contribute new theoretical insights; (2) to help you in actual stock market transactions; and (3) to provide the most thorough research to date on the relationship between the Fed's actions and the stock market's behavior.

NOTES

1. Milton Friedman, and Anna J. Schwartz, *A Monetary History of the United States, 1867–1960*. Princeton, N.J.: Princeton University Press, 1963; Ronald L. Teigen, "The Demand for and Supply of Money," in *Readings in Money, National Income and Stabilization Policy*, 3d ed., edited by W. L. Smith and Ronald L. Teigen, Homewood, Ill.: Irwin, 1974, pp. 68–103; and James Tobin, "Commercial Banks as Creators of Money," in *Banking and Monetary Studies*, ed. Deane Carson (Homewood, Ill.: Irwin, 1963), pp. 408–19. James Tobin is Sterling Professor of Economics, Yale University.
2. John M. Keynes, *The General Theory of Unemployment, Interest, and Money*. New York: Harcourt, Brace & World, 1936.
3. Between 1964 and 1974, the Dow Jones Utility Index dropped by 56 percent, from 155 to 68. This represents a good portion of the stock held by conservative investors (for example, retirees and widows), who often need income security. When this decline is adjusted for loss due to inflation, the real drop turns out to be 71.8 percent. (The cost price index was 94.5 in 1965 and 147.7 in 1974, based on an index of 100 for 1967.) While conservative stocks performed like speculations, most speculative stocks declined much more. The conservative investor had reason to believe that there was no safe stock market investment—that every sector of the stock market was, at best, a risk. Even though the average cash dividend for utility stocks rose over 40 percent during this period, its buying power suffered a net loss of 10 percent after adjustment is made for inflation.
4. The following table shows the decline in offerings and capital raised for companies having a net worth of $5 million or less. While availability of

Year	Number of Offerings	Total Dollar Amount (in millions)
1969	548	1457.7
1970	209	383.7
1971	224	551.5
1972	418	918.2
1973	69	137.5
1974	8	13.1
1975	4	16.2

[SOURCE: U.S. Small Business Administration, *Report of the Small Business Adminstration Task Force on Venture and Equity Capital for Small Business.* January 1977, p. 13.]

equity capital to small businesses declined dramatically, new money raised for all corporations in the public securities market increased from $28 billion in 1972 to over $41 billion in 1975, or almost 50 percent.

5. Warren Greene, interview held by telephone, March 3, 1976.

6. Monte Gordon, interview held by telephone, February 13, 1976.

7. Edson Gould, appearing on Public Broadcasting System (PBS), "Wall Street Week," November 12, 1976.

8. "A Fed Heavyweight Sizes up Monetary Policy," *Business Week*, August 11, 1975, p. 52.

9. Wilfred R. George to Arthur Burns, August 6, 1976.

10. Normand Bernard, Special Assistant to the Federal Reserve Board, to Wilfred R. George, August 16, 1976.

11. One Federal Reserve economist who insisted on anonymity refused to act as an advisor on this book because he believed that if he became involved with a book describing the Fed's role in creating tight money, his job and 20-year seniority might be at stake.

12. Charles J. Elia, "Short-Term Rates Seen Rising as Recovery Resumes Though Analysts' Timetables Differ," *Wall Street Journal*, October 13, 1976, p. 43; and James Bohan and Robert J. Farrell, *Interest Rates and Stock Prices*. New York: Merrill Lynch, Pierce, Fenner & Smith, Securities Research Division, September 22, 1976, pp. 9–11.

13. Michael W. Keran, "Forecasting Stock Prices," *Journal of Portfolio Management* 1 (Winter 1975):52–60.

14. Arthur A. Merrill, "Delayed Reaction," *Barron's National Business and Financial Weekly*, December 13, 1965, p. 9.

15. Arthur A. Merrill, *Behavior of Prices on Wall Street*. Chappaqua, N.Y.: Analysis Press, 1966, pp. 36–38, 159–60.

16. Merrill, "Delayed Reaction," p. 9.

17. A. Hamilton Bolton, *Money and Investment Profits*. Homewood, Ill.: Dow Jones-Irwin, 1967, pp. 155–86.

18. "Look Before You Leap—to Conclusions," *Forbes*, January 1, 1977, p. 207.

19. Stephen B. Packer, "Flow of Funds Analysis—Its Uses and Limitations," in *CFA Readings in Financial Analysis*, 2d ed. Homewood, Ill.: Irwin, 1970, pp. 118–19.

20. Beryl W. Sprinkel, *Money and Stock Prices*. Homewood, Ill.: Irwin, 1964; Michael W. Keran, "Expectations, Money, and the Stock Market," *Review*, St. Louis, Mo.: Federal Reserve Bank of St. Louis, January 1971, pp. 16–31; reprint ed., Reprint Series No. 63, St. Louis, Mo.: Federal Reserve Bank of St. Louis, Mo.; and Kenneth E. Homa and Dwight M. Jaffee, "The Supply of Money and Common Stock Prices," *Journal of Finance,* 26, December 1971:1045–66.

21. Robert D. Auerbach, "'Money and Stock Prices," *Monthly Review*, Federal Reserve Bank of Kansas City, September–October 1976, p. 11.

22. Appendix A provides a detailed explanation of interest and of the reasons why interest rates differ.

23. Douglas Greenwald et al., *The McGraw-Hill Dictionary of Modern Economics*. New York: McGraw-Hill, 1973, pp. 184, 588–89.
24. Free reserves are defined in Chapter 2.
25. Lindley H. Clark, Jr., "Calming the Fears," *Wall Street Journal*, March 8, 1976, p. 1.

TIGHT MONEY
TIMING

1

TIGHT MONEY TIMING

In this chapter I'm going to define tight and easy money in terms of the practices of the investment industry. I'll begin by stating two *hypotheses* that define the central concepts of tight and easy money. Next I'll list eight *TMT signals* and show, by means of historical evidence, how each one correlates with the movements of the stock market. I'll present a separate monthly chart for each signal covering the period 1966 to 1976. In a separate section I'll explain why tax changes don't provide an accurate TMT signal. Then I'll present a single chart that shows the combined effect of all eight signals. TMT signals are either overt or covert, depending on whether they are easy or difficult to use. The overt signals can have a devastating effect on the stock market, and I'll discuss this phenomenon as well. The chapter closes with a set of conclusions based on the ideas introduced here.

TMT: TWO HYPOTHESES AND EIGHT SIGNALS

The theory of Tight Money Timing (TMT) is based on two hypotheses:
Hypotheses 1: When money is tight, the stock market goes down. Money is tight when short-term interest rates rise and money becomes less available.
Hypotheses 2: When money is easy, the stock market goes up. Money is easy when short-term interest rates decline and money becomes more available.
Eight signals tell the investor when money is becoming tight or easy. These TMT signals fall into two groups. The first group indicates changes in interest rates. The second group indicates changes in the availability of money.
Changes in interest rates are indicated by changes in:

1

1. *Discount rate*—the interest a bank pays on money it borrows from the Fed;
2. *Federal funds rate*—the interest a bank pays on money it borrows from other banks in the Federal Reserve System;
3. *Prime rate*—the interest banks charge their best customers for short-term loans;
4. *Regulation Q*—the maximum interest rates banks pay on time and savings deposits;
5. *U.S. Treasury bill rates*—the interest paid on the shortest-term securities issued by the U.S. government;

Changes in the availability of money are indicated by changes in:

6. *Margin requirements*—the percentage of the total cost of securities that must be paid in cash;
7. *Free reserves*—the total reserves of all banks in the Fed, less required reserves, less member bank borrowings from the system; and
8. *Reserve requirements*—the percentage of deposits that banks are required to set aside as reserves.[1]

Because the stock market is affected by hundreds of events, none of these eight signals in itself is likely to be the sole cause of a change in prices. More often, several signals appear at once. It is this conjunction of signals that you can use to forecast the behavior of the stock market.

To determine the validity of the Tight Money Timing hypotheses, I plotted all eight TMT signals on ten-year time series charts of the Standard and Poor's 500 Stock Index.[2] On these charts you will see the symbol ↓. It signifies downward pressure on the stock market, which

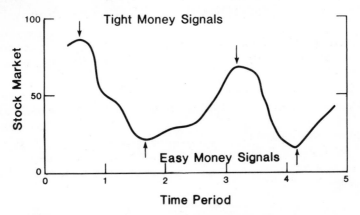

FIGURE 1-1. **Tight money signals—a conceptual chart.**

means that money becomes *tighter*, and constitutes a "Sell" signal. The symbol ↑ signifies upward pressure on the stock market, which means that money became *easier*, and constitutes a "Buy" signal.

To evaluate each TMT signal, take a look at the reaction of the stock market following the symbol ↓ or ↑. These TMT signals would be useless for timing and forecasting purposes if the stock market reacted instantaneously—that is, if it were discounted immediately and completely. However, the stock market reacts gradually, not instantaneously. If it moves gradually up after an easy money signal ↑ or down after a tight money signal ↓, these signals prove to be valid, especially if they hold over a long period. In an ideal typical situation, the stock market would react as shown in Figure 1-1.

HOW DOES EACH SIGNAL AFFECT THE MARKET?

In this section, each of the eight TMT signals is plotted on its own separate chart. The charts are presented in alphabetical order. Each is accompanied by a brief explanation and one or more observations. The last chart of the series (see Fig. 1-10), in which all eight TMT signals are combined, is accompanied by a few general observations. Once again, the arrow indicates *the direction of the pressure on the stock market*, not the direction of interest rates.

Discount Rate

Tighter money (↓) is indicated when the discount rate is increased, making it more expensive for banks to borrow from the Federal Reserve System. Easier money (↑) is indicated when the discount rate is decreased. An arrow inside a circle (①) indicates a reversal of the previous trend. For example, if the discount rate has been decreasing, an increase is shown as ① (Fig. 1-2).

Observation: The bull markets of 1970–71 and 1974–75 were driven up by a series of lower discount rates. Conversely, a series of higher discount rates in 1973–74 forced the stock market down into what turned out to be the biggest percentage drop in 36 years.

Federal Funds Rate

Rising Federal funds rates make it more costly for banks to borrow. This drives the market down (↓); declining rates tend to drive it up (↑). The

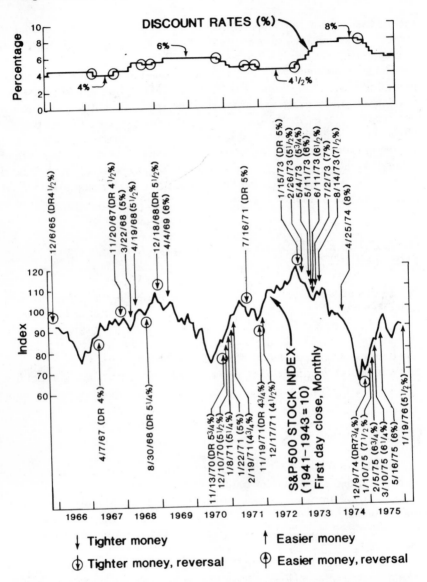

FIGURE 1-2. Discount rates of the Federal Reserve Bank of New York. [*SOURCES:* Discount rates: U.S. Federal Reserve Board, Division of Administrative Services, Publications Services, *Annual Statistical Digest 1971–75,* October 1976, p. 35; and U.S. Federal Reserve Board, Division of Administrative Services, Publication Services, *Banking and Monetary Statistics 1941–1970,* September 1976, p. 667. S&P 500 Stock Index: Standard & Poor's Corp., *Security Price Index Record 1976.* Orange, Conn.: Standard & Poor's Corp., 1976, p. 121.]

Federal funds rate is *rising* when it moves above its ten-week moving average by 10 percent and holds above this moving average for two weeks. It is *declining* when it moves below its ten-week moving average by 10 percent and holds below this moving average for two weeks. Figure 1-3 shows where the Federal funds rates would have told the investor to buy (↑) or sell (↓).

Observation: Since 1971, there has been a relatively good correlation between changes in the Federal funds trend and the intermediate-to long-term changers in the stock market. Before 1971, the correlation was less obvious.

Margin Requirements on Common Stock

Tighter money (↓) is indicated when stock margin requirements are raised—when more money must be advanced to buy securities. Easier money (↑) is indicated when stock margin requirements are lowered (Fig. 1-4).

Observations: With one major exception, this signal has proved valid since 1966. The exception occurred in late 1973, when the brokerage industry urged the Fed to lower margin requirements in order to increase brokerage business. Margin requirements were lowered on January 3, 1974. On that day, U.S. Treasury bills were yielding then historically-high rates—between 7 and 9 percent. Clearly, money was tight. The result of its action should have been obvious to the Fed. By lowering margin requirements, it allowed many unsophisticated investors to buy into a major bear market—a bear market brought about by severe tight money conditions. The Fed could not make money easy in one financial market while keeping it tight in all the others. Had the Fed pursued a consistent policy by making money easier in other markets as well, the stock market probably would have risen instead of continuing to decline.

Free Reserves

Net free reserves (low net borrowed reserves) indicate easy money. Negative free reserves (high net borrowed reserves) indicate tight money. Money becomes tight (↓) at the point where net borrowed reserves (negative free reserves) exceed $500 million. Money becomes easy (↑) at the point where net borrowed reserves (negative free reserves) are less than $500 million (Fig. 1-5).

Observations: On the chart, this signal is closely correlated with the market. However, the figure of $500 million was fitted to achieve best results during this period. It will not necessarily produce the same results in the future.

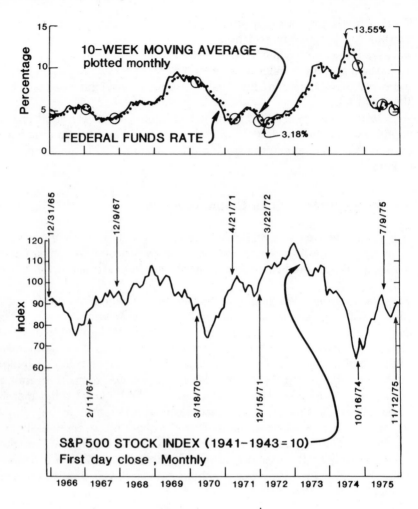

↓ Tighter money   ↑ Easier money

FIGURE 1-3. Federal funds rates and ten-week moving average.
[SOURCES: Federal funds rates: U.S. Federal Reserve Board, Division of Administrative Services, Publications Services, Annual Statistical Digest 1971–1975, October 1976, pp. 122–25; and U.S. Federal Reserve Board, Division of Administrative Services, Publications Services, Banking and Monetary Statistics 1941–1970, September 1976, pp. 691–92. S&P 500 Stock Index: Standard & Poor's Corp., Security Price Index Record 1976. Orange, Conn.: Standard & Poor's Corp., 1976, p. 121.]

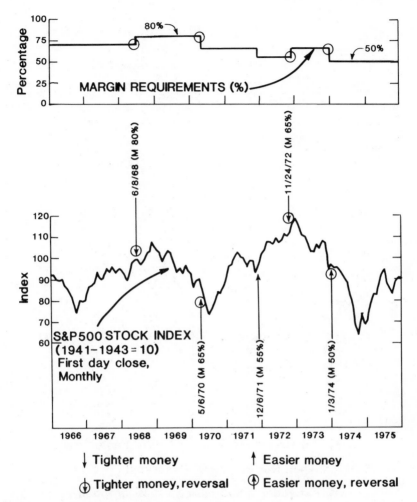

FIGURE 1-4.   **Margin requirements.**   [*SOURCES:* Margin requirements: U.S. Federal Reserve Board, Division of Administrative Services, Publications Services, *Annual Statistical Digest 1971–1975*, October 1976, p. 39; and U.S. Federal Reserve Board, Division of Administrative Services, Publications Services, *Banking and Monetary Statistics 1941–1970*, September, 1976, p. 799. S&P 500 Stock Index: Standard & Poor's Corp., *Security Price Index Record 1976*. Orange, Conn.: Standard & Poor's Corp., 1976, p. 121.]

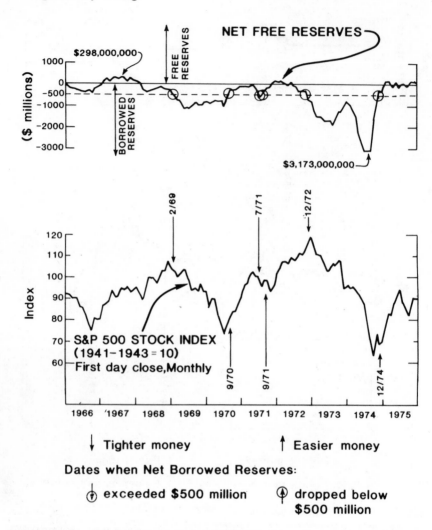

FIGURE 1-5.   **Net free reserves.**   [*SOURCES*: Free reserves: National Bureau of Economic Research, Computer Service, 261 Madison Avenue, New York. S&P 500 Stock Index: Standard & Poor's Corp., *Security Price Index Record 1976*, Orange, Conn.: Standard & Poor's Corp., 1976. p. 121.]

Prime Rate

A rise in the prime rate makes borrowing less attractive and indicates tighter money (↓). A drop in the prime rate after one or more increases indicates easy money (↑). In 1975 alone there were 21 changes in the prime rate. However, Figure 1-6 shows only 13 reversals for the period

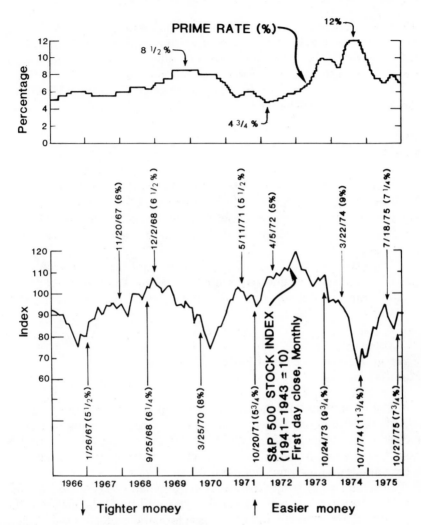

FIGURE 1-6. Prime rate. [*SOURCES*: Prime rate: U.S. Federal Reserve Board, Division of Administrative Services, Publications Services, *Annual Statistical Digest 1971–1975*, October 1976, p. 39; and U.S. Federal Reserve Board, Division of Administrative Services, Publications Services, *Banking and Monetary Statistics 1941–1970*, September 1976, p. 673. S&P 500 Stock Index: Standard & Poor's Corp., *Security Price Index Record 1976*. Orange, Conn.: Standard & Poor's Corp., 1976, p. 121.]

1966–76. A reversal in the trend of the prime rate should be considered more important than a change that continues in the direction of the previous trend. This is because a reversal often indicates a change in the trend of interest rates and of the stock market.

Observation: A reversal in the trend of the prime rate has often been a good stock market forecaster.

Regulation Q

Tighter money (↓) is indicated when the maximum interest rates on bank deposits are increased. This increase makes it more attractive to invest money in savings accounts than in stocks. Easier money (↑) is indicated when the maximum interest rates on deposits are decreased (Fig. 1-7).

Observation: Regulation Q is the least accurate of the eight TMT signals. Perhaps the incentives it represents are too small to attract money to and from the stock market. Or perhaps savers and investors simply have different objectives.

Reserve Requirements of Federal Reserve Member Banks

Tighter money (↓) is indicated when bank reserve requirements are raised, making money less available for loans. Easier money (↑) is indicated when bank reserve requirements are lowered. In Figure 1-8, note the reversals of trend (①). Any such reversal is more important than a continuation of the previous trend (↑).

Observation: Changes in reserve requirements have a strong influence on the stock market. One analyst has said that a reduction in the reserve requirement on demand deposits for large city banks is the single most bullish event that can occur on the market.[3]

U.S. Treasury Bill Rates Versus Long-Term Government Bond Rates

Money becomes tight (↓) at the point where U.S. Treasury bill interest rates exceed long-term government bond rates. Money becomes easy (↑) at the point where long-term government bond rates exceed U.S. Treasury bill rates (Fig. 1-9).

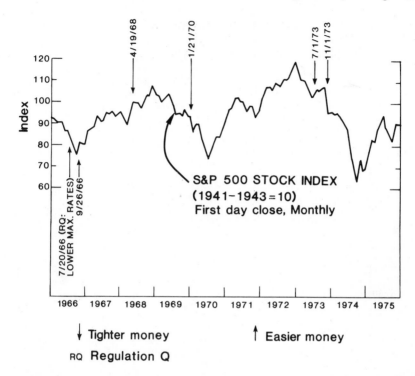

↓ **Tighter money**   ↑ **Easier money**

RQ **Regulation Q**

FIGURE 1-7. Regulation Q. [*SOURCES*: Regulation Q: U.S. Federal Reserve Board, Division of Administrative Services, Publications Services, *Annual Statistical Digest 1971–1975*, October 1976, p. 39; and U.S. Federal Reserve Board, Division of Administrative Services, Publications Services, *Banking and Monetary Statistics 1941–1970*, September 1976, p. 673. S&P 500 Stock Index: Standard & Poor's Corp., *Security Price Index Record 1976*. Orange, Conn.: Standard & Poor's Corp., 1976, p. 121.]

Observation: Money is tight when the interest rate curve is inverse—that is, when short-term yields exceed long-term yields. I use U.S. Treasury bill versus long-term government bond rates for this signal. The stock market reacted particularly well to these signals between 1970–76. Perhaps this was because there were extreme swings in interest rates during this period.

WHAT ABOUT INCOME TAX POLICIES?

Tight money and easy money are also caused by changes in income tax policies. However, during the period 1931–81, these changes were

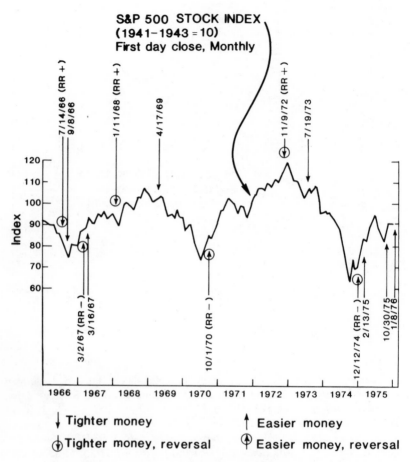

FIGURE 1–8.   Changes in reserve requirements of Federal Reserve member banks.   [SOURCES: Reserve requirements: U.S. Federal Reserve Board, Division of Administrative Services, Publications Services, *Annual Statistical Digest 1971–1975*, October 1976, p. 38; and U.S. Federal Reserve Board, Division of Administrative Services, Publications Services, *Banking and Monetary Statistics 1941–1970* September 1976, p. 608. S&P 500 Stock Index: Standard & Poor's Corp., *Security Price Index Record 1976*. Orange, Conn.: Standard & Poor's Corp., 1976, p. 121.]

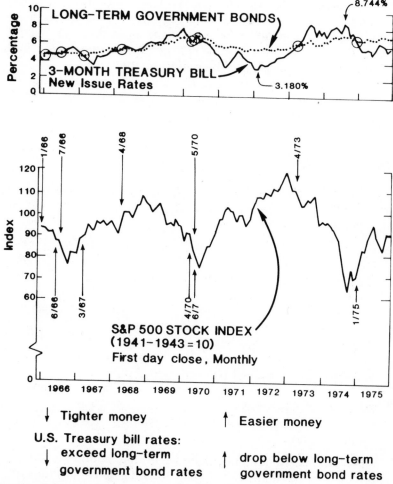

FIGURE 1-9. Treasury bill versus long-term government bond rates.
[*SOURCES:* Three-month Treasury bill and long-term government bond rates:
U.S. Federal Reserve Board, Division of Administrative Services, Publications
Services, *Annual Statistical Digest 1971–75*, October 1976, p. 121; and U.S.
Federal Reserve Board, Division of Administrative Services, Publications Services,
Banking and Monetary Statistics 1941–70, September 1976, pp. 460, 726–27.
S&P 500 Stock Index: Standard & Poor's Corp., *Security Price Index Record
1976*. Orange, Conn.: Standard & Poor's Corp., 1976, p. 121.]

not correlated with changes in the market. This is not surprising, however: tax changes are discussed and revised for many months before they are implemented. By the time they take effect, therefore, the stock market has adjusted to them. In addition, some changes merely shift the tax burden, making it difficult to determine their effect on the market.[4]

Changes in income tax policies do influence the market. But when, and to what extent? It is impossible to say. That is why I do not consider tax changes to constitute an accurate TMT signal.

THE TMT COMPOSITE

Figure 1-10 represents the Tight Money Timing composite. All eight TMT signals are combined in this figure, which uses the following abbreviations:

D = *Discount rate* of the Federal Reserve Bank of New York was increased (↓)/decreased (↑);

F = *Federal funds rates* turned up (↓)/down (↑);

M = *Margin requirements* were increased (↓)/decreased (↑);

N = *Free reserves* of Federal Reserve member banks were *higher than* (↑)/*lower than* (↓) a negative $500 million;

P = *Prime rate* charged by banks was increased (↓)/decreased (↑);

Q = *Regulation Q*—maximum interest rates payable on time and savings accounts were increased (↓)/decreased (↑);

R = *Reserve requirements* on Federal Reserve member banks were increased (↓)/decreased (↑);

T = *U.S. Treasury bills exceeded* (↓)/*dropped below* (↑) long-term government bond rates.

Observations: Tight money signals clustered around the major market tops of 1968–69 and 1972–73 and around intermediate tops such as that of 1971. Easy money signals clustered around the major bottoms of 1970 and 1974 and the intermediate bottoms of 1967 and 1971.

The correlation of Federal Reserve action and stock market reaction is obvious. Tight money signals are followed by intermediate- and long-term stock market declines. In the presence of easy money, the stock market rises. Figure 1-11 shows why the Fed acts—and the market reacts—as it does. In fact, as this figure makes plain, the Fed reacts to changes in the national economic environment—it does not *initiate* them.

Four of the TMT signals are *covert*. These signals are fairly difficult to use. The moving average of the Federal funds rate should be calculated every week. Net borrowed reserves should be smoothed, perhaps by using a five-week moving average, because they tend to fluctuate widely

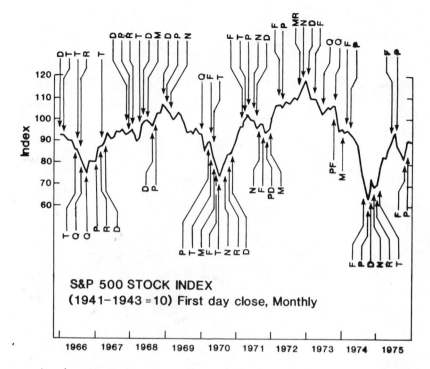

S&P 500 STOCK INDEX
(1941–1943 = 10) First day close, Monthly

↓ Tighter money	↑ Easier money
D Discount Rate	P Prime Rate
F Federal Funds Trend	Q Regulation Q
M Margin Requirement	R Reserve Requirements
N Free Reserves	T Treasury Bill vs. Government Bond Rates

FIGURE 1–10. Composite analysis of TMT signals. [*SOURCES:* D F M   P   Q   R   T : U.S. Federal Reserve Board, Division of Administrative Services, Publications Services, *Annual Statistical Digest 1971–1975*, October 1976, pp. 35; 112–25; 39; 117; 39; 38; 121; and U.S. Federal Reserve Board, Division of Administrative Services, Publications Services, *Banking and Monetary Statistics 1941–1970*, September 1976, pp. 667; 691–92; 799; 707; 673; 608; 693–96; 726–27. N : National Bureau of Economic Research, Computer Service, 261 Madison Avenue, New York. S&P 500 Stock Index: Standard & Poor's Corp., *Security Price Index Record 1976*, Orange, Conn.: Standard & Poor's Corp., 1976, p. 121.]

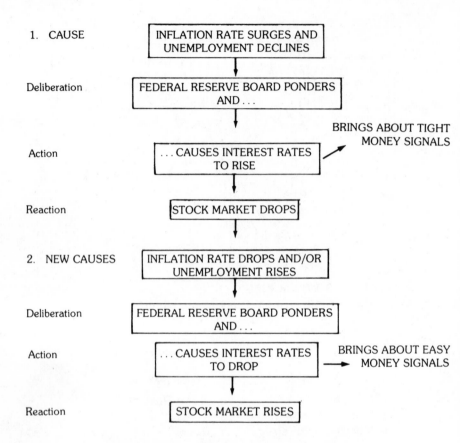

FIGURE 1-11.   TMT conceptual flowchart.

from one week to the next. Treasury bill rates must be compared to a long-term government bond index. Regulation Q is especially complex. It involves 14 different maximum interest rates payable on time and savings accounts. These rates are based on net demand deposits; the size of bank deposits; and the size, maturity, and type of time deposits.

The other TMT signals are *overt*. These are easy to use. Changes in the discount rate, the prime rate, margin requirements, and bank reserve requirements are reported immediately in the financial press. They require no interpretation; the investor only needs to understand the general hypotheses. If interest rates or cash requirements go up, money will get tighter; if they go down, it will get easier.

Overt TMT signals can have a devastating effect on the stock market. Look at Figure 1-12. The Value Line Composite Index measures the price change of a "typical" stock. The Standard and Poor's 500 Stock Index measures the market value of larger company or "institutional" stocks. These two indexes are plotted over the period 1966–75. Notice how their rise and fall is correlated with the four overt TMT signals.

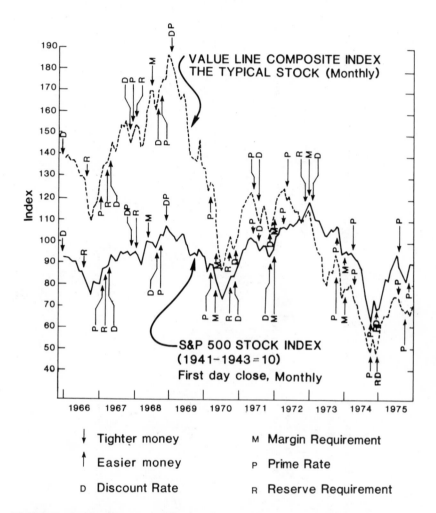

↓ Tighter money   M Margin Requirement

↑ Easier money   P Prime Rate

D Discount Rate   R Reserve Requirement

FIGURE 1–12. Overt TMT signals. [SOURCES: D M P R : U.S. Federal Reserve Board, Division of Administrative Services, Publications Services, *Annual Statistical Digest 1971–1975*, October 1976, pp. 35; 39; 39; 38; and U.S. Federal Reserve Board, Division of Administrative Services, Publications Services, *Banking and Monetary Statistics 1941–1970*, September 1976, pp. 667; 799; 673; 608. Value Line Composite Index: Arnold Bernhard & Co., *The Value Line Stock Market Averages, 1962 to 1974*, part 4, vol. 30, no. 15. New York: Arnold Bernhard & Co., 1975, pp. 4–18.]

TABLE 1-1. Number of times the stock market was higher by any percentage after easy money signals and lower after tight money signals.

	Until Signal Reversed or to 1/1/76	After Signal Reversed				
		1 Month	3 Months	6 Months	12 Months	24 Months
Discount rate	9 out of 10	7 out of 10	10 out of 10	7 out of 9	5 out of 6	—
Federal funds	10/10	9/10	7/9	4/7	2/4	2/2
Margin requirements	3/4	1/4	1/4	2/4	2/4	2/3
Free reserves	5/6	4/6	3/5	5/5	4/4	1/1
Prime rate	10/13	8/13	10/13*	4/7	2/2	—
Regulation Q	1/1	2/1	1/1	1/1	1/1	—
Reserve requirements	5/6	5/6	5/6	4/6	3/4	3/3
UST bills/LTG bonds	7/10	6/10	6/7	4/5	4/5	2/2
Grouping of three signals, same direction	6/7	5/7	6/7	6/7	4/4	1/1

*Thus, for example, 10 out of 13 prime-rate signals were correct in forecasting whether the direction of the stock market would be up or down three months after the prime-rate change.

The correlation is closest in the case of the Value Line Composite Index. This index seems to be particularly sensitive to two or more overt signals pointing in the same direction. Notice how tight money signals forced the market down from its high points in 1968 and 1972, while easy money signals forced it up from its low points in 1967, 1970, and 1974.

In early 1972, the prime-rate signal of tight money had little effect on the S&P 500 Index, which went up. However, it had considerable effect on the Value Line Composite Index, which went down.

Finally, notice how the Value Line Composite Index collapsed in 1969–70 and again in 1973–74, in each case after several tight money signals.

CONCLUSIONS

What conclusions can we draw from all this? First, tight and easy money signals do tend to predict the subsequent direction of the stock market. From 1966 to 1976, the market reacted generally according to the hypotheses that I stated at the beginning of this chapter.

Second, an investor who used TMT signals to forecast the stock market would have made money in the period 1966 to 1976. This conclusion is based on the data in Table 1-1. These data suggest just how accurate the TMT signals are.

Third, it would be possible to compose a numerical weighting for each TMT signal. However, this would probably make the signals look more accurate than they are. And I feel it is unjustifiable to establish a mathematical model based on premises that may require periodic revision. Mathematical models are inherently rigid; they cannot deal with constantly changing and unforeseen variables. Furthermore, they are based on the assumption that history will repeat itself exactly. That is why mathematical models have a poor record in terms of economic and stock market forecasting.[5]

In this chapter, I have listed the eight TMT signals and showed that these signals are correlated with the movement of the stock market. In the next chapter, I will discuss each TMT signal in greater detail. Then we will see what the experts say about the factors that are used in tight money timing.

NOTES

1. The Federal funds rate, U.S. Treasury bill rate, and net borrowed bank reserves can usually be found in the Monday edition of the *Wall Street Journal*. Changes in the discount rate, prime rate, Regulation Q, margin

requirements, and reserve requirements are reported in the financial news as they occur.

2. The Standard and Poor's 500 Stock Index reflects the market value of a representative 500 out of 1500 common stocks listed on the New York Stock Exchange. It is a base-weighted aggregative expressed in terms of the average market value for the base period (1941–43) equal to 10.

3. Normal G. Fosback, *Stock Market Logic*. Ft. Lauderdale, Fla.: Institute for Economic Research, 1976, p. 33.

4. Changes in the tax structure are recorded in U.S. Bureau of Census, *Statistical Abstract of the United States*, 1960, and U.S. Bureau of Census, *Historical Statistics of the United States, Colonial Times to 1957*, 1960.

5. Jane Quinn, "Harmful to Investor Health," *Oakland Tribune*, August 17, 1978, p. 49.

THE WALL STREET JOURNAL

"Interest rates are peaking . . . interest
rates are peaking . . ."

2
THE TMT SIGNALS

In this chapter I'm going to analyze the eight TMT signals in depth. I'll begin by defining and discussing each signal. Then I'll survey the existing research and the opinions of other experts concerning the impact of these and other related signals on the stock market.

DISCOUNT RATE

The discount rate (formerly called the rediscount rate) is the interest a commercial bank pays when it borrows from the Federal Reserve System. Although this rate is set by regional Fed banks, it must be approved by the Fed's Board of Governors.

When the Fed wants to prevent inflation, it raises the discount rate. When business is lagging, the Fed lowers the discount rate. Here is what happened when the discount rate was lowered at the end of 1976:

> Capped by today's cut in the discount rate from 5½% to 5¼%, the Fed's move toward ease is having a profound impact on expectations of the money market. The best gauge of these expectations is the movement in the rates on Treasury bill futures. In effect, the yield on those futures reflects the interest rate that the market expects will prevail on the day the futures expire. Today the implied yield for December, 1976, futures, which expire at midmonth, fell 48 basis points to 4.46%, while the yield on March, 1977, futures fell 31 basis points to 4.95%. With expectations moving downward, it appears Burns has had significant impact in lowering anticipated interest rates. That is an effective way to combat the business lull.[1]

If banks are short of cash reserves, lowering the discount rate is usually effective. However, if they already have sufficient cash reserves to lend, lowering the discount rate may not do much to stimulate loans and investments.

The discount rate fluctuates less than other interest rates. It has ranged from a low of 0.50 percent during World War II to a high of 14 percent in 1981. Changes in the discount rate are reported in the *Wall Street Journal*, in *Barron's*, and in the financial sections of most metropolitan newspapers. Long-term levels in the discount rate are published in the *Annual Statistical Digest* and in *Banking and Monetary Statistics*.[2] Figure 2-1 shows the discount rate over the period April 1980 to June 1981, and compares it with two other short-term interest rates—those for Federal funds and Treasury bills.

In Figure 2-2, the discount rate is compared with the Treasury bill and Federal funds rates for the period 1929 to 1981. Although commercial banks can borrow directly from the Fed and pay the discount rate, they are more likely to borrow Federal funds and pay the Federal funds rate. Let us see why.

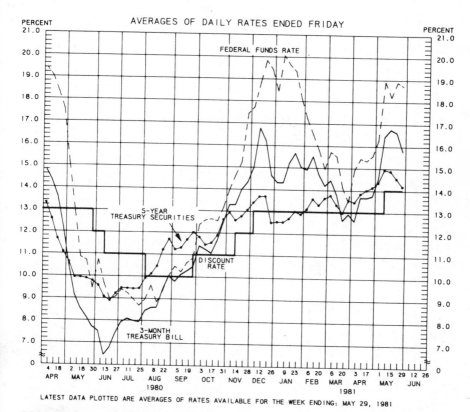

LATEST DATA PLOTTED ARE AVERAGES OF RATES AVAILABLE FOR THE WEEK ENDING: MAY 29, 1981

FIGURE 2-1. Selected short-term interest rates (averages of daily rates ended Friday). [*SOURCE:* Reproduced from *U.S. Financial Data,* Federal Reserve Bank of St. Louis, St. Louis, Mo., week ending May 27, 1981, released May 29, 1981, p. 7.]

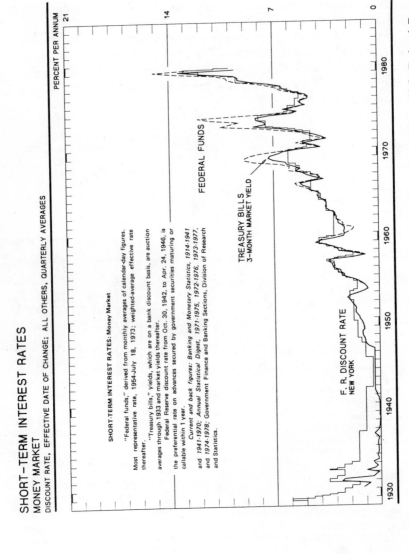

FIGURE 2-2. Short-term interest rates, 1929–80. [*SOURCE:* Reproduced from U.S. Federal Reserve Board, Division of Administrative Services, Publications Services, *Historical Chart Book* 1980 p. 98.]

FEDERAL FUNDS RATE

Federal funds are excess reserves held at the regional Federal
Reserve bank and credited to member banks in the Federal Reserve
System. The Federal funds market is an informal network that links these
member banks to one another. Banks with deposits over their legal
requirements can lend these deposits (in multiples of $1 million, and
usually for one day at a time) to other banks with too few reserves. The
money that one bank lends to another is called *Federal funds* because it is
legally in the hands of the Federal Reserve System; it merely is transferred
from the account of one commercial bank to that of another. This
arrangement allows banks to hold only the legal minimum of noninterest-
earning reserves. The Federal Reserve System does not participate in the
Federal funds market except by transferring the reserves it holds on its
books in the manner just described.

The Federal funds rate is the rate of interest that is charged on
Federal funds. It acts as a kind of base from which most other short-term
interest rates are scaled upward. This is because it represents the cost of
short-term money to a bank. The Federal funds rate is usually lower than
the discount rate except when money is tight. If the Federal funds rate
were higher than the discount rate, banks could borrow from the Federal
Reserve System for less than it would cost them to borrow from private
sources—a practice that the Fed discourages. The Federal funds market
becomes more active when money is tight. During these periods, daily
transactions usually run between $2 and $3 billion.

Although the market sets the rate for Federal funds, the Federal
Reserve System has a strong indirect influence on what that rate is. If, for
example, bank deposits and credit are expanding too fast, the Fed
instructs the manager of its Open Market Committee not to supply
reserves to the full extent of the increase in reserve requirements. This
forces banks to borrow more Federal funds, which, in turn, bids up the
Federal funds rate. On the other hand, if bank deposits and credit are too
low, the manager is authorized to provide nonborrowed reserves more
freely. This provision has the effect of lowering the Federal funds rate.

In Chapter 1, I said that the Federal funds rate is characterized as
rising when it moves above its ten-week moving average by 10 percent
and holds above this moving average for two weeks, and as *declining*
when it moves below its ten-week moving average by 10 percent and
holds below this moving average for two weeks. Table 2-1 offers an
additional definition: The Federal funds rate is defined as rising on the
basis of a three-week, rather than a two-week, lag. The data used in this
table came from the Dow Jones Industrial Index (which measures primarily blue-chip stocks), the S&P 500 Index (which measures institutional

TABLE 2-1. Buy/sell signals based on Federal funds rate trends (ten-week moving average with three-week lag).

Date	Action	Stock Market Indexes					
		DJI	P/L (%)	S&P 500	P/L (%)	Value Line Composite (weekly close)	P/L (%)
01-29-70	Sell	737.39		81.81		105.93	
05-13-70	Buy	693.84	+ 6	76.53	+ 6	97.92	+ 7
08-31-71	Sell	904.37	+30	100.31	+31	121.50	+24
10-06-71	Buy	900.55	+ 0	99.82	+ 0	113.56	+ 6
08-15-72	Sell	937.31	+ 4	107.75	+ 8	123.96	+ 9
10-10-73	Buy	960.57	– 2	109.22	– 1	96.58	+22
03-21-74	Sell	875.47	– 9	97.34	–11	81.29	–16
08-14-74	Buy	740.54	+15	76.73	+21	59.51	+27
06-25-75	Sell	872.73	+18	94.62	+23	77.77	+30
10-08-75	Buy	823.91	+ 6	87.94	+ 7	69.26	+11
04-28-76	Sell	1,000.71	+21	114.89	+30	86.49	+25
08-11-76	Buy	986.79	+ 1	104.06	+ 9	87.70	– 1
12-31-76		(1,004.65)	+ 2	(107.46)	+ 3	(93.47)	+ 7
Cumulative gain			2.29X		3.07X		3.81X

[SOURCE: *Daily Stock Price Record, New York Stock Exchange.* New York: Standard & Poor's Corp. (published quarterly).]

stocks), and the Value Line Composite Index (which measures typical stocks).

Although the difference between these two definitions is too slight to be important, the observation it leads to is quite important: The more volatile the stock group, the more accurate a signal the Federal funds rate is. In other words, the typical stock (as measured by the Value Line Index) seems to be affected more strongly by changes in this rate than does the blue-chip stock. In addition, perhaps holders of blue-chip stocks are less sensitive to changes in the Federal funds rate. One possible reason is that when the Federal funds rate increases substantially, smaller or more highly leveraged companies are more likely to suffer, which, in turn, renders their stock more volatile when money is tight.

The Federal funds rate is one of the most sensitive money market indicators.[3] A rise or fall of 0.25 percent in this rate may not mean much, but if the Federal funds rate has been declining for some time and then rises, this movement may be one of the first signs that money is growing tighter. Figure 2-3 compares the Federal funds rate with three other short-term interest rates over an 11-month period. Notice that changes in the Federal funds rate precede changes in the prime rate by a matter of weeks. They also precede, or coincide with, changes in the rates for Treasury bills and commercial paper. In December 1980, the drop in the Federal funds rate led the drop in the prime rate by one week. In March and April 1981, the rise in the Federal funds rate led the rise in the prime rate by several weeks.

MARGIN REQUIREMENTS

The margin requirement is the percentage of the total purchase price of securities that, according to the Federal Reserve, must be put up in cash. It represents the difference between the market value of a stock and the maximum legal loan that can be made on that stock. Because excessive use of credit (borrowing to buy securities) was one factor leading to the stock market collapse of 1929–32, the U.S. Congress gave the Federal Reserve Board the power to regulate the required margin. Margin requirements have ranged from 40 percent to 100 percent since they were instituted in 1934 (Fig. 2-4).

The Fed changes the margin requirement as conditions warrant. If the debt used to borrow securities (margin debt) is increasing, the Fed may lower the loan value by raising the margin requirement. If margin debt is decreasing, the Fed may raise the loan value by lowering the margin requirement.[4]

The Fed can make money tighter or easier by raising or lowering the

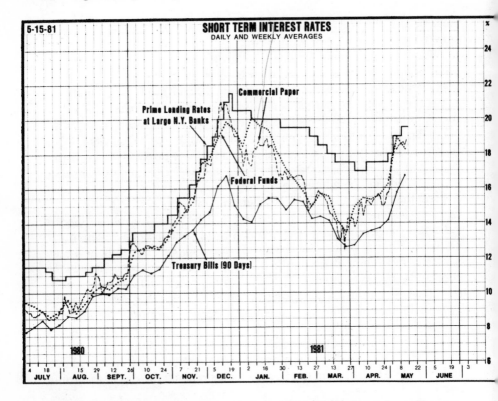

FIGURE 2-3. Short-term interest rates, 1980–81 (daily and weekly averages). [SOURCE: Reproduced from *Commodity Chart Service*, 1 Liberty Plaza, New York, N.Y. 10016, May 15, 1981, p. 16.]

margin requirement. When the margin requirement is raised, credit (money) is tightened. This usually happens after the market has risen to a relatively high point. On the other hand, when the margin requirement is lowered, credit is eased. This usually happens after the market has sunk to a relatively low point. Figure 2-5 charts the history of margin requirements and the growth of security credit over the period 1934–76.

When the margin requirement is lowered, it is often an excellent time to buy stocks. This was the case in 1949, 1953, 1958, 1960, 1962, and 1970. However, there is one major exception to this rule, which the following example illustrates. In late 1973, the securities industry urged the Fed to lower the margin requirement, so it did—from 65 to 50 percent. This allowed investors to borrow more and to buy additional stock in a major bear market. As stocks declined, brokers and banks made

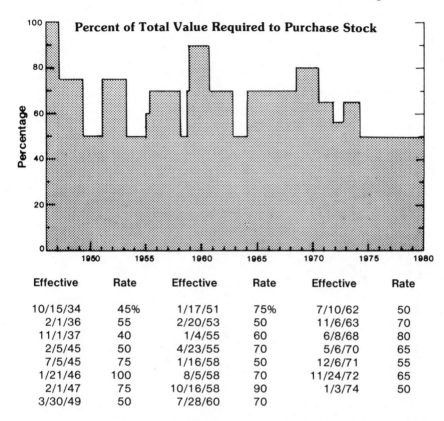

Effective	Rate	Effective	Rate	Effective	Rate
10/15/34	45%	1/17/51	75%	7/10/62	50
2/1/36	55	2/20/53	50	11/6/63	70
11/1/37	40	1/4/55	60	6/8/68	80
2/5/45	50	4/23/55	70	5/6/70	65
7/5/45	75	1/16/58	50	12/6/71	55
1/21/46	100	8/5/58	70	11/24/72	65
2/1/47	75	10/16/58	90	1/3/74	50
3/30/49	50	7/28/60	70		

FIGURE 2-4. Initial margin requirements. [SOURCE: Reproduced from Barbara Wheeler, ed., *The New York Stock Exchange 1980 Fact Book*, 25th ed. New York: New York Stock Exchange, 1980, p. 44.]

thousands, perhaps millions, of margin calls. If investors did not put up more cash or collateral when their stocks declined a certain amount, their stocks were sold to cover their margin debts. These forced sales put more pressure on an already falling market. Investors' equity dropped substantially. In many cases, investors on margin were ruined.

When the margin requirement is raised, the effect is not usually immediate, since investors can continue to hold their stocks. However, when the margin requirement is lowered, the market may rise almost immediately. This is because a lower margin requirement permits investors to buy more stocks with less cash, or to use their present stocks to

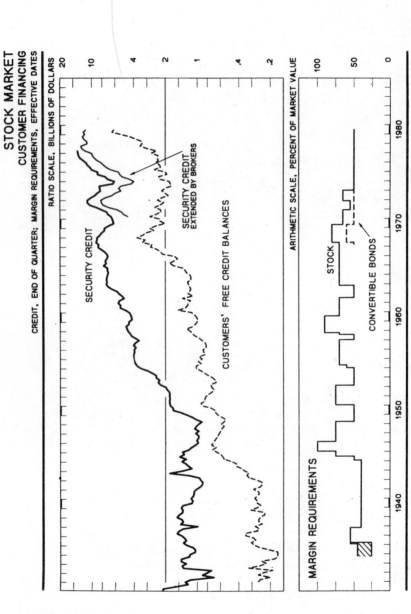

STOCK MARKET
CUSTOMER FINANCING
CREDIT, END OF QUARTER; MARGIN REQUIREMENTS, EFFECTIVE DATES

RATIO SCALE, BILLIONS OF DOLLARS

SECURITY CREDIT

SECURITY CREDIT
EXTENDED BY BROKERS

CUSTOMERS' FREE CREDIT BALANCES

ARITHMETIC SCALE, PERCENT OF MARKET VALUE

MARGIN REQUIREMENTS

STOCK

CONVERTIBLE BONDS

1940 1950 1960 1970 1980

"Security credit" is a composite of credit to purchase or carry securities at brokers and at banks. The brokers' component consists of end-of-month debit balances in margin accounts of customers of New York Stock Exchange (NYSE) member firms. For November 1931 to December 1965, credit extended by brokers consisted of customers' net debit balances with member firms of the NYSE excluding debt collateralized by U.S. government securities. From January 1966 to June 1970, this figure was estimated from reports by a sample of firms accounting for about 70 percent of margin credit extended by member firms.

The bank component of "Security credit" includes all loans to purchase or carry securities, whether or not subject to margin requirements under Regulation U, and is currently estimated from end-of-month reports by 70 large suppliers of security credit. Before January 1971, the bank component consisted of bank loans to others—other than brokers and dealers—to purchase or carry securities, excluding U.S. government securities, as reported by weekly reporting member banks on the last Wednesday of each month. The level of this series was affected from time to time by minor revisions.

"Customers' free credit balances" are end-of-quarter figures on customers' balances subject to withdrawal at member firms of the NYSE and include credit balances in cash as well as margin accounts.

"Margin requirements" refer to the Federal Reserve Regulations G, T, and U, prescribed in accordance with the Securities Exchange Act of 1934, limiting the amount of credit to purchase or carry margin stocks that may be extended on securities collateral by prescribing maximum loan values, which are specified percentages of the market value of the collateral at the time the credit is extended. "Margin requirements" are the difference between the market value—100 percent—and the maximum loan value. On March 11, 1968, "Convertible bonds" became subject to regulated maximum loan value prescriptions.

FIGURE 2-5. Security credit. [SOURCE: Reproduced from U.S. Federal Reserve Board, Division of Administrative Services, Publications Services, *Historical Chart Book*, 1980, p. 93.]

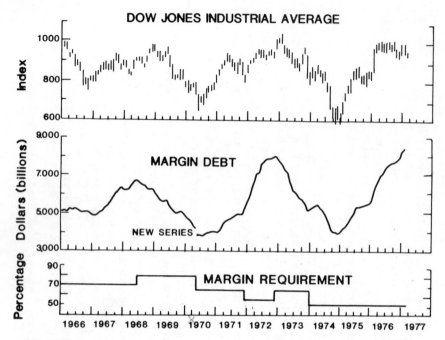

FIGURE 2-6.   Margin requirements and related items. [*SOURCE*: Reproduced from U.S. Federal Reserve Board, Division of Administrative Services, Publications Services, *Monthly Chart Book*, 1976, pp. 70, 71.]

buy more on margin without putting up additional cash (provided they are not already overmargined).

The margin debt figure represents the amount that margin buyers are borrowing to invest or speculate in common stocks. It tends to move up and down with the market (Fig. 2-6). Usually, bear markets bottom out when margin debt stops declining. A rise in margin debt over several consecutive months often signals the beginning of a new bull market. A decline in margin debt often signals the onset of a bear market.

FREE RESERVES

Free reserves are the difference between excess bank reserves and money borrowed at Federal Reserve Banks.[5] A negative free-reserve figure is called *net borrowed reserves*. Figure 2-7 shows free reserves and net borrowed reserves for the period 1969–77.

X The more free reserves in the banking system, the more dollars the bank can lend and invest. By manipulating the net free-reserve position of member banks, the Fed indicates the direction of its monetary policy. If the Fed wants to implement a policy of aggressive ease, it pumps reserves into the banking system. So it stimulates a sluggish economy: Each dollar of free reserves can support more than a dollar's worth of loans and investments. For example, with an average of 15 percent in legal reserve requirements, banks can (theoretically) expand their loans and investments up to six and two-thirds times, or $6.66 for every $1.00 of free reserves. However, if the Fed wishes to stop a business boom that is creating inflationary pressures, it can make money tight by forcing free reserves down. The current free-reserve position of the banking system is published once a week in the *Wall Street Journal* (Fig. I-2).

As I explained in Chapter 1, I choose a free-reserve figure of $500 million for the purpose of stock market timing. Money becomes tight when free reserves exceed $500 million, and easy when free reserves drop below a negative $500 million. I chose the figure $500 million by X induction, using the monthly data published in the *Federal Reserve Bulletins*.[6] "Buy" and "Sell" signals based on these criteria are shown in Table 2-2. On the whole, if you as an investor had followed the free-reserve signal, you would have made money from 1957 on. You would also have avoided the major decline of 1972–74.

PRIME RATE

The free-reserve figure indicates the availability of funds. The prime rate indicates the cost of funds to the banking system's best customers— that is, those who have the highest credit ratings. The prime rate is the interest rate commercial banks charge these favored customers for short-term loans.[7] Figure 2-8 shows the fluctuation of the prime rate over a 14-month period, from November 1975 through December 1977. Figure 2-9 shows its fluctuations over a period of 51 years (1929–80).

X The prime rate is usually lower than other commercial rates. The difference between the prime rate and the rate actually charged for a commercial loan represents the additional risk involved in lending to a given customer.

It was an offhand remark by a securities investor that first gave me the idea of using the prime rate as a TMT signal. William Q. Steinmetz believed that an investor could make money in the stock market by following two rules: (1) *buy stocks the first time the prime rate goes down*

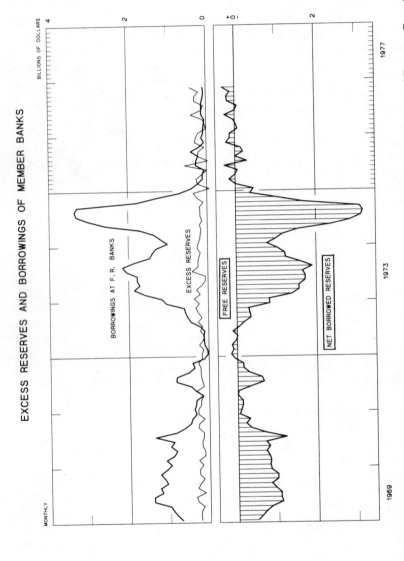

FIGURE 2-7. Free and net borrowed reserves. [SOURCE: Reproduced from U.S. Federal Reserve Board, Division of Administrative Services, Publications Services, *Monthly Chart Book*, 1976, p.3.]

TABLE 2-2.   Free reserves, 1955–77.

Free Reserves Rose Above a Minus $500 Million ("Buy" Signal)		Free Reserves Dropped Below a Minus $500 Million ("Sell" Signal)		
Date	S&P Stock Market Index	Date	S&P Stock Market Index	Gain (%)
		April 1956	48	
June 1956	47	April 1957	46	-2%
May 1957	47	June 1957	47	-0%
July 1957	47	June 1959	59	+26%
September 1959	57	February 1969	99	+74%
September 1970	84	July 1971	96	+14%
September 1971	99	December 1972	115	+16%
December 1974	70	December 31, 1976	(107)	(+53%)

following one or more increases (an indication that money was becoming easier); and (2) *sell stocks the first time the prime rate goes up following one or more decreases* (an indication that money was becoming tighter).[8] A series of signals might go like this: 6 percent, 6.25 percent, 6.75 percent, 7 percent, 6.75 percent ("Buy"); 6.25 percent, 6 percent, 5.50 percent, 5.75 percent ("Sell").

Table 2-3 lists the gains or losses you would have realized for the period 1954 to 1977 if your investments had performed like the S&P 500 Index, and if you had used the prime-rate reversal as a TMT signal.

As you can see, this signal gave pleasing results. From March 1954 to July 1976, it produced profits about 90 percent of the time on the long side and 57 percent of the time on the short side. In fact, from 1954 to 1967 it produced profits 100 percent of the time on the long side and 67 percent of the time on the short side. However, after 1967, other TMT signals gave better results. Prime-rate reversal points are correlated with the NYSE Composite Index in Figure 2-10. Compare this with Figure 1-6, in which the prime rate is correlated with the S&P 500 Stock Index.

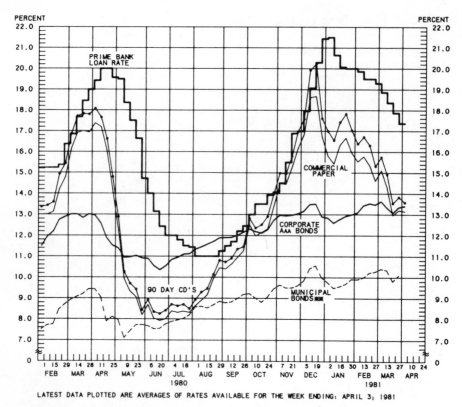

PERCENT

LATEST DATA PLOTTED ARE AVERAGES OF RATES AVAILABLE FOR THE WEEK ENDING: APRIL 3; 1981

FIGURE 2-8. Yields on selected securities (averages of daily rates ended Friday). [SOURCE: Reproduced from *U.S. Financial Data.* St. Louis, Mo.: Federal Reserve Bank of St. Louis, week ending April 3, 1981, released April 5, 1981, p. 6.]

REGULATION Q

Regulation Q sets the maximum rate of interest that U.S. commercial banks can pay on time deposits. This regulation was initiated by the Banking Act of 1933.

The rate of interest specified by Regulation Q fluctuates very little. It remained constant from 1936 to 1957. However, what fluctuations there are sometimes have dramatic sequels. In 1957, Regulation Q was raised from 2.50 to 3 percent. During the next ten months the stock market dropped almost 15 percent. In January 1962, Regulation Q was raised again, from 3 to 4 percent. Within five months the stock market had declined 20 percent.

TABLE 2-3. Prime rate as a TMT signal.

Date Prime Rate First Decreased ("Buy" Signal)	S&P 500 Index*	Date Prime Rate First Increased ("Sell" Signal)	S&P 500 Index*	Gain or Loss (%)
03-17-54 (3.25 to 3.0%)	27	08-04-55 (3.0 to 3.25%)	43	+59%
01-22-58 (4.5 to 4.0%)	42	09-11-58 (3.5 to 4.0%)	50	+19%
08-23-60 (5.0 to 4.5%)	57	12-06-65 (4.5 to 5.0%)	92	+61%
01-26-67 (6.0 to 5.5%)	87	11-20-67 (5.5 to 6.0%)	95	+9%
09-25-68 (6.5 to 6.25%)	102	12-02-68 (6.25 to 6.5%)	104	+2%
03-25-70 (8.5 to 8.0%)	90	05-11-71 (5.25 to 5.0%)	101	+12%
10-20-71 (6.0 to 5.75%)	92	04-05-72 (4.75 to 5.0%)	107	+16%
10-24-73 (10.0 to 9.75%)	108	03-22-74 (8.75 to 9.0%)	93	-14%
10-07-74 (12.0 to 11.75%)	74	07-18-75 (7.0 to 7.25%)	88	+19%
10-27-75 (8.0 to 7.75%)	88	07-1-76 (6.75 to 7.0%)	100	+14%

*Stock market index was computed as of the first of the month following the prime-rate signal.

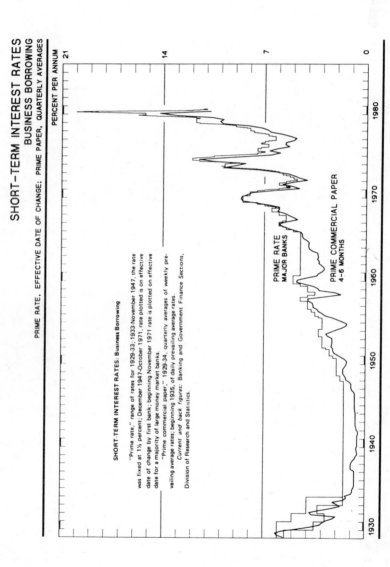

FIGURE 2-9.   Prime rate. [SOURCE: Reproduced from U.S. Federal Reserve Board, Division of Administrative Services, Publications Services, *Historical Chart Book*, 1980, p. 99.]

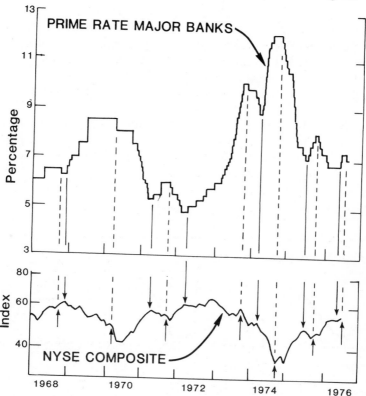

FIGURE 2-10. Prime rate versus NYSE Composite Index. [SOURCE: Redrawn from U.S. Federal Reserve Board, Division of Administrative Services, Publications Services, *Monthly Chart Book*, 1976, pp. 70, 72.]

The financial industry offered two reasons for the 1962 decline: (1) stock prices were too high (stock was selling at an average of 22 times earnings); and (2) President Kennedy had reprimanded the steel industry for raising prices in defiance of his inflation-curbing guidelines. Nobody seems to have blamed the decline on the change in Regulation Q, even though this change allowed savings deposits held for one year or more to receive 4 percent interest instead of 3 percent—a 33 percent increase. This fact must have encouraged some investors to sell stocks, which yielded an average of 2.97 percent, and put their cash into savings accounts. The change occurred on January 1, 1962. Had investors heeded this TMT signal, they would have had plenty of time to liquidate their stocks before the decline, which resulted in increased stock yields to 3.78 percent within six months.

Regulation Q was raised again for certain deposits in July 1963. For our purposes, this increase is not significant because it did not affect savings, only other 90-day to one-year time deposits. There were further increases: The increase of November 24, 1964 resulted in a six-month trendless market; the increase of December 6, 1965 signaled the top of the market just before a 20 percent drop.

The Fed is in a position to alter the flow of money without altering the supply, just by changing the rate of interest specified by Regulation Q. Raising the maximum interest rate payable on time deposits increases the flow of cash into commercial banks (Fig. 2-11). These funds are reinvested so that they compensate for the higher rates paid on saving

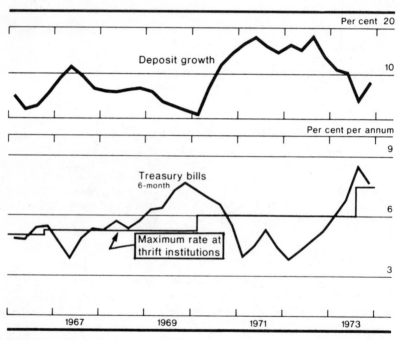

Interest rates: Quarterly data. Treasury bills, averages of daily rates. Thrift institutions, averages of highest ceiling rates payable on consumer-type deposits at mutual savings banks and savings and loan associations. During the period July 1–Oct. 31, 1973, when the rate ceiling on 4-year, $1,000 minimum-denomination consumer-type certificates of deposit was suspended, most institutions offered rates no higher than 7½ per cent on these deposits.

Deposit growth: Quarterly changes, at seasonally adjusted annual rates, in total deposits at mutual savings banks and in savings capital at savings and loan associations.

FIGURE 2-11.   Deposit growth at thrift institutions and selected interest rates. [SOURCE: Reproduced from U.S. Federal Reserve Board, Division of Administrative Services, Publications Services, *The Federal Reserve System— Purposes and Functions*, 6th ed., 1974, p. 84.]

accounts. A change in Regulation Q also affects the interest rates paid on U.S. T-bills, notes, commercial paper, and other investment media.

RESERVE REQUIREMENTS

Required reserves are the percentage of deposits commercial banks must set aside, either as reserves at their regional Federal Reserve bank or as cash in their vaults. Reserve requirements are set by the Federal Reserve System and vary with the size of the bank. They are changed only once or twice a year, if at all.

The reserve requirement enables the Fed to control the behavior of member banks by controlling the amount of money they have available for loans and investments. For example, as of December 31, 1975, member banks were required to hold reserves equal to 7.5 percent of their first $2 million of demand deposits; 10 percent of the next $2 to $10 million; 12 percent of the next $10 to $100 million; 13 percent of the next $100 to $400 million; and 17.50 percent of any demand deposits over $400 million. Member banks were also required to keep reserves equal to 3 percent of savings deposits and various percentages of other time deposits.

When reserve requirements are lowered, member banks can make more loans and investments, a signal of easier money. This situation encourages the stock market to rise. When reserve requirements are raised, member banks must make fewer loans and investments. This signals tighter money and encourages the stock market to decline.

U.S. TREASURY BILL RATES VERSUS LONG-TERM GOVERNMENT BOND RATES

Three types of U.S. Treasury bills are available: (1) T-bills that mature in 90 days; (2) T-bills that mature in 180 days (both the 90-day and the 180-day bills are the shortest-term securities issued by the U.S. government, and are sold at weekly auctions); and (3) one-year T-bills (which are sold at monthly auctions).[9] The government's high credit rating makes T-bills an exceptionally secure, attractive investment, particularly for domestic banks and corporations, foreign central banks, and other investors who want to earn interest on temporary idle cash without worrying about default.

T-bill *prices* do not fluctuate as much as the prices of other U.S. securities, because their maturities are so short. However, because the Fed frequently buys and sells huge quantities of T-bills, their *rates* do fluctuate widely. This, in turn, affects the cost and availability of bank loans.

As of September 30, 1976, more than $161 billion worth of T-bills were outstanding. Also outstanding were over $39 billion worth of government bonds[10] (securities that mature in ten or more years) and over $206 billion worth of Treasury notes (securities that mature in one to ten years).[11] By comparing T-bill rates with the rates paid on long-term government bonds, we obtain the eighth and last TMT signal. The best source of data for making this comparison is *U.S. Financial Data*, published by the Federal Reserve Bank of St. Louis (Table 2-4).

On pages xxvi–xxvii I gave you the classic definitions of tight and easy money. Actually, however, these definitions are useful to the economist but of little use to the investor. They do not say at what specific point

TABLE 2-4. Treasury bills versus long-term government securities.

1977	Federal Funds†	Three-Month Treasury Bills	One-Year Treasury Bills	Three- to Five-Year Government Securities	Long-Term Government Securities
Nov. 5	5.06	4.83	5.12	6.51	7.57
12	4.98	4.92	5.19	6.55	7.57
19	5.02	4.80	5.05	6.44	7.58
26	4.90	4.60	4.79	6.09	7.44
Dec. 3	4.78	4.42	4.66	5.92	7.31
10	4.67	4.41	4.66	5.94	7.22
17	4.68	4.33	4.66	5.99	7.23
24	4.63	4.27	4.60	5.96	7.18
31	4.69	4.34	4.62	5.98	7.11
Jan. 7*	4.47	4.45	4.71	6.05	7.10
14					
21					
28					

Source: U.S. Financial Data, Federal Reserve Bank of St. Louis, St. Louis, MO, week ending January 7, 1977, released January 9, 1977, p. 7.

*Average of rate available.

†Seven-day averages for week ending Wednesday two days earlier than date shown.

money becomes tight or easy (or tighter or easier). If, as an investor, you
wish to time actual stock market transactions, you must be able to
determine when money becomes easy (so you can buy low) and when it
becomes tight (so you can sell high). Here I would like to propose the
following hypothesis, based on the relationship between short-term and
long-term interest rates.

*Money becomes easy at the point where the interest rate of new 90-
day U.S. Treasury bills drops below that of long-term U.S government
bonds.* This point represents the best time to sell stocks. buy

*Money becomes tight at the point where the interest rate yield of
new 90-day U.S. Treasury bills rises above that of long-term U.S.
government bonds.* This point represents the best time to sell stocks.

This hypothesis is based upon two assumptions. First, long-term
interest rates normally are higher than short-term rates (Fig. 2-12). This is
because when investors commit their funds for the long term, they assume
the added risk of loss of market value due to rising interest rates. The rates
paid on U.S. government bonds and T-bills are used for comparison
because these securities are the two safest possible investments. The only
difference between them is that of maturity.

Second, there are abnormal times when short-term interest rates are
higher than long-term rates. Figure 2–13 shows the inverted yield curves
that result when money is tight and many borrowers seek loans. Because

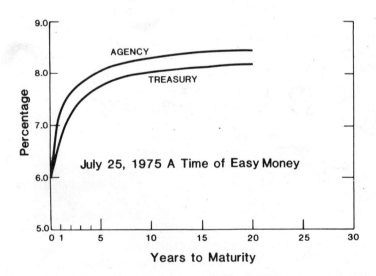

FIGURE 2-12. **Easy money yield curves.** [SOURCE: *Weekly Monetary
Summary*. San Francisco, Calif.: Bank of America, Bank Investment Services
Division, July 25, 1975, p. 2.]

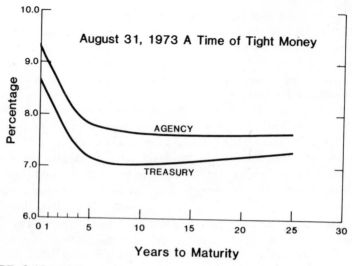

FIGURE 2-13. Tight money yield curves. [*SOURCE*: *Weekly Monetary Summary*. San Francisco: Bank of America, Bank Investment Services Division, August 31, 1973, p. 2.]

short-term loan and investment money is scarce, interest rates skyrocket. Short-term borrowers must pay more—and this includes the U.S. government, when it issues new three-month T-bills. These bills are very sensitive to money rates, and their yields are volatile, ranging from a negative yield in 1940 to approximately 17 percent in December 1980.

In testing this and the other hypotheses proposed in this book, I have ignored tax consequences, dividends, and transaction costs. I have assumed that the average price of stocks rose and fell in proportion to the stock market indexes used.

The foregoing hypothesis may also be stated as follows: *Money becomes easy when yield curves first show that short-term Treasury and federal agency rates are less than long-term rates. Money becomes tight when yield curves first show that short-term rates are greater than long-term rates.* Figure 2-14 illustrates yield curves for one tight money period and four easy money periods.

You may wonder why I define tight money in terms of the relationship between short- and long-term government securities, rather than in terms of a specific level of interest. I do so because this relationship automatically adjusts for inflation. For example, in 1967, short- and long-term interest rates crossed at about 4.50 percent to give a "Buy" signal. In 1970 and 1974, the "Buy" signal occurred when the rates crossed at 6.50 to 7 percent. The difference between these percentages is due to inflation.

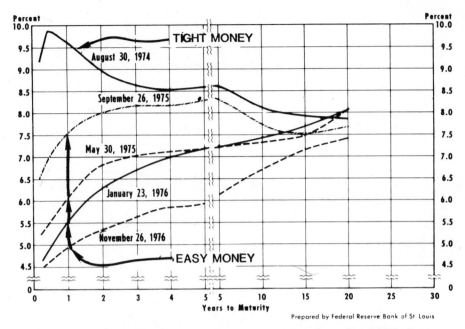

Prepared by Federal Reserve Bank of St Louis

FIGURE 2-14.   Yields on U.S. government securities.   [*SOURCE*: Reproduced from *U.S. Financial Data*. St. Louis: Federal Reserve Bank of St. Louis, (week ending December 8, 1976,) released December 10, 1976, p. 1.]

I tested this eighth and last TMT signal for the 57-year period from 1920 to 1977 for a historical comparison. The results are summarized in Figures 2-15a through 2-15e. If you look at these figures, you will notice that eight tight money "Sell" signals occurred at the points where 90-day U.S. T-bill yields moved above yields for long-term U.S. government bonds. You will also see that eight easy money "Buy" signals occurred at the points where 90-day U.S. T-bill yields moved below yields for long-term U.S. government bonds. I have listed the S&P 500 Stock Index at each "Buy" and "Sell" point and the compiled results in Table 2-5.

If you had invested in the stock market in January 1920, your total profits from capital appreciation as of January 1976 would have been about 900 percent, or 4.0 percent compounded annually, excluding dividends and transaction costs. This assumes that you followed a buy and hold policy. It also assumes that your investment approximated the performance of the indexes used in the charts.

However, if you had bought and sold common stocks, using the "Buy" and "Sell" signals mentioned above, your total profits would have been 2217 percent from long trades (6.0 percent compounded annually), 42 percent from short trades (0.7 percent compounded annually), and

TABLE 2-5. TMT signal results (using three-month T-bills versus government bonds).

Date	Signals		Approx. % Gain (Loss)[a]		Cumulative Value		
	Buy	Sell	Long	Short	Long	Short	Both Long & Short
Jun. 1920		7.9			1.0	1.0	1.0
Apr. 1921	6.9			+13		1.13	1.13
Jan. 1928		17.5	+153		2.53		2.86
Dec. 1929	21.4			-22		.88	2.23
Oct. 1959		57.0	-166		6.73		5.92
Feb. 1960	55.8			+2		.90	6.06
Jan. 1966		93.3	+67		11.24		10.12
Jun. 1966	86.1			+8		.97	10.90
Jul. 1966		85.8	-1		11.13		10.80
Feb. 1967	87.4			-2		.95	10.57
Apr. 1968		95.7	+9		12.13		11.52
Apr. 1970	85.9			+10		1.05	12.74
May 1970		76.1	-11		10.79		11.33
Jun. 1970	75.6			+1		1.06	11.44
Apr. 1973		110.0	+46		15.76		16.71
Jan. 1975	72.6			+34		1.43[c]	22.38
(To Jan. 1976)		107.0	+47		23.17[b]		32.90[d]

[a]To provide comparable figures, the figure that was "invested" is used as the base for percentage figures for either the long or the short side.

[b]Compounded totals, long positions = +2217% or 6.0% compounded annually.

[c]Compounded totals, short positions = +42%, 0.7% compounded annually.

[d]Compounded totals, long and short positions = +3190%, 6.6% compounded annually.

46

3190 percent from both long and short trades (6.6 percent compounded annually). Since a buying-and-holding policy results in a 4.0 percent annualized gain whereas the use of these TMT signals results in a 6.0 percent gain, if you had used the signals your annualized results would have improved by approximately 50 percent.

Finally, you would have become fully invested in the stock market in January 1975, when the S&P 500 Stock Index was 73. You would still be holding these securities as of January 1977, when the same index was 107. This represents a gain of 46 percent.

From 1970 to 1975, tight money was a severe problem for the market. Between June 1970 and June 1975, the profit to be realized from Tight Money Timing would have been 91 percent on the long side, or 13.8 percent compounded annually, and 57 percent on the short side, or 9.4 percent compounded annually. Investing in both sides of the market would have produced a profit of 200 percent, or 24.6 compounded annually. Investing according to a buy-and-hold policy would have produced a profit of 26.6 percent, or 4.8 percent compounded annually.

Some institutions did not react to tight money during the 1973–74 bear market. For example, Morgan Guaranty Trust Company's three pooled stock funds dropped more than 50 percent in value—more than $1 billion—in the year ended September 30, 1974. This followed a 10 percent drop in the previous fiscal year. Morgan's performance was documented in a two-day series of articles in the *Wall Street Journal*, which shed considerable doubt on this company's ability to preserve capital. The article cited many examples of poor timing on Morgan's part, including buying Polaroid stock at a cost of $6.7 million (later valued at only $1.5 million), and buying MGIC Investment stock at a cost of $11.3 million (later valued at only $1.8 million).[12]

One last point. Look once more at Figures 2–15b through 2–15d. Note that between December 1929 and October 1959, the signals described in this section did not occur. Although the stock index appreciated 244 percent during this 30-year period, it dropped 78 percent between December 1929 and June 1932. It also dropped 45 percent in the 1937–38 decline, and 25 percent in the 1962 decline. That is why it is important to use other TMT signals to confirm changes in market trends.

WHAT DO OTHER EXPERTS SAY?

This section surveys the research done by experts other than myself. While it is both interesting and informative, it may go into greater depth than you require. If so, please feel free to go directly to Chapter 3.

FIGURE 2-15a-e. Treasury bill and government bond rates versus common stock index, 1914–76.

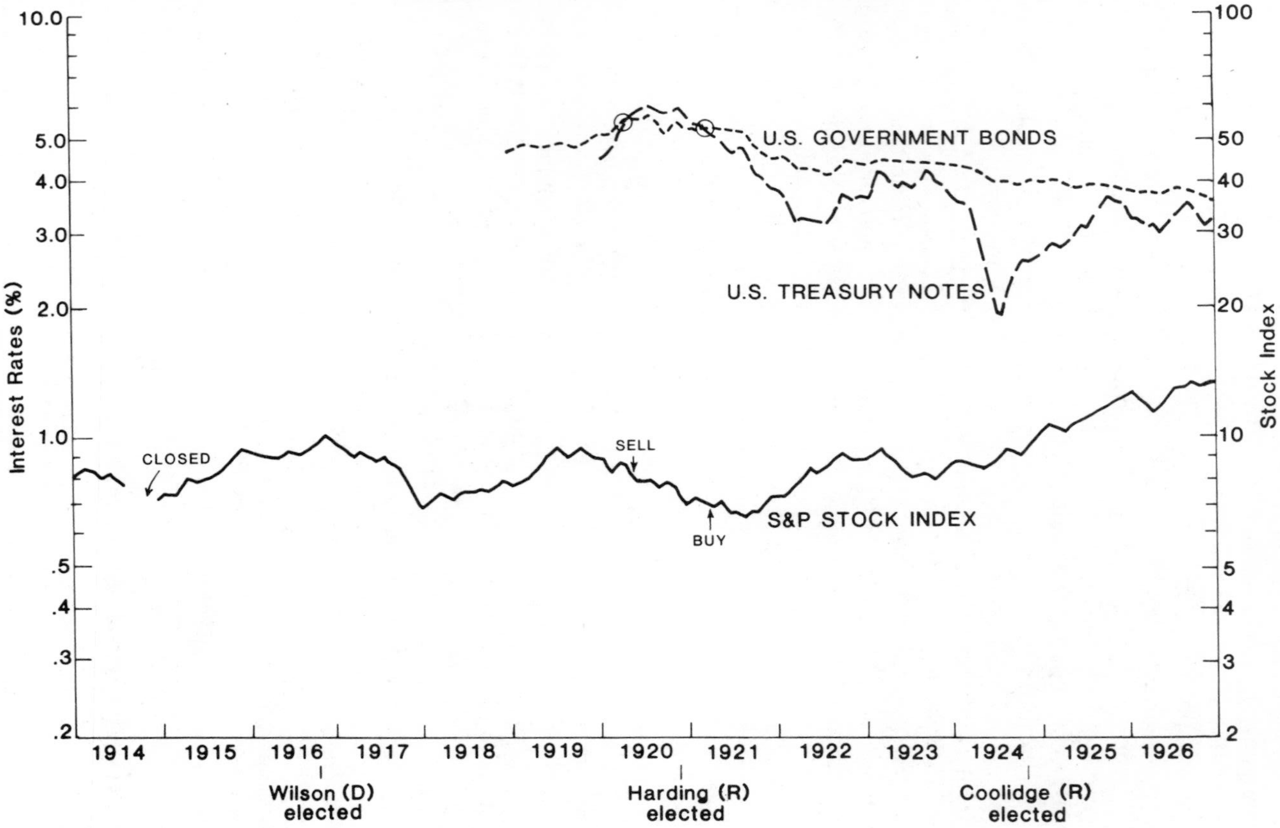

FIGURE 2-15a

48

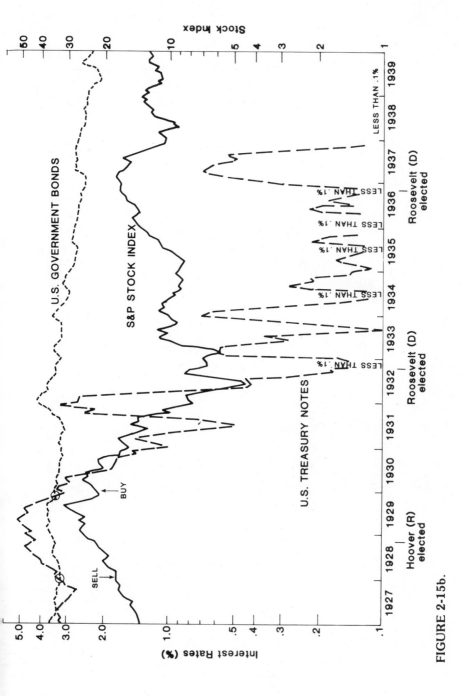

FIGURE 2-15b.

49

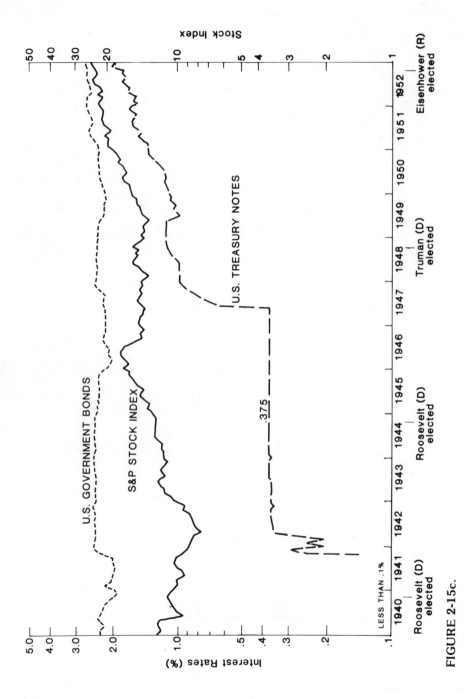

FIGURE 2-15c.

50

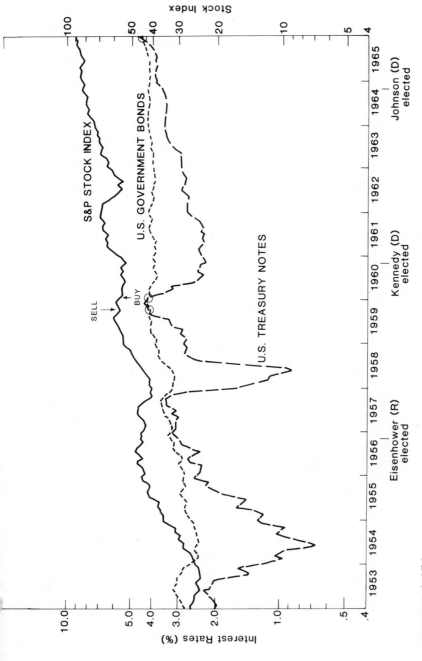

FIGURE 2-15d.

51

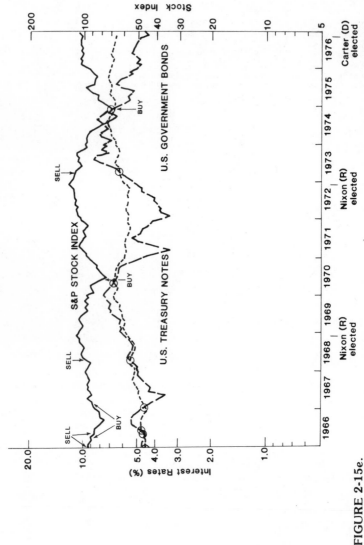

FIGURE 2-15e.

[SOURCES: Figures 2–15a-e. U.S. Federal Reserve Board, Division of Administrative Services, Publications Services, *Banking and Monetary Statistics 1914–41,* November 1943, pp. 479–81; U.S. Federal Reserve Board, Division of Administrative Services, Publications Services, *Supplement to Banking and Monetary Statistics for the Period January 1941 to July 1964,* 1966, sec. 12; and U.S. Federal Reserve Board, Division of Administrative Services, Publications Services, *Federal Reserve Bulletin,* 1964–76, pp. A-27, A-28, A-29.]

Research by other writers in the field of finance tends to support the ideas I have presented in this book. However, this material must be weighed against certain reservations. Investment advisors tend to espouse sound premises in theory, but in practice their research is often shallow—they test their premises over periods too short to permit the drawing of accurate conclusions. The premises espoused by academicians, on the other hand, sometimes are actually unsound. For example, one academician asserts that moving averages are not useful in defining trend changes. However, he bases this conclusion on *monthly* data,[13] when almost all investors who employ moving averages use *daily* or *weekly* data. Monthly moving averages miss most of the profitable trends in the market.

Some of the investment rules described below were developed from data that are now obsolete. Others are highly theoretical because they have only been tested over short periods.

As you read this section of reserach done by others, keep these reservations in mind.

Conversations with Other Authorities

I asked several senior economists and investment managers to define tight money. I also asked them what, in their opinion, constituted accurate market-timing signals. Finally, I asked them to comment on the TMT hypothesis. In this section I will summarize their replies.

"What is tight money?" is not an easy question to answer. There is no standard definition. (However, when confronted with the definitions offered in this book, most authorities accepted them.) Therefore it is not surprising that some answers were vague. For example, when Paul Volcker, then President of the Federal Reserve Bank of New York, was asked, "How will you tell whether money is tight or easy?" he replied, "You have to look at a variety of indicators and inevitably compromise among them."[14]

The definition offered by Joe Wahead, a senior economist of a large Western bank, was only slightly more useful. He said that money was tight when it was difficult to borrow and easy when it was easy to borrow. I asked him for a "light switch" definition—one that would define money as either tight or easy, with no gray areas. He offered this: Money is tight when 90-day U.S Treasury bills rise to 6.5 or 7 percent, or when money starts to flow out of savings and loan associations. He added that he would expect the stock market to decline under these conditions.[15]

Neither of these definitions of tight money constitutes a practical TMT signal. The T-bill levels specified are too inflexible to cover all markets. The data on savings flows would have to be smoothed via moving averages, and these data often are obsolete by the time they become available.

Will the Fed continue to make money tight and easy in the future? Wahead believed it would. He also thought the Fed would move faster in the future to correct the course of the economy. And on the basis of what has happened since 1976, he was right.

I talked at length with Dr. Sherman Maisel, a former member of the Federal Reserve Bank Board who is now an economics professor at the University of California, Berkeley. He defined tightness as the relationship between the supply and the demand for money.[16] My talk with Maisel was highly illuminating. I will have more to say about it later on.

I asked William M. Burke, a senior economist of the Federal Reserve Bank of San Francisco, to define tight and easy money. His reply indicated that this book's definition, which is based on free reserves, is currently out of favor with Federal Reserve economists. He himself believed that money becomes tight when the rate of growth of money supply (M_1 or M_2) falls below its respective long-term rate.[17] This definition, covered on pages 66–71, does not seem to be useful in timing stock market moves.

The role of money supply as a market-timing signal was touched upon by Monte Gordon, the research director of a large mutual fund. Gordon, who has followed the Fed's actions closely for years, makes investment decisions involving billions of dollars. He told me that since the 1960s the stock market has become more sensitive to interest rates and less sensitive to money supply. This opinion was later confirmed by my own research. Later in this chapter I shall explain why I believe that changes in the money supply are of dubious value in forecasting changes in the stock market.[18]

Dr. Michael W. Keran, Director of Research of the Federal Reserve Bank of San Francisco, has stated that money supply is a factor in the interest rate equation, but that it has no direct bearing on stock prices. Keran's model for forecasting the stock market uses two variables: (1) interest rates, and (2) corporate earnings. He believes that interest rates depend on four factors: (1) the long-term price of money; (2) the demand and supply of money; (3) risk; and (4) inflation.

Keran's opinions on forecasting are somewhat ambiguous. He lists many factors that have correlated with the market in the past. At the same time, however, he expresses no confidence that they will correlate with future markets.[19]

No book on TMT would be complete without an opinion from a chairman of the Federal Reserve Board. Dr. Arthur F. Burns was chairman of the Fed from 1970 to 1978. I asked him for his definition of tight money.[20] Normand Bernard, Burn's special assistant, responded as follows: "Stock market reactions to changes in the money and capital markets vary over time, so that there is no specific point at which stock prices become vulnerable to tight money."[21] In one sense this is a true and safe answer. At the same time, it is misleading. TMT is unique in that it does deal with specific points to show when stock prices are vulnerable to tight or easy money.

I also asked various experts to evaluate the role that the Federal Reserve plays in the stock market. As you can imagine, answers to this question varied according to the position of the respondent. Professional investment managers tend to be sensitive to the Fed's actions. In general, they feel that the Fed exerts a powerful influence over the stock market, even though they may not always understand the results of its actions. Warren Greene, the manager of an aggressive mutual fund, told me, "I don't fight the Fed anymore. It doesn't pay. When the Fed tries to choke off money, I would rather be out of the market."[22] James B. Morse, a former chief investment manager for Bank of America, described investors in spring 1976 as being "mesmerized by what the Federal Reserve has been doing."[23] He was referring to increases in the Federal funds rate, which had raised the cost of borrowing.

As you will see, this book suggests that investors would have been wise to heed the Fed's actions for the past 67 years—especially since 1934, when the Fed gained even greater power over financial markets. It also suggests that investors who use the TMT signals will get rich—at the expense of investors who ignore them.

When approached, employees of the Federal Reserve had quite a different set of insights to offer. Certain questions were so sensitive that I had to pose them as tactfully as possible. Representative "sensitive" questions included, "With your knowledge of Federal Reserve actions, could you and your associates make large sums of money in the stock market?" (read on for one expert's answer to this question), and "Is there a point where the U.S. debt burden becomes uncontrollable?" One Fed economist told me that this burden can be controlled only as long as the percentage of debt of GNP remains relatively small or on the decline. I asked this same economist whether the Fed *really* always puts public interest first, as it is supposed to do, in light of the apparent coincidence that money has been eased and that the stock market has gone up two years prior to every presidential election since 1962. His answers were not completely objective, and I feel they were too noncommittal to be worth quoting here.[24]

I got more illuminating answers from Dr. Sherman Maisel. A former seven-year member of the Federal Reserve Bank Board, Maisel is now a professor of applied economics and finance at the University of California, Berkeley. Maisel's long tenure on the board makes his opinion well worth listening to.

I asked Maisel if it really is a coincidence that the stock market goes up two years before every presidential election. I also asked, "Is there a real conflict between what actually happens before elections and putting public interest first?" Maisel answered both questions by saying that the Fed's actions had indeed been coincidental. He added that the Fed would probably postpone any necessary actions until after the November 1976 elections in order to stay neutral. He was right. The Fed made no overt changes until after the election. Then it made money easier by lowering the discount rate and bank reserve requirements. In the meantime, banks had lowered their prime rates several times.

I pointed out to Maisel that interest rates had become much more erratic since 1966, and I asked him whether this was a result of the Fed's more concise and formal forecasts, which had been initiated around that time. He replied that the Fed's actions were based on the unique circumstances current at the time (presumably referring to President Johnson's guns-and-butter program, which had increased inflation).

I next suggested that the Fed controls the destiny of the stock and bond markets, and that the average investor is completely unaware of this fact. Maisel did not deny this outright, but he pointed out that the Fed can control short-term interest rates only to a certain extent—an extent that is limited by other variables. He agreed, however, that the Fed will continue to have a strong influence over future stock and bond markets.

I asked, "If you were a small investor, how would you invest in the stock and bond markets?" Maisel's advice was classic—he would diversify according to his particular needs. If liquidity, safety, or growth was the objective he would invest accordingly. He offered no secret formula.

I drew his attention to an article stating that officers of the Fed had personal investments of over $100 million in the stock market.[25] Maisel questioned this figure. He said he doubted that any board member had more than $200,000 total invested.

I asked, "With your knowledge of Fed actions, did you and your former associates make large profits in the stock markets?" He replied that his personal investments had been held in a blind trust. Some other board members, such as former chairman William Martin, had invested solely in U.S. government bonds. (In fact, this turned out to one of the best investment strategies—in terms of both performance and safety—for the ten-year period ending in 1974.)[26]

What are we to make of Maisel's answers? First, members of the Federal Reserve Board walk a tight line. They must remain neutral for political reasons—and this sometimes prevents them from taking necessary action. Such was the case in the nine months preceding the 1976 presidential election. If the Fed had made money easier during this period, it might have encouraged the stock market to rise. This, in turn, might have suggested that Gerald Ford (the incumbent) was managing the country very well, thus influencing the election in his favor. When the Fed is obliged to stay neutral for political reasons, it is prevented from doing its job—that is, tightening or easing money to serve the country's best long-term interests. Furthermore, if the Fed is prevented from taking action for some time, when it finally does act it must take more drastic action than would have been necessary if it could have acted gradually. Consider the six months after the 1972 election. During this period (which followed a long period of inaction) the Fed was obliged to tighten money severely. The result was the 1973–74 collapse.

Second, membership on the Federal Reserve Board entails a potential for conflict of interest. What board members would allow their trusts to be invested in common stocks or long-term bonds while knowing that money must soon be tightened? Board members who did such a thing would lose their assets as stock and bond prices declined.

Interest Rate Studies

Other writers have suggested various correlations between interest rates and stock market trends. Let's take a look at some of them.

Correlations Involving One or More Specific Rates

Federal funds rate.   The Federal funds rate is often used to predict stock market trends. Some market analysts maintain a constant comparison between the Federal funds rate and the prime rate. Since banks normally borrow Federal funds at interest rates lower than the prime rate, the Federal funds rate is usually lower than the prime rate. When banks pay a Federal funds rate that is higher than the prime rate, the prime rate is likely to be raised, indicating tighter money.

Other analysts compare the Federal funds rate and the discount rate. One financial service notes that between 1966 and 1976, the stock market was extremely vulnerable whenever the Federal funds rate held above the discount rate for very long. Since the Federal funds rate is influenced by the market, and the discount rate is set by the Fed, changes in the former usually precede changes in the latter.[27] The Federal funds rate is likely to stay above the discount rate for long periods only when money is tight. This indicates either that the Federal funds rate is rising faster than the discount rate, or that the Fed wants to help out certain banks by offering them lower rates on loans.

Discount rate. A few writers have studied the effect of changes in the discount rate. Arthur A. Merrill found that these changes affected stock prices for as long as several months after they occurred. He noted that when the discount rate goes down, stocks go up immediately. And when the discount rate goes up, stocks tend to go down; however, this effect is not strong enough to reserve a rising trend.[28]

T-bill rates. The cyclical aspect of savings flows is affected by T-bill rates (Fig. 2-16). Rising T-bill rates attract money away from savings held at savings and loan associations. This simply confirms that, all else being equal, money seeks the highest possible return.

T-bill rates have also been correlated with the discount rate. Market analyst David Upshaw offers these general timing rules:

- Buy when T-bill rates fall below the discount rate and the discount rate is reduced—usually after a bear market has ended.
- Sell when T-bill rates rise above the discount rate and the discount rate is increased. Do not sell, however, if the increase in the discount rate places that rate back above the T-bill rate.

Upshaw believes that these signals have worked best since 1968, because since 1968 the stock market has become hypersensitive to changes in interest rates. When portfolio managers feel that debt instruments are no longer an attractive alternative to owning stocks, Upshaw believes that these signals may lose their usefulness.[29]

Short-term interest rates. Some writers study the effect of changes in short-term interest rates. Analysts at Merrill Lynch believe that the direction of the trend in these rates is a crucial element in market timing. The most dynamic phase of a bull market usually occurs when short-term rates are falling sharply below long-term rates. This phase is signaled by a sharp increase in the ratio of long-term bond rates to short-term 90-day T-bill rates. When this ratio has peaked, it often has signaled an impending correction in the market. The level of the ratio must be considered, because the major trend usually holds firm until the indicator drops below a certain level. It is also important to consider the change in short-term rates in relation to the recent trend, rather than the absolute interest level.

Merrill Lynch adds that the market seldom peaks until well after T-bill rates have reached a low. Since World War II, bull markets have continued from 7 to 44 months after such a low.[30]

Some writers' definitions of tight money involve the relationship between long- and short-term interest rates. One of these definitions is based on a comparison that resembles my own comparison between T-bill rates and government bond rates. It goes like this. *Boardroom Reports* contends that rising interest rates are bad for business. Therefore, when

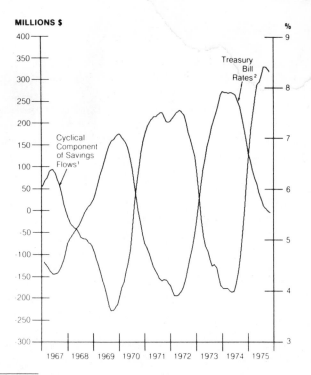

[1] Cyclical component of net new savings at California savings and loan associations, January 1967 through November 1975.
[2] Twelve-month centered moving average of the new issue rate on U.S. Government 3-month bills (auction average), percent per annum, January 1967 through November 1975.

FIGURE 2-16.   Cyclical component of savings flows and moving average of three-month Treasury bill rates (January 1967–November 1975). [*SOURCE:* Reproduced from *Commentary*, Federal Home Loan Bank of San Francisco, Calif., June 1976, p. 2.]

interest rates rise, stock prices fall. Conversely, stock prices rise when interest rates drop, on the premise that easier and cheaper loans are good for business. Thus the trend in interest rates anticipates trends in the stock market. The formula is as follows: Divide Barron's ten high-grade bond yield index by the 90-day U.S. T-bill yield. If the ratio is over 1.4 to 1, it is considered favorable. If the ratio drops below 1.4 to 1, this drop constitutes an initial "Sell" signal. If it drops below 1.2 to 1, the drop constitutes a strong "Sell" signal. Avoid stock ownership if the ratio stays below 1.2 to 1. However, if the ratio rises above 1.2 to 1, this constitutes an initial "Buy" signal. And if the ratio moves up through 1.4 to 1, become fully invested.[31]

General Correlations

The investment rules I have just described are based on correlations between specific rates. Some writers have also formulated rules based on more general correlations.

Keran model. Michael W. Keran, a Federal Reserve Bank economist, has developed a model to forecast stock prices. It is based on two variables: (1) expected earnings, and (2) expected interest rates. Keran points out that since stock prices affect interest rates and earnings, there is a two-way causation. It follows, however, that both of his variables may be biased.

Keran maintains that actual inflation helps the stock market, because it increases earnings. Expected inflation, however, hurts the stock market, because it increases interest rates.[32]

Three-step-and-stumble rule. The three-step-and-stumble rule was formulated by Arthur Weisenberger & Co., an advisory service. It states: "Whenever three successive rises occur in any of the three rates set by the monetary authorities, the investor should beware, for some time thereafter the market is likely to suffer a substantial—perhaps serious—setback."[33]

This rule signaled trouble on six different occasions: November 3, 1919; July 13, 1928; August 13, 1948; September 9, 1955; March 6, 1959; and December 6, 1965.[34] However, there was considerable variation as to how long it took stocks to react, how badly they fell, and how long the downward trend lasted. The 1919 signal was followed by a steep drop, which did not bottom out until mid-1921. I discussed the 1928 signal earlier; it resulted in a generally rising market to September 1929, followed by another steep drop. The 1948 signal was followed by a relatively slight decline. The 1955 signal was followed by a wavering market until the break in 1957.[35] The 1959 signal was followed by a sharp decline, ending in fall 1960.

The three-step-and-stumble rule gave no warning of the 1937 decline. It completely overlooked one very important TMT signal—the reserve requirement. If you look ahead at Figure 3-5b in Chapter 3, you will see that an increase in the margin requirement in February 1936, followed by two increases in the reserve requirement, would have given a three-step signal at the top on March 1, 1937; just before a 50 percent decline. This rule deals with only three TMT signals; for that reason, I believe it is less accurate than the rule proposed in this book.

The three-step-and-stumble rule is consistent with the TMT hypotheses. However, I would like to propose a corollary. It might be called the "three-step" (easier money) "-and-a-jump" (bull market) rule. This corollary would be as useful in indicating when to buy as the three-step-and-stumble rule is in indicating when to sell.

Fed watching. Many investors make their decisions after observing the actions of the Federal Reserve. This is called *Fed watching.* The rule is to sell when the Fed seems about to tighten credit. "Sell" signals, then, are increases in: bank reserve requirements; the discount rate; or margin requirements. One writer points out that the Fed raised the discount rate six times between January and July 1973, and that investors who engaged in timely Fed watching could have taken their profits near the peak.[36]

Financial analyst Arthur Merrill has studied the effect of changes in discount rates, margin requirements, and bank reserve requirements on the stock market. He believes that changes in these rates encourage a trend to continue. For example, the easing of credit encourages a bull market; the tightening of credit encourages a bear market. Merrill writes that when the Fed wants to strengthen the economy, it acts to bring about the early stages of a bull market.[37]

Finally, Ben Weberman, the economics editor of *Forbes* magazine, describes what he calls an "overlooked message" from the Fed:

> What was the signal from the Fed? It appeared in the last week of December [1976], and few money-market pundits recognized it. It was a subtle signal, but for the careful Fed-watcher, there was no mistaking its impact.
>
> It appeared in the tightly edited summary of the November 16 meeting of the Fed's Open Market Committee. The summary read as follows:
>
> "It was observed that nominal long-term interest rates were still high by postwar standards and that—the rate of inflation notwithstanding—current levels of interest rates tended to discourage some business managers from undertaking or enlarging commitments to make capital investments and consumers from undertaking commitments to buy houses.
>
> "Modest downward pressure on short-term interest rates, it was argued, would be communicated in some degree to longer term rates, as managers of the portfolios of financial institutions lengthened the average maturities of those portfolios in an effort to maintain a satisfactory overall return."
>
> Stop and read that statement again. It is dynamite to any experienced Fed-watcher . . . .
>
> Quite clearly, most money-market managers missed this signal . . . .
>
> At the risk of sounding monotonous, I repeat: *Long-term interest rates are going to continue their downward path.* The oracle has spoken—however obliquely—and no investor should ignore his message.[38]

It is true that the Fed had signaled easier money, but this news was two months old when it was reported. By comparison, two TMT signals (lowered discount rate and reserve requirements) were reported instantly. Weberman's findings—and his conclusions—confirm the TMT hypotheses.

Bond and Stock Market Trends

Managers of large portfolios are always wondering what to invest in. This book does not address the various alternatives or suggest which stocks to buy. However, TMT implies that when interest rates are up and money is tight, short-term investments, such as U.S. Treasury bill, certificates of deposit, and short-term bonds, are prudent, attractive alternatives. And when money is easy, the best investments are long-term bonds or stocks.

Many analysts have compared bond market and stock market trends. A rising bond market usually predicts a rising stock market. Richard A. Hanan, a seasoned investment manager, told me that the bond market and the stock market generally move in the same direction. Between 1955 and 1975, he said, there have been only two exceptions to this rule: The first occurred in 1959, when the stock market moved up while the bond market moved down, and the second occurred in 1962, when the reverse came about.[39]

Merrill Lynch has computed a bond/stock ratio that compares the interest yield on the S&P High-Grade Bond Index with the earnings-to-price ratio of the S&P 400 Industrial Index. In the late 1920s, bond yields were higher than stock earnings. In the depression years 1929–32, stock earnings rose to more than three times the yield on bonds. The return of confidence in the 1960s and early 1970s produced an approximate one-to-one bond/stock ratio.[40]

Other Trends Correlated with Interest Rates

Various writers have described other trends that seem to be correlated with interest rates. Market cycles are what one investment manager uses to base his investments on:

> Historically, we have invested in stocks during periods of easing monetary conditions, decelerating recessions and early economic expansions. We want to liquidate our stock positions in the late stages of an economic uptrend, when money markets significantly tighten, and offer our clients attractive yields in fixed income securities. We typically roll-over short maturity discount paper until the yield curve peaks out and returns to a positive relationship between short-term and long-term rates. At this point, we shift major portions of our assets into the bond market, and as soon as interest rates reach a level conducive to better business conditions, we return to the stock market. This portfolio cycle has been successfully used for decades in the United States.[41]

Certain groups of stock are particularly sensitive to interest rates, including insurance, financial, savings and loan, bank, and utility stocks. According to investment manager Ricardo Cortez, these groups have gone up in the past when interest rates seemed to be heading down.[42]

One stock market analyst, Norman G. Fosback, claimed that utility stocks are so sensitive to interest rates that developments in the bond and money markets are often reflected in the Dow Jones Utility Average long before they are reflected in the stock market as a whole. For this reason, utility stocks can be quite a useful leading indicator of general market trends.[43] Since utility stocks are affected by changes in interest rates, their direction serves to signal tight or easy money. For example, when utility stock prices are trending up, this means that money is growing easier and that the market for other stocks should rise.

Edson Gould, the well-known market analyst and financial writer, has said, "Monetary indicators are always early."[44] This view coincides with my own: Monetary indicators—that is, tight and easy money signals—are usually visible early enough to let an investor become properly invested before the stock market rises or falls significantly.

One financial service monitors several dozen stock market indicators, including six that are worth mentioning here because they indicate interest rate trends and availability of money. These indicators are:

1. The "Alert" indicator, a ratio of AAA bonds divided by 13-week T-bills;
2. The level and trend of the margin debit;
3. The percentage, level, and trend of cash held by mutual funds;
4. The net free reserves and whether this figure is in the net free or net borrowed area;
5. The trend and level of T-bills;
6. The trend of the government bond 4.25 percent maturing in 1987–92.[45]

Money Availability Studies

Many experts have examined the effect that the availability and growth of money has on the stock market. Some of their studies are discussed below.

Money Availability: Approaches to Tight Money Timing

Bank debit/loan ratio. The *Bank Credit Analyst* is a monthly investment service with a sophisticated approach to tight money timing.[46]

According to A. Hamilton Bolton, the service's former editor, the bank debit/loan ratio is not only fundamental to any study of bank credit but it is also the single most useful index of economic data for interpreting the stock market economic environment. Bolton claims that it has signaled every major decline in the stock market (except the declines of 1929 and 1962), as well as every major rise. However, he says this accuracy depends on being able to interpret the data accurately.[47]

Net loanable funds. Bolton proposes other approaches to timing. One is to track the net loanable funds. For example, if loans gain rapidly in relation to deposits, it means that money and credit are tightening, which in turn means that the business cycle will soon be in trouble. Since stock prices usually anticipate trouble in the business cycle, clear indications of a decline in net loanable funds mean "Sell."[48] Another of Bolton's approaches is to monitor bank liquidity—that is, bank deposits and excess reserves minus loans and borrowings.[49]

Free reserves. Irvin L. Kellner, Economist and Vice-president of Manufacturers Hanover Trust Co., uses Federal Reserve credit policy to forecast share price trends. "When the banking system gets more reserves from the Fed," Kellner says, "the stock market is heading for a rise within three months."[50] Figure 2-17 illustrates this correlation.

Market analyst Arthur A. Merrill says that of all his indicators, bank free reserves are most accurate in forecasting market swings of 10 percent or more. However, they forecast 5 percent swings less effectively. Merrill gets his "Buy" signal when free reserves go above a minus $80 million, and his "Sell" signal when they drop below a minus $940 million in quartiles. He chose these limits because past figures proved that they had given the best performance. Therefore, these limits might produce similar results in the future.[51]

One financial service observes that the market is vulnerable when the five-week moving average of bank reserves reaches a net borrowed figure of $500 million or more[52]—a figure that coincides with the TMT signal defined here.

Net deposit flow into savings and loan associations. Tight money affects savings and loan statistics. Figure 2-18 shows the net savings gains realized by savings and loan associations from 1966 to 1974. In late 1966, net savings spurted upward, indicating easy money, near the low point of the stock market. In late 1968, net savings gave no real positive signal near the top of the market to indicate tight money. The next market bottom occurred in June 1970, just after net savings had spurted upward (again indicating easy money). Net savings declined sharply in early 1973, near a major market top, indicating tight money. According to the 1974 edition of the *Savings and Loan Fact Book*, "The sharp drop in 1973 was

Federal Reserve credit policy, as reflected in the relative availability of bank reserves, is a major force behind stock market rises and falls. Irwin L. Kellner, economist and vice president of Manufacturers Hanover Trust Co., uses this to forecast share price trends.

It works like this: When the banking system as a whole gets more reserves from the Federal Reserve, the stock market is heading for a rise within three months. Since reserves are a leading indicator, the reserve curve is shown on the chart three months ahead of actual timing.

The Dow Jones industrials followed the reserve curve to a high of 1015 last September before election, oil and economic uncertainties pulled the rate back. As these concerns fade, the stock market should return to the 1000-to-1500 zone this winter, Kellner believes.

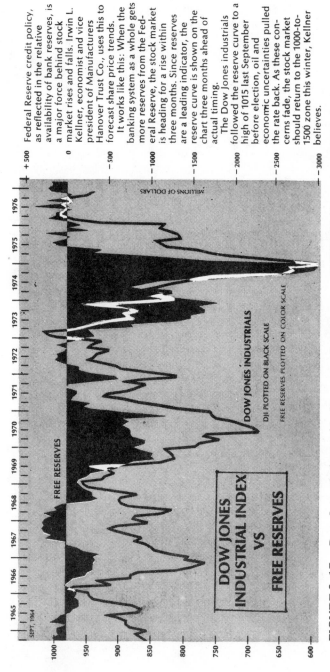

FIGURE 2-17. Dow Jones Industrial Index versus free reserves. [SOURCE: Reproduced from "Look Before You Leap—to Conclusions," Forbes, January 1, 1977, p. 207, reprinted by permission.]

Billions of Dollars

FIGURE 2-18. Net savings gains at associations (seasonally adjusted). [SOURCE: Reproduced from United States League of Savings Associations, '74 Savings & Loan Fact Book. Chicago: United States League of Savings Associations, 1974, p. 73.]

caused by the imposition of tight money policies and the resulting sharp rise in interest rates."[53]

The period 1966 to 1974 has a relatively good correlation between major changes in net savings and major changes in the trend of the stock market. So we can conclude that tight money not only makes the stock market decline, but also makes savings into savings and loan associations decline.

Flow of funds analysis. The Federal Reserve Board's flow of funds analysis offers a good picture of the entire U.S. financial economy. This analysis, an invaluable source of statistics, appears quarterly and presents seasonally adjusted data.[54] Because these data may be up to six months old by the time they are published, they form an impractical basis for making investment decisions.[55] Therefore, I have not attempted to analyze them for tight and easy money conditions.

Growth of Money Supply

Many studies have examined the growth rate of money and how this growth rate affects the stock market. The generally accepted theory is that when money supply is increasing, stock prices tend to rise. When new money is invested in the stock market, higher stock prices result almost immediately. In contrast, money invested in business takes much longer to bring profits; it must first be invested in new machinery, personnel, raw materials, and advertising. This is one reason why the stock market has been such a good forecaster of the economy.

Money supply growth and inflation. There is a close relationship between money supply growth and inflation, as Dr. Beryl Sprinkel's insightful study demonstrates. Sprinkel shows that growth in money supply divided by real gross national product (GNP) parallels the growth in the consumer price index (CPI). In other words, if the government prints 20 percent more dollars in a period when the GNP is going sideways, an inflation of approximately 20 percent will result.[56]

Figure 2-19 shows the S&P 500 Index for the period 1966 to 1976, before and after adjusting for inflation.

According to the Bank of America's *Weekly Monetary Summary,* the variation in the long-term inflation rate is substantially due to the long-term growth rate in money. From 1954 to 1964, the money growth rate ranged from 1.25 to 3.5 percent, while the inflation rate ranged from 1.5

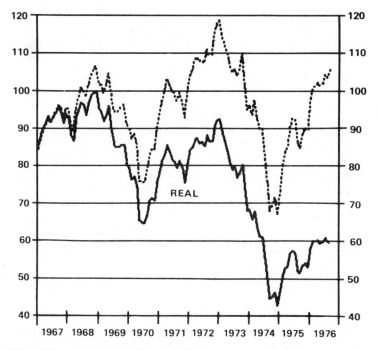

FIGURE 2-19. Standard & Poor's 500—nominal (1976) and real (1967) dollars. [SOURCE: Reproduced from *Monthly Investment Strategy.* New York: Bache Halsey Stuart & Co., October 1976, p. 23.]

to 3 percent. Over the next ten years, the money growth rate increased steadily, reaching a range of 5.8 to 6.2 percent from late 1972 to mid-1975. This drove up the long-term inflation rate, which peaked at 6.8 percent in late 1975.[57]

According to the Harris Bank's *Barometer of Business*, "Inflation is primarily the result of the government creating too much money."[58] The *Barometer* cites a correlation similar to the one mentioned by the Bank of America (Table 2-6).

Money supply growth and the stock market. The Sprinkel study also suggests a relationship between growth in money supply and the stock market.[59] Unfortunately, this is one of those relationships that, with hindsight, can be explained clearly, but that cannot be used to forecast the stock market. Why not? Because money supply growth occasionally lags the stock market at critical turning points in the market.

The *Wall Street Journal* tends to emphasize the importance of money supply growth to the economy. For example, "The money supply is considered a key economic determinant. Too fast a growth in the supply, economists say, could heat inflationary fires, while too slow a growth could slow the economy."[60]

The relationship between money supply growth and business growth is mentioned by the editors of the Bank of America's *Weekly Monetary Summary*. "In the past," they say, "declines in real money (M_1) have signaled business downturns with a lead, on average, of roughly 10 months."[61] The Sprinkel study claims that a change in the rate of money supply growth has consistently preceded a turning point in the business cycle, with an average lead time of 15 to 16 months. By contrast, a change in stock prices leads a change in the business cycle by an average of five to six months. More specifically, growth in money supply leads a business *upturn* by an average of eight months. A rise in stock prices leads a business upturn by an average of four to five months. And changes in monetary growth lead changes in stock prices by an average of nine months prior to a bear market, and by two or three months prior to a bull market.[62]

These lead times are *averages*. Actually, for the period 1918 to

TABLE 2-6. Money and inflation (annual rates of change).

	Money (%)	Consumer Prices (%)
1955–65	2.2	1.7
1965–75	5.6	5.5

[SOURCE: *Weekly Monetary Summary*. San Francisco: Bank of America, Bank Investment Services Division, August 20, 1976, p. 1.]

1969, bear market lead times for changes in money supply ranged from minus 1 month to plus 21 months. And bull markets lead times ranged from minus 2 months to plus 11 months, depending on how the figures are interpreted.[63]

According to Sprinkel, major bull and bear markets cannot develop without affecting money supply growth; however, the lead time in such cases varies considerably. Therefore, the monetary theory of stock price fluctuation appears to be a good, but imperfect, predictor.[64] I, for one, agree: Changes in money supply growth may have some degree of predictive power, but they barely help the investor, who must decide exactly when to buy or sell.

Another expert who has examined the effect of money supply growth on the stock market is economist Michael Keran. His conclusion? Changes in nominal money stock have little direct influence on stock prices. However, they do have a major indirect effect, in that they influence the investor's expectations about inflation and corporate earnings.[65]

The doubts I've expressed thus far about the existence of a simple link between money supply growth and stock prices are shared by economist Robert D. Auerbach of the Federal Reserve Bank of Kansas City. According to his findings, changes in stock prices are related to both current and future changes in money supply, but not to past changes. If this is true, then the stock market might be a better forecaster of future money supply than money supply is a forecaster of the stock market.[66] Economist Richard V. L. Cooper's study also concluded that significant money supply lead and lag relationships can't really be evaluated on the basis of regression analysis.[67]

Auerbach questions the statistical methodologies and techniques used by Sprinkel, Keran, and Kenneth E. Homa and Dwight M. Jaffee to investigate the relationship between money supply rates and the stock market. His own tests indicate an absence of relationship between changes in money supply rates and future stock yields, and a weak relationship between yields from stocks and current and future changes in money supply rates.[68]

There is no good correlation between interest rates and the stock market, says one financial advisory service.[69] At first this statement seems to conflict with the use of interest rates as TMT signals. However, such TMT signals deal primarily with *changes* in interest rates, not with interest rate levels (which are initiated by the Fed). This service also finds a good broad correlation between changes in the money supply and the stock market.[70] I agree; however, this correlation is much too broad to be useful for most investors.

The Fed watchers on Wall Street were reportedly having a hard time

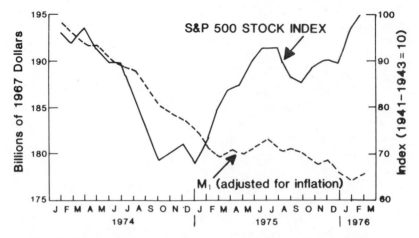

FIGURE 2-20. S&P 500 Index versus M_1 adjusted for inflation.

making a profit from watching the money supply, according to a recent article in *Fortune*.[71] There was, in fact, an excellent correlation between the annual rate of growth in money supply and the annual rate of stock market returns; however, the stock market often leads the money supply.

On the basis of such data, we can draw the following conclusions:

- Money supply growth is highly overrated as a forecaster of stock market trends. We can't even be sure that it has any predictive value at all. For example, changes in money supply (M_1) in no way helped forecast the 1975 bull market (Fig. 2-20).
- There is a rough correlation between the money supply (deflated by the consumer price index) and the stock market (Fig. 2-21). When real money supply is growing, the stock market is likely to continue upwards. When real money is declining, the stock market is vulnerable. This correlation may contain the chief value of the money-supply variable.
- Peaks in money growth have occurred up to three years before a major decline. Such a time lag could mislead anyone with the daily responsibility of managing securities. A major uptrending market can occur even after money-supply growth has turned down.

Despite the many studies that have been done to determine the relationship between the growth of money and the stock market, the results are vague, at best. However, the aforementioned body of literature seems unopposed to the Tight Money Timing hypothesis.

Two methods for monitoring TMT signals appear in the next chapter,

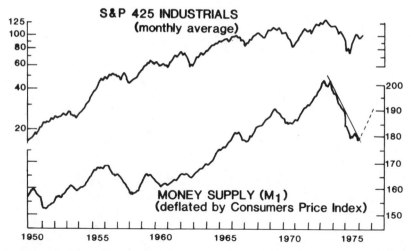

FIGURE 2–21. The stock market and the trend of real money supply. [*SOURCE*: Reproduced from *Bank Credit Analyst*. Montreal: December 1975, p. 26.]

as well as a weekly analysis for the period 1966 to 1981 and a monthly overview for the period 1914 to 1981.

NOTES

1. "Stimulus Becomes the Inevitable Policy," *Business Week*, December 6, 1976, p. 20.
2. Both of these documents are published by the U.S. Federal Reserve Board, Division of Administrative Services, Publications Services. The Federal Reserve Bank discount rates for the period November 1914 through December 1980 are listed in Appendix C.
3. The Federal funds rates for the period 1960 to 1981 are listed in Appendix B.
4. The New York Stock Exchange sets the margin requirements for U.S. government securities and municipal bonds. Brokerage houses may set higher margin requirements for their customers than the minimum required by the Fed or the New York Stock Exchange.
5. Free reserves for the period January 1946 to January 1981 are listed in Appendix B.
6. U.S. Federal Reserve Board, Division of Administrative Services, *Federal Reserve Bulletin* (published monthly).

7. Prime rates charged by banks on short-term business loans for the period 1929 to 1981 are listed in Appendix C.

8. William Q. Steinmetz, business consultant, interview held in Piedmont, Calif., May 15, 1976.

9. Treasury bill rates for the period January 1920 through December 1980 are listed in Appendix B.

10. U.S. government bond yields for the period January 1919 through December 1980 are listed in Appendix B.

11. Detailed statistics are published in U.S. Department of Treasury, Office of the Secretary, Superintendent of Documents, *Treasury Bulletin* (published monthly).

12. Charles J. Elia, "Heard on the Street," *Wall Street Journal*, December 9, 1974, p. 35; ibid., *Wall Street Journal*, December 10, 1974, p. 45.

13. F. F. James, "Monthly Moving Averages—An Effective Investment Tool?" *Journal of Financial and Quantitative Analysis* 3 (September 1968):315–26.

14. "A Fed Heavyweight Sizes up Monetary Policy," *Business Week*, August 11, 1975, p. 52.

15. Joe Wahead, Economist, Wells Fargo Bank, San Francisco, Calif., interview held by telephone, February 25, 1976.

16. Sherman Maisel, Professor of Applied Economics and Finance, University of California, Berkeley, interview held in Berkeley, Calif., April 15, 1976.

17. William M. Burke, Senior Economist and Director of Public Information, Federal Reserve Bank of San Francisco, interview held in San Francisco, Calif., February 10, 1976.

18. Monte Gordon, Director of Research, Dreyfus Corp., interview held by telephone, February 13, 1976.

19. Michael W. Keran, "Expectations and the Stock Market," paper presented at the meeting of the Technical Securities Analysts of San Francisco, San Francisco, Calif., March 18, 1976.

20. Wilfred R. George to Arthur F. Burns, August 6, 1976.

21. Normand Bernard, Special Assistant to the Federal Reserve Board, to Wilfred R. George, August 16, 1976.

22. Warren Greene, Vice-President, American Investors Fund, interview held by telephone, March 3, 1976.

23. Dan Dorfman, "The Next Big Market Play: The View from B of A," *New West Magazine*, June 7, 1976, p. 14.

24. Burke, interview, February 10, 1976.

25. Gary Allen, "Federal Reserve: The Trillion-Dollar Conspiracy," *American Opinion*, February 1976, p. 79.

26. Sherman J. Maisel, interview, April 15, 1976. Dr. Maisel's knowledge of this subject is recorded in Sherman J. Maisel, *Managing the Dollar*. New York:Norton, 1973.

27. *Chartist*, Long Beach, Calif., October 1976, p. 2.

28. Arthur A. Merrill, "Delayed Reaction, *"Barron's National Business and Financial Weekly*, December 13, 1965, p. 9.

29. Charles J. Elia, "Moves in Treasury-Bill Yields, Discount Rates Correlated by

Analyst to Major Market Swings," *Wall Street Journal*, May 26, 1976, p. 39.
30. Charles J. Elia, "Short-Term Rates Seen Rising as Recovery Resumes, Though Analysts' Timetables Differ," *Wall Street Journal*, October 13, 1976, p. 43; and James Bohan and Robert J. Farrell, *Interest Rates and Stock Prices*. New York:Merrill Lynch, Pierce, Fenner & Smith, Securities Research Division, 1976, pp. 9–11.
31. "Investment Decisions," *Boardroom Reports*, February 29, 1976, p. 6.
32. Michael W. Keran, "Forecasting Stock Prices," *Journal of Portfolio Management* 1 (Winter 1975):52–60.
33. Arthur A. Merrill, "Delayed Reaction," p. 9.
34. Ibid.
35. These signals are illustrated in Figures 3–5a through 3–5d.
36. Barbara G. Quint, "When To Bail Out of Your Stocks," *Money Magazine*, December 1976, pp. 36–38.
37. Arthur A. Merrill, *Behavior of Prices on Wall Street* (Chappaqua, N.Y.: Analysis Press, 1966, pp. 36–37.
38. Ben Weberman, "The Oracle Has Spoken," *Forbes*, January 15, 1977, p. 78.
39. Richard A. Hanan, interview held in San Francisco, Calif., March 3, 1976.
40. Bohan and Farrell, *Interest Rates*, pp. 3–4.
41. Stephenson & Co., Denver, Colo., response to a survey conducted by Bache & Co., San Francisco, Calif., ca. 1975.
42. Charles J. Elia, "'Top Growth Stocks, Third Period Resurgence Seen as Sign of Adjustment to Economic Shifts," *Wall Street Journal*, October 27, 1976, p. 47.
43. Norman G. Fosback, *Stock Market Logic*. Ft. Lauderdale, Fla.:Institute for Economic Research, 1976, p. 11.
44. PBS, "Wall Street Week," November 12, 1976.
45. *Professional Tape Reader*. New York: Radcap, September 23, 1976, pp. 6–7.
46. *Bank Credit Analyst*, Montreal (published monthly).
47. Arthur H. Bolton, *Money and Investment Profits*. Homewood, Ill.: Dow Jones-Irwin, 1967, p. 169.
48. Ibid., pp. 155–57.
49. Ibid., pp. 164–65.
50. "Look before You Leap—to Conclusions," *Forbes*, January 1, 1977, p. 207.
51. Arthur A. Merrill, *Indicator Accuracy*, paper presented at the meeting of the Market Technicians Association and the New York Society of Security Analysts, New York, October 5, 1977 (Chappaqua, N.Y.: Analysis Press, n.d.).
52. *Chartist*, October 21, 1976, pp. 2–3.
53. United States League of Savings Associations, *'74 Savings & Loan Fact Book*. Chicago: United States League of Savings Associations, 1974, p. 73.
54. U.S. Federal Reserve Board, Division of Research and Statistics, *Flow of Funds* (published quarterly).
55. Stephen B. Packer, "Flow of Funds Analysis—Its Uses and Limitations," in *CFA Readings in Financial Analysis*, 2d ed. Homewood, Ill.: Irwin, 1970,

pp. 118–19.

56. Beryl Sprinkel, *Money and Markets: A Monetarist View*. Homewood, Ill.:Irwin, 1971, pp. 167–73.
57. *Weekly Monetary Summary*. San Francisco, Calif.:Bank of America, Bank Investment Services Division, August 20, 1976, p. 1.
58. *Barometer of Business*. Chicago: Harris Bank, June 1976, p. 1.
59. Sprinkel, *Money and Markets*, pp. 217–41.
60. "Money Supply Surged in October 27 Week, Putting Growth Rate Near Fed Maximum," *Wall Street Journal*, November 5, 1976, p. 22.
61. *Weekly Monetary Summary*, San Francisco, Calif.:Bank of America, Bank Investment Services Division, November 19, 1976, p. 1.
62. Sprinkel, *Money and Markets*, pp. 224–25.
63. Ibid., p. 225.
64. Ibid., p. 241.
65. Michael W. Keran, "Expectations, Money, and the Stock Market," *Review*, Federal Reserve Bank of St. Louis, January 1971, pp. 16–31; reprint ed., Reprint Series No. 63, St. Louis, Mo.:Federal Reserve Bank of St. Louis, n.d.
66. Robert D. Auerbach, "Money and Stock Prices," *Monthly Review*, Kansas City, Mo.:Federal Reserve Bank of Kansas City, September–October 1976, pp. 3–11.
67. Richard V. L. Cooper, "Efficient Capital Markets and the Quantity Theory of Money," *Journal of Finance*, June 1974:887–908, as cited in *Monthly Review*, Kansas City, Mo.:Federal Reserve Bank of Kansas City, September–October 1976, p. 7.
68. Robert D. Auerbach, "Money and Stock Prices," p. 11.
69. *Findings and Forecasts*, Anemetrics, New York, November 17, 1976, p. 44.
70. Ibid.
71. A. F. Ehrbar, "How the Money Supply Drives the Stock Market," *Fortune*, October 1975, pp. 105–109.

3

MONITORING TMT SIGNALS

You can use either of two methods to monitor TMT signals, both of which give a running history of monetary changes. The first method uses the TMT Worksheet, the second the TMT Workchart.

THE TMT WORKSHEET

If you're the kind who prefers statistical tabulation to charts, the TMT Worksheet is for you (see Tables 3-1 and 3-2 to get an idea of the Worksheet format).

The TMT Worksheet distinguishes *overt* TMT signals from *covert* TMT signals. In Chapter 1 we discussed these two categories of signals briefly, and mentioned that the five overt TMT signals are relatively easy to trace. These are:

- Discount rate;
- Margin requirement;
- Prime rate;
- Regulation Q; and
- Reserve requirement.

As changes in these signals occur, they are recorded from data published in financial newspapers such as the *Wall Street Journal* or *Barron's*.[1]

There are three covert TMT signals: (1) the Federal funds rate; (2) the free-reserves rate; and (3) the T-bill rate versus long-term government bond rate. Up-to-date figures for the first three rates are published weekly in the *Wall Street Journal* (Fig. 3-1). The long-term government bond index is published in the *Federal Reserve Bulletin*.

Although the covert TMT signals are relatively difficult to trace, they tend to confirm the direction of the overt signals. To trace the Federal funds rate and free reserves, a trend-defining technique such as a moving average must be used.[2] The T-bill and long-term government bond rates can be compared by using data published in the *Federal Reserve Bulletin*:

TABLE 3-1. TMT worksheet, 1974.

1974 Date	Overt Signals					Covert Signals			
	Discount Rate (↓ 7.5%)*	Margin Req. ↑65 to 50%	Prime Rate (↑ 9.75%)*	Regulation Q (↓ Raised)*	Reserve Requirements (↓ Raised)*	Federal Funds (↓ Trend: Up)*	Net Borrowed Reserves (↓ > $500M)*	US T-Bills/ LT Gov't. Bonds (↑ Bills > Bond Rates)*	S&P 500 Index
1– 4									98.90
–11									93.66
–18									95.56
–25									96.63
2– 1			↑ 9.75 to 9.5%						95.32
– 8									92.33
–15			↑ 9.5 to 9.25%						92.27
–22			↑ 9.25 to 9.0%						95.39
3– 1									
– 8			↑ 9.0 to 8.75%						95.53
–15									97.78
–22			ⓐ 8.75 to 9.0%						99.28 High
–29			↓ 9.0 to 9.25%						97.27
4– 5			↓ 9.25 to 9.75%						93.98
–12			↓ 9.75 to 10.0%						93.01
–19			↓ 10.0 to 10.25%						92.12
–26	7.25 to 8.0%		↓ 10.5 to 10.5%						93.75
5– 3			↓ 10.5 to 10.75%						90.18
–10			↓ 10.75 to 11.25%						91.29
–17			↓ 11.25 to 11.5%						91.47
–25									88.21
–31									88.58
									87.28

76

Date		Value
6- 7		92.55
-14		91.30
-21		87.46
-28		86.00
7- 5	↓ 11.5 to 11.75%	83.66
-12	↓ 11.75 to 12.0%	83.15
-19		83.54
-26		82.40
8- 2		78.59
- 9		80.86
-16		75.67
-23		71.55
-30		72.15
9- 6		71.42
-13		65.20
-20		70.14
-27		64.94
10- 4	⊕12.0 to 11.75% ⊕ Trend: Down	62.34 Low
-11	↑ 11.75 to 11.5%	71.14
-18		72.28
-25		70.12
11- 1	↑ 11.5 to 11.25%	73.88
- 8	↑ 11.25 to 11.0%	74.91
-15	↑ 11.0 to 10.75%	71.91
-22		68.90
-29	↑ 10.75 to 10.5%	69.97
12- 6	⊕8.0 to 7.75% ⊕ Lowered ⊕ <$500M	65.01
-13		67.07
-20	(No change in Reg. Q all year)	66.91
-27		67.14

(T-bills were higher than bond rates all year)

NOTES: Asterisks * indicate status as of 1 January 1974.
Circled arrows ⊕⊕ indicate trend reversals.
Arrows indicate tighter money ↓ and easier money ↑.

77

TABLE 3-2. TMT worksheet, 1975.

| | Overt Signals | | | | Covert Signals | | | | |
	Discount Rate	Margin Req.	Prime Rate	Regulation Q	Reserve Requirements	Federal Funds	Net Borrowed Reserves	US T-Bills/ LT Gov't. Bonds	S&P 500 Index
1975 Date	(↑ 7.75%)*	(↓50%)*			(↑Lowered)*	(↑Trend: Down)*	(↑ < $500M)*	(↓Bills > Bond Rates)* ⊕ Bills < Bond Rates	
1- 3	↑7.75 to 7.25%		↑10.5 to 10.25%						70.71
-10			↑10.25 to 10.0%						72.61
-17			↑10.0 to 9.75%						70.96
-24			↑9.75 to 9.5%						72.98
-31									76.98
2- 7	↑ 7.25 to 6.75%		↑9.5 to 9.25%						78.63
-14			↑9.25 to 9.0%						81.50
-21			↑9.0 to 8.75%		Lowered				82.62
-28			↑8.75 to 8.5%						81.59
3- 7	↑ 6.75 to 6.25%		↑8.5 to 8.25%						84.30
-14			↑8.25 to 8.0%						84.76
-21			↑8.0 to 7.75%						83.39
-28			↑7.75 to 7.5%						83.85
4- 4									80.88
-11									84.18
-18									86.30
-25									86.62
5- 2									89.22
-9	↑ 6.25 to 6.0%								90.53
-16			↑7.5 to 7.25%						90.43
-23									90.58
-30									91.15

Date	Rate Change	Trend	High/Low
6- 6	↑7.25 to 7.0%		92.48
-13			90.52
-20			92.61
-27			94.81 High
7- 4		⊕ Trend: Up	94.36
-11	⊕7.0 to 7.25%		94.66
-18			93.20
-25			89.29
8- 1	↓7.25 to 7.5%		87.99
- 8			86.02
-15	↓7.5 to 7.75%		86.36
-22			84.28
-29			86.88
9- 5			85.62
-12			83.30 Low
-19	↓7.75 to 8.0%		85.88
-26			86.19
10- 3			85.95
-10			88.21
-17			88.86
-24	↑ Lowered		89.83
-31	⊕8.0 to 7.75%		89.04
11- 7	↑7.75 to 7.5%	⊕ Trend: Down	89.33
-19			90.97
-21			89.53
-28			91.24
12- 5	↑7.5 to 7.25%		86.82
-12			87.83
-19	(No change in		88.80
-26	Reg. Q all year)		90.25

NOTES: Asterisks * indicate status as of 1 January 1975.
Circled arrows ⊕ indicate trend reversals.
Arrows indicate tighter money ↓ and easier money ↑.

Federal Reserve Data

KEY ASSETS AND LIABILITIES OF 10 WEEKLY REPORTING MEMBER BANKS IN NEW YORK CITY
(in millions of dollars)

		- - Change from - -	
	Sept. 15	Sept. 8	Sept. 17
ASSETS:	1976	1976	1975
Total assets	128,819	+ 604	+ 2,777
Total loans and investments	88,027	+1,785	− 3,498
Included:			
Loan loss reserve	1,724	+ 8	− 77
Fed funds sold and like assets	2,511	+1,245	+ 989
Commercial and indust loans	32,711	+ 85	− 5,041
U.S. Treasury securities	9,656	− 93	+ 1,639
Municipal securities:			
Short-term	1,467	− 23	− 160
Long-term	6,226	+ 39	− 26
Other key assets:			
Cash items in proc of collection	12,847	+1,368	+ 2,037
Reserves with F.R. bank	5,638	−2,239	+ 1,218
Currency and coin	740	− 6	+ 29
LIABILITIES:			
Total demand deposits	50,060	+4,488	+ 3,648
Demand deposits adjusted (a)	24,890	+1,843	+ 308
Time & savings deposits	40,688	− 382	− 7,703
Includes negotiable CDs			
of $100,000 or more	21,738	− 439	− 7,288
Federal funds purchased and			
similar liabilities	15,113	−4,489	+ 4,378
Other key liabilities:			
From own foreign branches	2,790	− 187	+ 919
Borrowings from F.R.	0	0	0
Total capital plus certain debt	11,480	+ 6	+ 1,586

(a) All demand deposits except U.S. Government and domestic commercial banks, less cash items in process of collection.

MEMBER BANK RESERVE CHANGES

Changes in weekly averages of member bank reserves and related items during the week and year ended September 15, 1976 were as follows (in millions of dollars)

		Chg fm wk end	
	Sept. 15	Sept. 8	Sept. 17
Reserve bank credit:	1976	1976	1975
U.S. Gov't securities:			
Bought outright	87,175	−3,324	+ 6,104
Held under repurch agreement	....	− 107	− 783
Federal agency issues:			
Bought outright	6,760	− 18	+ 1,365
Held under repurch agreemt	....	− 4	− 37
Acceptances − bought outright	253	− 4	− 401
Held under repurch agreemt	....	− 9	− 52
Member bank borrowings	33	+ 17	− 233
Seasonal bank borrowings	28	− 2	− 33
Float	3,542	+1,072	+ 1,688
Other Federal Reserve Assets	3,716	+ 211	+ 619
Total Reserve Bank credit	101,507	−2,168	+ 8,238
Gold stock	11,598	....	− 1
SDR certificates	700	....	+ 200
Treasury currency outstanding	10,735	+ 15	+ 946
Total	124,540	−2,153	+ 9,382
Money in circulation	90,344	+ 458	+ 8,178
Treasury cash holdings	425	− 25	+ 71
Treasury dpts with F.R. Bnks	3,768	−2,967	+ 2,587
Foreign deposits with F.R. Bnks	262	− 5	− 64
Other deposits with F.R. Banks	1,197	+ 135	+ 251
Other F.R. liabilities & capital	3,200	+ 105	+ 131
Total	99,195	−2,300	+11,154
Member bank reserves			
With F.R. Banks	25,345	+ 147	− 1,771
Cash allowed as res.	8,393	+ 161	+ 957
Total reserves held	33,894	+ 315	− 658
Required reserves	33,570	+ 263	− 715
Excess reserves	324	+ 52	+ 57
Free reserves	291	+ 35	

MONETARY AND RESERVE AGGREGATES
(four-week daily avg., seasonally adj., in billions)

	Sept. 8	Aug. 4
Money supply (M1)	305.9	305.6
Money supply (M2)	715.0	710.1
Adjusted bank deposits	522.2	524.3
Bank time deposits	472.2	471.9
Reserves available to support	Sept. 15	Aug. 18
private, nonbank deposits	z	z

KEY INTEREST RATES
(weekly averages)

	Sept. 15	Sept. 8
Federal funds	5.22	5.25
Treasury bill (90 day)	5.12	5.10
Commercial paper (dealer, 90 day)	5.38	5.38
Certifs of Deposit (resale, 90 day)	5.35	5.34
Eurodollars (90 days)	5.58	5.54

FIGURE 3-1. Federal Reserve data as of September 15, 1976. [SOURCE: Reproduced from the *Wall Street Journal*, September 17, 1976, p. 25.]

however, this information often is two months old by the time it becomes available. A more current source, *U.S. Financial Data*, is published weekly by the Federal Reserve Bank of St. Louis. Currently, a subscription to this service can be had free of charge.[3]

THE TMT WORKCHART

In contrast to the TMT Worksheet, the TMT Workchart (Figs. 3-2a through 3–2h) helps you monitor TMT more precisely, because it express-es such factors as time, market cycles, and the magnitude and level of the market more precisely. For example, by looking at the Workchart, you can see that easy money signals seem to have the greatest effect on a market that has dropped to a very low level, as occurred in fall 1974 (Figure 3-2e). The Workchart also shows you the stock market's immediate reaction to TMT signals. Take a look at Figures 3-2a through 3-2h. Here, changes in each TMT signal are shown for the week during which they occurred, for the period 1966 through 1980.

The TMT Workcharts shown in Figures 3-2a through 3-2h provide a basis for forecasting the direction of the stock market. An examination suggests the following observations:

TMT Signals in 1966

Four tight money signals occurred in December 1965, and a fifth occurred in January 1966 (Fig. 3-2a), resulting in a downtrending market. Four more tight money signals occurred in July, with the same result. (Actually, it's impossible to prove conclusively that any specific factor caused any specific market to drop. The cause-and-effect relationship presented here is purely deduction.)

The only clue that the market might turn occurred in September 1966, when maximum interest rates payable on savings deposits (Regulation Q) were lowered. This made stocks relatively more attractive as investments.

You don't need to understand what causes TMT signals in order to benefit from them. But it is an area of interest for many investors. Paul Meek, Assistant Vice-President of the Federal Reserve Bank of New York, describes the 1966 situation:

> The large commitment of U.S. forces in Vietnam, that began in mid-1965, imposed major demands on an economy already growing at near the maximum rate attainable without inflation. The decision

FIGURE 3–2a-h.　TMT workchart, 1966–80.

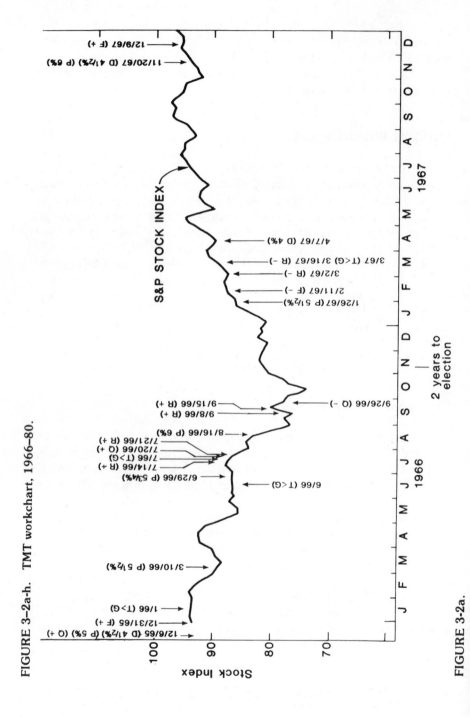

FIGURE 3-2a.

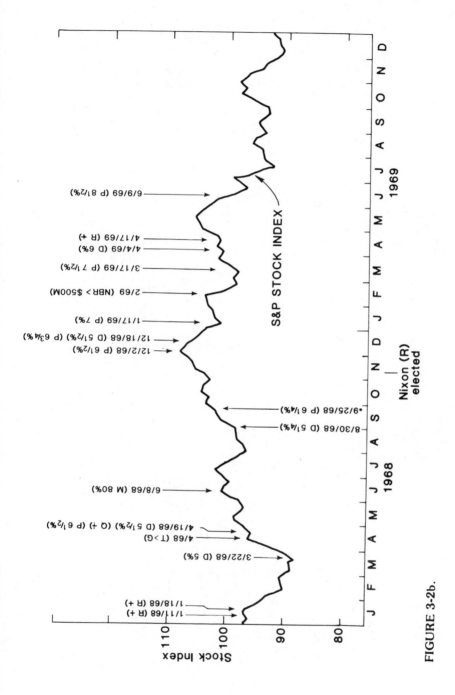

FIGURE 3-2b.

83

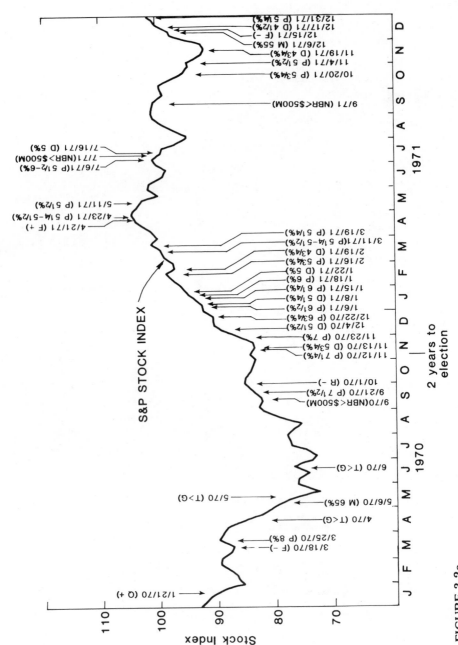

FIGURE 3-2c.

84

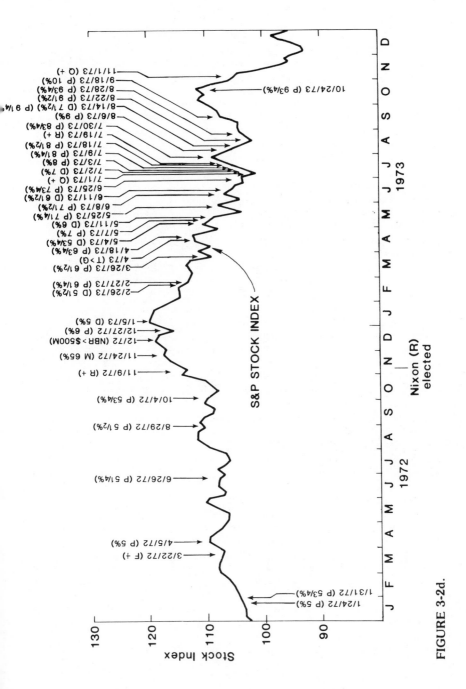

FIGURE 3-2d.

85

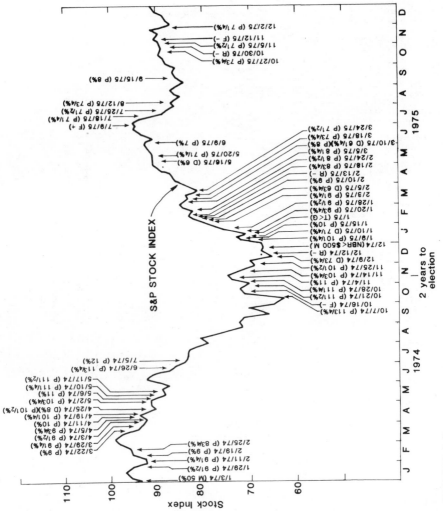

FIGURE 3-2e.

86

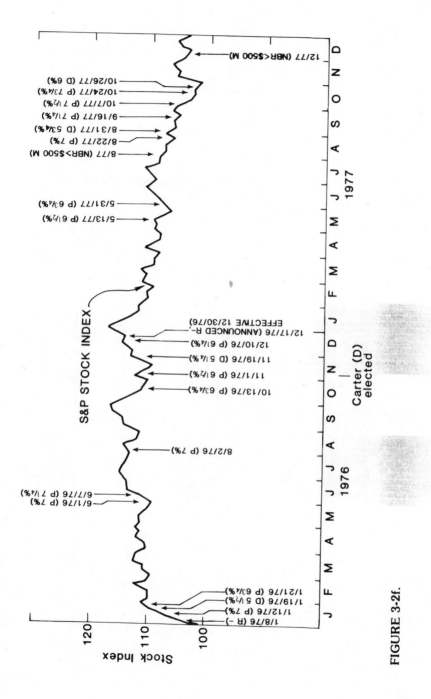

FIGURE 3-2f.

87

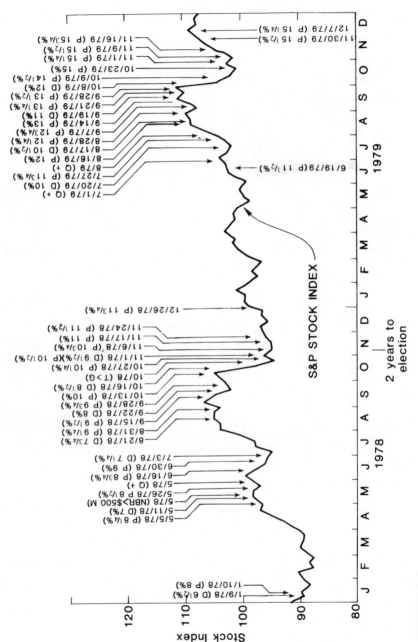

FIGURE 3-2g.

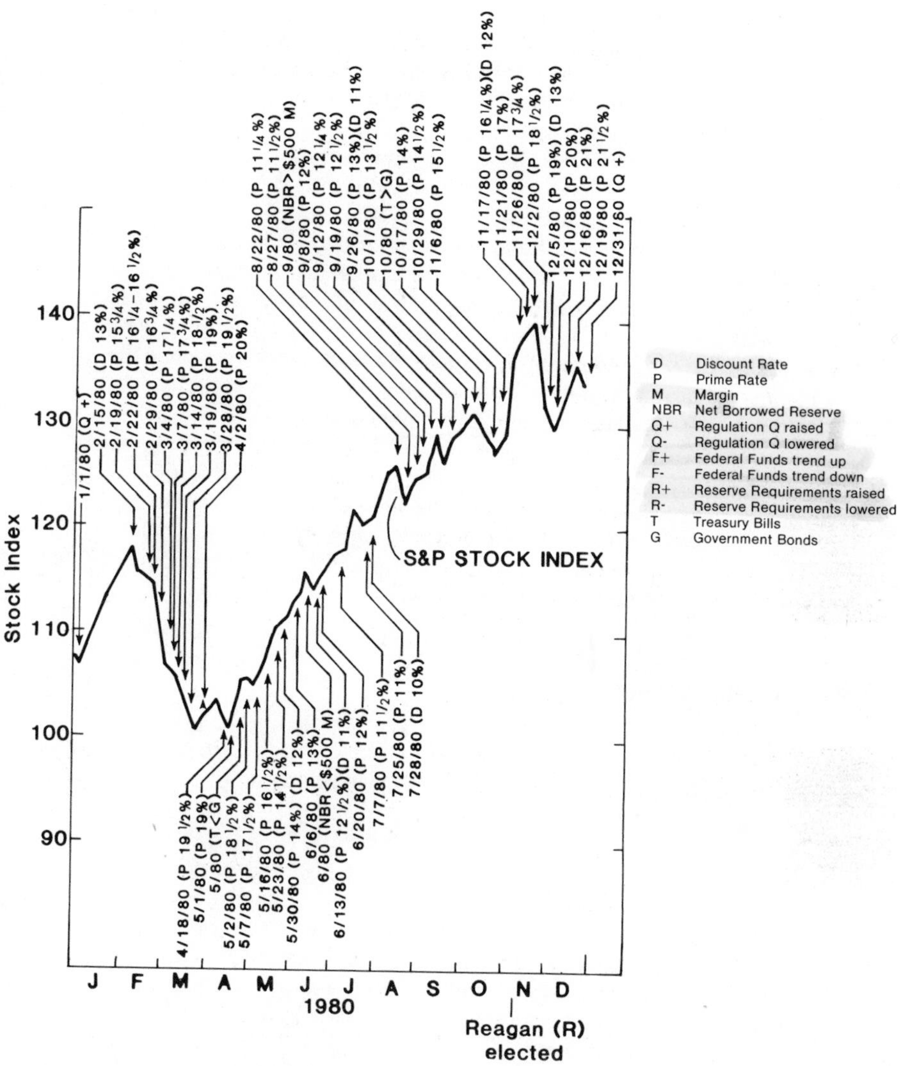
Stock Index
140
130
120
110
100
90
1/1/80 (Q +)
2/15/80 (D 13%)
2/19/80 (P 15 3/4 %)
2/22/80 (P 16 1/4 – 16 1/2 %)
2/29/80 (P 16 3/4 %)
3/4/80 (P 17 1/4 %)
3/7/80 (P 17 3/4 %)
3/14/80 (P 18 1/2 %)
3/19/80 (P 19%)
3/28/80 (P 19 1/2 %)
4/2/80 (P 20%)
4/18/80 (P 19 1/2 %)
5/1/80 (P 19%)
5/80 (T<G)
5/2/80 (P 18 1/2 %)
5/7/80 (P 17 1/2 %)
5/16/80 (P 16 1/2 %)
5/23/80 (P 14 1/2 %)
5/30/80 (P 14%) (D 12%)
6/6/80 (P 13%)
6/80 (NBR<$500 M)
6/13/80 (P 12 1/2 %)(D 11%)
6/20/80 (P 12%)
7/7/80 (P 11 1/2 %)
7/25/80 (P 11%)
7/28/80 (D 10%)
8/22/80 (P 11 1/4 %)
8/27/80 (P 11 1/2 %)
9/80 (NBR>$500 M)
9/8/80 (P 12%)
9/12/80 (P 12 1/4 %)
9/19/80 (P 12 1/2 %)
9/26/80 (P 13%)(D 11%)
10/1/80 (P 13 1/2 %)
10/80 (T>G)
10/17/80 (P 14%)
10/29/80 (P 14 1/2 %)
11/6/80 (P 15 1/2 %)
11/17/80 (P 16 1/4 %)(D 12%)
11/21/80 (P 17%)
11/26/80 (P 17 3/4 %)
12/2/80 (P 18 1/2 %)
12/5/80 (P 19%) (D 13%)
12/10/80 (P 20%)
12/16/80 (P 21%)
12/19/80 (P 21 1/2 %)
12/31/80 (Q +)
S&P STOCK INDEX
J F M A M J J A S O N D
1980
Reagan (R) elected
D Discount Rate
P Prime Rate
M Margin
NBR Net Borrowed Reserve
Q+ Regulation Q raised
Q- Regulation Q lowered
F+ Federal Funds trend up
F- Federal Funds trend down
R+ Reserve Requirements raised
R- Reserve Requirements lowered
T Treasury Bills
G Government Bonds

FIGURE 3-2h.

FIGURES 3-2a-h. [*SOURCE*: see pages 103–104.]

not to increase federal taxes sufficiently to balance the new impetus given by defense spending and rising incomes shifted the burden of restraint to monetary policy. The Federal Reserve raised the discount rate on advances to member banks to 4.50 percent in December 1965 and sought to restrict credit flows through open market operations as 1966 progressed. Interest rates rose sharply as government, business, the housing industry, and consumers competed for funds to carry out their spending plans. The economy raced ahead with production and prices rising and unemployment falling below 4 percent by mid-1966. However, in late summer near-crisis conditions emerged in financial markets. New housing starts fell by more than a third as savings banks and savings and loan associations curtailed their mortgage lending in the face of savings deposit losses to higher yielding commercial bank deposits and marketable securities. Industrial production began to dip before the end of 1966, but price inflation was already in motion and steeply rising imports were erasing all of the fundamental progress made earlier in correcting the balance-of-payments deficit. Even a tightly restrictive monetary policy with its harsh impact on housing could not compensate for the lack of adequate restraint from the government's tax and spending policies.

Once the economy began to slow down in the fall of 1966, the Federal Reserve reversed direction, using open market operations to pump in bank reserves, revive housing, and avoid a snowballing decline in economic activity. Bank credit and the money supply rose and the economy resumed its advance.[4]

TMT Signals in 1967

Six bursts of easy money occurred in 1967 (Fig. 3-2a), each of which seemed to lift the market more. Paul Meek explains why:

> Interest rates, after falling abruptly in early 1967, began to ratchet higher as the Treasury financed a huge deficit and businessmen, recalling the drying-up of credit the previous summer, borrowed a record volume in the bond markets. The need for a broad tax increase to blunt the inflationary thrust of rising federal defense and other expenditures, and to restore balanced economic growth, was urged by the Administration. Congressional discussion dragged on while the boom gathered steam, unemployment dropped to 3.5 percent, wages and prices rose, the balánce of trade deteriorated further, and the international monetary system was exposed to a severe crisis in the wake of the devaluation of sterling. Federal Reserve policy once more moved to restrain the excessive demands at work in the economy and interest rates shot up, reaching in May 1968 the highest levels seen in some cases since the Civil War.[5]

As a means of forecasting the stock market, this statement is fairly complex compared with the relative simplicity of TMT signals. Investors in 1967 would have profited more from observing the Fed's actions than from listening to its explanations.

TMT Signals in 1968

Five tight money signals drove the market down in late 1967 and early 1968 (Figs. 3-2a and 3-2b). In the March–April rally, the market appeared to ignore the Fed's actions. Once the Fed increased margin requirements, however, the market was stunned into a sideways movement that lasted several months. In late August, the Fed gave an easy money signal and the market moved upward again. After Richard Nixon was elected president, the market rose for three weeks. Then the Fed and the banks raised interest rates, bringing an end to the two-year bull market with three tight money signals. Meek continues:

> Passage of a large federal tax increase coupled with a mandatory spending cut in mid-1968 for the time relieved fears of unchecked inflation and financial crisis at home and of devaluation of the dollar and economic turmoil abroad.[6]

TMT Signals in 1969

Three more tight money signals occurred in 1969 (Fig. 3-2b). For the rest of that year, the market floundered in a generally downward direction. According to Meek:

> The inflationary momentum built up in the previous three years proved difficult to check. Increased monetary stimulus on the heels of the tax surcharge proved a mistake and monetary policy shifted progressively toward restraint during 1969. Interest rates moved up to record highs, reflecting not only a slowing in the growth of the money stock and bank credit but also a premium that investors began to expect to protect themselves against rising prices.[7]

TMT Signals in 1970

In 1970, one more tight money signal occurrred, lowering the market (Fig. 3-2c). There were four easy money signals in the spring, including a lowering of margin requirements. These actions indicated that the Fed really meant to reverse the 18 month decline in the stock market. However, short-term T-bill yields rose above long-term government bond yields, indicating that money was becoming easier. Between June and December, *seven easy money signals* appeared to drive the market up. The stock market index rose from 73 in June 1970 to 104 in April 1971 — a 42 percent gain in ten months. Meek explains these events as follows:

> The system's braking action took hold, slowing the economy's growth below its full employment potential and eliminating excessive demand. As unemployment rose toward 6 percent in 1970, the monetary authorities shifted to a policy of moderate stimulation, seeking to reinvigorate the economy while avoiding excesses that might lead to a new round of inflation. Prices continued to rise, however, as labor sought, and won, settlements that more than made up for past increases in the cost of living. Continuing national concern with inflation led to increasing interest in possible ways of exerting public influence on the bargaining process.[8]

TMT Signals in 1971

In 1971, two tight money signals occurred at the peak of the market and sent it down (Fig. 3-2c). In the fall, three easy money signals drove the market up for a substantial year-end rally.

Meek's explanation:

> The economic recovery remained sluggish through mid-summer 1971, but prices were continuing to rise and the dollar was under a massive speculative attack in foreign exchange markets. The administration responded with tax measures to spur the economy, a wage-price program to try to curb inflation, and a severance of the link between the dollar and gold. The economy responded to the stimulus of the new program and accompanying monetary expansion. The rate of inflation slowed, but remained a source of concern. The negotiation of revised currency parities was concluded in December 1971 as an essential first step to the reshaping of the world's monetary machinery.[9]

As these analyses show, there are two ways to study tight and easy money signals: (1) by plotting them on the TMT Workchart as they occur; or (2) by viewing them as the result of complex economic situations. While professional investors may make good use of the second approach, relatively few lay investors need to understand why TMT signals occur. What does need to be understood, however, is that *an increase in interest rates is generally bad for the stock market, while a decrease in interest rates is generally good for it.*

TMT Signals in 1972

While the two tight money signals that occurred in 1972 weren't strong enough to send the market down, they were strong enough to send it sideways for eight months (Fig. 3–2d). *The Fed created no TMT signals until after the election,*[10] when it raised the bank reserve requirement and increased margin requirements. Net borrowed bank reserves rose above $500 million. Banks continued to raise their prime rates. The market peaked in January 1973—and *the stock market would not see this level again for seven years!*

TMT Signals in 1973

The Fed continued to tighten money in 1973 (Fig. 3-2d), *raising the discount rate seven times*, raising T-bill rates above government bond rates, raising Regulation Q once, and *raising bank reserve requirements three times. The 27 tight money signals that appeared indicated, as a group, that the stock market would probably decline substantially.* The market index lost 17 percent in 1973, and this bear market lasted through the following year.

Why didn't the press blame the Fed's tight money policy for the market decline? Because, for the most part, it doesn't understand the effect of tight money or regard it as particularly newsworthy. Since dividends and earnings kept increasing, the media ignored the Fed and instead focused the blame on Watergate. This scandal made investors pessimistic, because it lowered their confidence in the government and because for some time the outcome of the scandal itself was uncertain. In the fall of 1973, the press then shifted the blame to the oil boycott and the energy crisis, inflation, and the tighter money policies resulting from inflation.[11]

TMT Signals in 1974

The Fed had been urged to lower margin requirements by the stock brokerage industry in December 1973. On January 3, 1974, the Fed succumbed, lowering margin requirements 15 percent—from 65 percent to 50 percent (Fig. 3-2e). But the extreme tightness of money caused this action to have the opposite effect from what investors were expecting. The lower margin requirements allowed investors to buy more stock in what turned out to be a major bear market. Investors who used margin to buy stock lost heavily (as Chap. 2 explained). The Fed's attempts to fight inflation drove the market down from an S&P 500 Stock Index of 99 to 62—*a loss of 37 percent—in only seven months.* In fact, more stock market dollars were lost during this seven-month period than during the great crash of 1929–32.

The first easy money signal came almost at the exact bottom of the market. On October 7, 1974, the prime rate was lowered from a high point of 12 percent to 11.75 percent. By the end of the year, ten easy money signals had occurred. These stopped the momentum of the bear market and reversed the trend.

TMT Signals in 1975

Six more easy money signals occurred in January 1975, helping to turn the market into a bull market (Fig. 3-2e). From the bottom of the market in October 1974 to June 1975, the S&P 500 Stock Market Index rose from 62 to 94, a gain of 51 percent. During this period there were 30 easy money signals and no tight money signals.

In June, three tight money signals occurred. These signals drove the market down; perhaps the memory of the 1973–74 bear market was still fresh in investors' minds. Late in 1975, five easy money signals occurred, which laid the groundwork for a short bull market that lasted from December 1975 through January 1976.

TMT Signals in 1976

Four easy money signals occurred early in 1976 (Fig. 3-2f). After that, the Fed kept a low profile—this was a presidential election year and presumably the Fed didn't want to take any action that might have been construed as political.[12]

This completes the analysis of TMT signals for the period 1966 to 1977. Figures 3-2f through 3-2h cover the period 1977 to 1981.

HOW TO INTERPRET TMT SIGNALS

If, as an investor, you want to learn how to interpret TMT signals, try the following exercise. Open the book to the first TMT Workchart (Fig. 3-

2a). Now take a piece of paper and use it to conceal the period from February 1966 on. Now make a forecast for the immediately ensuing month. Then uncover the relevant section of the chart and compare your forecast with the actual market. You can keep doing this through Figure 3-2h. This exercise should give you a hypothetical 15-year experience in Tight Money Timing. For additional practice, use Figures 3-3 and 3-4.

These workcharts cover a relatively short period. In the next section, however, we will examine the TMT signals over a period of 67 years— from 1914 to 1981.

TMT HISTORY: 1914–80

Here we will explore the effect of TMT signals on the market since the Federal Reserve was established in 1913.

At that time, none of the TMT signals existed. Not until the next year did these signals* begin to be developed and put into effect:

- 1914—Changes in the discount rate (Appendix C);
- 1917—Initiation of reserve requirements;
- 1920—Compilation of data on T-bill rates versus government bond rates (Appendix B);
- 1933—Initiation of Regulation Q;
- 1934—Initiation of margin requirements;
- 1934—Availability of exact data on the prime rate (Appendix C);
- 1946—Availability of data on free reserves (Appendix B); and
- 1966—Monitoring of Federal funds rate figures (Appendix B).

The 67-year history of TMT signals is plotted below on a series of monthly charts (Fig. 3-5a through 3-5e). These charts are presented on a semilog scale so that you can measure and compare changes in the market.

Let's examine these data by first looking at Figure 3-5a. From December 1914 to March 1915, the newly formed Federal Reserve System reduced its discount rate in four steps, from 6 to 4 percent. The Standard and Poor's 500 Stock Index rose 40 percent over the next 20 months. This sequel agrees with my TMT hypothesis: Lower interest rates indicate easy money and forecast a rising stock market.

From late 1916 through 1917, the market dropped by 33 percent. We can assume that the major cause of this drop was the uncertainty

---

*For a statistical history of the eight TMT signals, refer to Chapter 2.

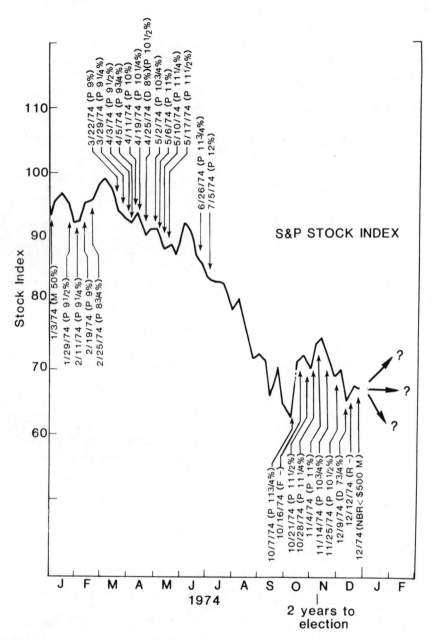

FIGURE 3-3.   Background for forecasting 1975–76 market. *The Question:* What will happen to the stock market in 1975? (Note the 11 easy money signals in late 1974.)

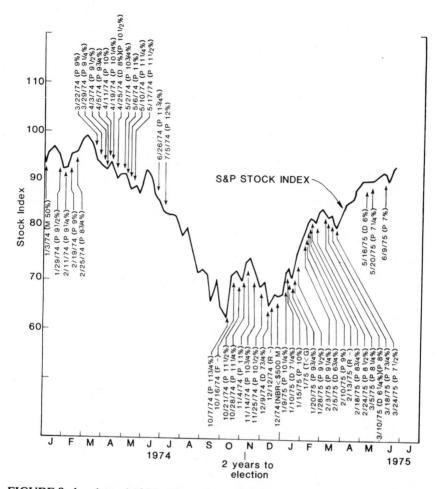

FIGURE 3–4.   Actual 1975–76 market. *The Answer:* The market will go up in 1975!

created by World War I.[13] However, the Fed did initiate member bank reserve requirements in June 1917—probably to make money tighter, since there was no existing requirement.

Further tight money signals occurred in December 1917 and April 1918. These signals were not strong enough to lower the already depressed market, but the market's recovery in 1918 was mild, at best.

The market dropped 33 percent in the period 1919–21 (Fig. 3-5a). Three increases in the discount rate occurred early in the decline; the first two alone totaled an increase of 50 percent. The size of this increase (from 4 to 6 percent) indicates that the Fed moved with a very heavy hand

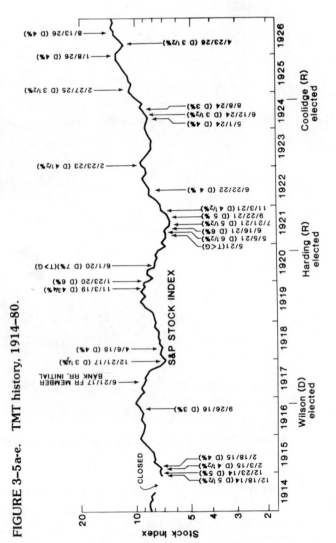

FIGURE 3-5a-e. TMT history, 1914–80.

FIGURE 3-5a.

98

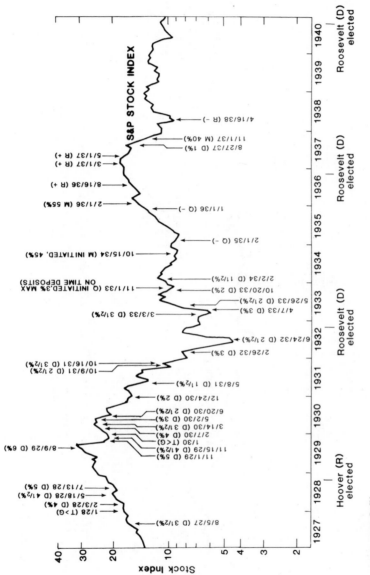

FIGURE 3-5b.

99

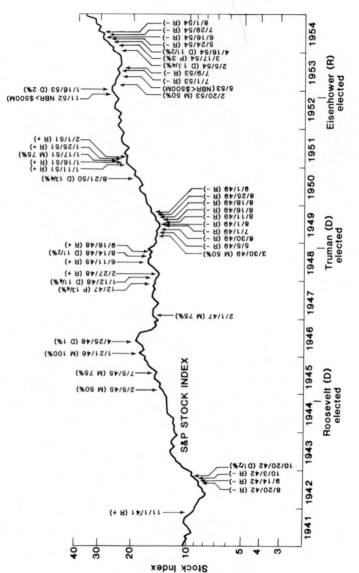

FIGURE 3-5c.

100

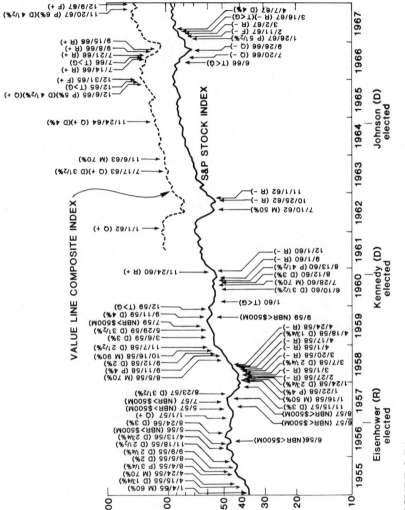

FIGURE 3-5d.

101

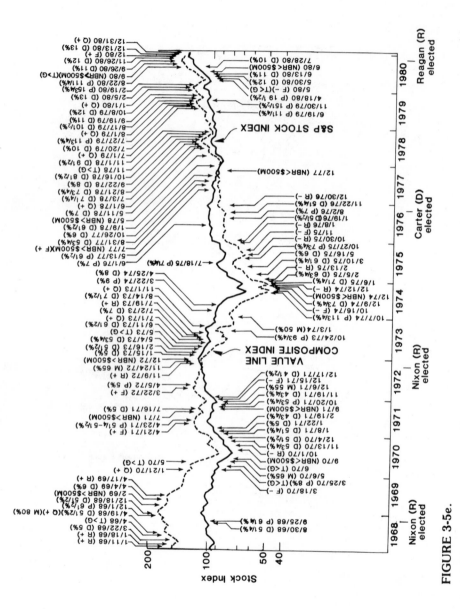

FIGURE 3-5e.

102

D   Discount Rate

P   Prime Rate

M   Margin

NBR   Net Borrowed Reserve

Q+   Regulation Q raised

Q–   Regulation Q lowered

F+   Federal Funds trend up

F–   Federal Funds trend down

R+   Reserve Requirements raised

R–   Reserve Requirements lowered

T   Treasury Bills

G   Government Bonds

[SOURCES: Figures 3-5a–3-5e: S&P Stock Index: Standard and Poor's Corp., *Security Price Index Record 1976.* Orange, Conn.: Standard & Poor's Corp., 1976, first trading day close each month, and *Security Price Index Record 1980.* Orange, Conn.: Standard & Poor's Corp., 1980.

Discount rates: U.S. Federal Reserve Board, Division of Administrative Services, Publications Services, *Banking and Monetary Statistics 1914–1941,* November 1943, pp. 439–42; U.S. Federal Reserve Board, Division of Administrative Services, Publications Services, *Banking and Monetary Statistics, 1941–1970,* September 1976, p. 667; and U.S. Federal Reserve Board, Division of Administrative Services, Publications Services, *Annual Statistical Digest 1971–1975,* October 1976, p. 35.

Federal funds trends: U.S. Federal Reserve Board, Division of Administrative Services, Publications Services, *Banking and Monetary Statistics 1941–1970,* September 1976, pp. 691–92; and U.S. Federal Reserve Board, Division of Administrative Services, Publications Services, *Annual Statistical Digest 1971–1975,* October 1976, pp. 122–25.

Margin requirements: U.S. Federal Reserve Board, Division of Administrative Services, Publications Services, *Banking and Monetary Statistics 1941–1970,* September 1976, p. 799; and U.S. Federal Reserve Board, Division of Administrative Services, Publications Services, *Annual Statistical Digest 1971–1975,* October 1976, p. 39.

Free reserves: National Bureau of Economic Research, Computer Service, 1050 Massachusetts, Mass. 01238

103

Prime rates: U.S. Federal Reserve Board, Division of Administrative Services, Publications Services, *Banking and Monetary Statistics 1941–1970*, September 1976, p. 707; and U.S. Federal Reserve Board, Division of Administrative Services, Publications Services, *Annual Statistical Digest 1971–1975*, October 1976, p. 117.

Regulation Q: U.S. Federal Reserve Board, Division of Administrative Services, Publications Services, *Banking and Monetary Statistics 1941–1970*, September 1976, p. 673; and U.S. Federal Reserve Board, Division of Administrative Services, Publications Services, *Annual Statistical Digest 1971–1975*, October 1976, p. 39.

Reserve requirements: U.S. Federal Reserve Board, Division of Administrative Services, Publications Services, *Banking and Monetary Statistics 1941–1970*, September 1976, p. 608; and U.S. Federal Reserve Board, Division of Administrative Services, Publications Services, *Annual Statistical Digest 1971–1975*, October 1976, p.38.

Treasury bill rates: U.S. Federal Reserve Board, Division of Administrative Services, Publications Services, *Banking and Monetary Statistics 1914–1941*, November 1943, p. 460; U.S. Federal Reserve Board, Division of Administrative Services, Publications Services, *Banking and Monetary Statistics 1941–1970*, September 1976, pp. 693–96; and U.S. Federal Reserve Board, Division of Administrative Services, Publications Services, *Annual Statistical Digest 1971–1975*, October 1976, p. 121.

Long-term government bond rates: U.S. Federal Reserve Board, Division of Administrative Services, Publications Services, *Banking and Monetary Statistics 1914–1941*, November 1943, pp. 468–71; U.S. Federal Reserve Board, Division of Administrative Services, Publications Services, *Banking and Monetary Statistics 1941–1970*, September 1976, pp. 720–27; and U.S. Federal Reserve Board, Division of Administrative Services, Publications Services, *Annual Statistical Digest 1971–1975*, October 1976, p. 126.

Value Line Composite Index: Arnold Bernhard & Co., *The Value Line Stock Market Averages, 1962 to 1974,* part 4, vol. 30, no. 15 (New York: Arnold Bernhard & Co., 1975), pp. 4–18.

Notes: Periods covered: discount rates from 1913; reserve requirements from 1916; T-bill versus long-term government bond rates from 1919; Regulation Q from 1932; margin requirements from 1934; prime rates from 1933; free reserves from 1946; Federal funds trends from 1965. S&P 500 Indexes for 1926–27 are based on Friday closing prices of first week of month, e.g., January index = S&P 500 Index at first week's Friday close. S&P 500 Indexes for 1928–76 are based on closing prices of first trading day of each month. Value Line Composite Indexes for 1961–76 are based on Friday closing prices of first week of month.]

and provides an excellent clue to the subsequent stock market decline. This decline was accelerated by the two tight money signals that occurred in June 1920.

During 1921, in the bottom of the market, the discount rate was lowered five times, and T-bill rates dropped below government bond rates. This total of six easy money signals accurately forecast the rising market that followed. However, in the second half of 1922 and through-out 1923, there were only two TMT signals, and there was little move-ment in the market.

In 1924, three easy money signals correctly forecast a rising market. This proved to be the first year of a five-year bull market that topped out in 1929. Discount rates were lowered a total of 33 percent in three steps—from 4.50 to 3 percent—indicating easier money.

From 1925 through 1927, TMT signals occurred rarely, and were significant when they did (Figs, 3–5a and 3–5b). However, each TMT signal did have an immediate—though short-lived—effect on the market.

In the first half of 1928, four TMT signals indicated that money was tight (Fig. 3-5b); yet the market continued to rise another 50 percent, apparently influenced less by TMT signals than by public optimism and low margin requirements. At this time, the Fed had no power to set margin requirements to control stock market speculation.

On August 9, 1929, the Fed raised the discount rate by 20 percent, from 5 to 6 percent. This discount rate increase was the fifth and largest since January 1928 and constituted a very important TMT signal during this crucial period. One month later, the market topped out. In the next three months it dropped a startling 33 percent; within three years it had dropped 87 percent! From late 1929 to the low point in the market in June 1932, there were 11 easy money signals and two tight money signals. Obviously, TMT signals did not forecast market conditions accu-rately during this period of economic collapse.[14]

In 1932, the discount rate was lowered twice, signaling easier money. The market fluctuated violently in 1933, reaching the final bottom in March and then rising abruptly (Fig. 3-5b). The establishment of Regula-tion Q, which set the maximum interest payable on time deposits at 3 percent, coincided with the beginning of a year-end rally. Its impact on the market was minor, however, compared to the impact of decreases in the discount rate—from 3.5 to 2 percent in three steps.

In 1934, margin requirements were initiated: investors had to make a minimum payment of 45 percent in order to purchase stocks. However, this new requirement had no serious effect on the stock market: it seemed reasonable, and most of the problems related to margin debt had been resolved during the 1929–32 decline.

In 1935, Regulation Q lowered the interest rates that could be paid on time deposits from 3 to 2.5 percent, which made stock dividends more attractive than savings accounts. When the stock market rose 45 percent that year, it was a sign not only of easier money but also of the public's renewed confidence in the market.

In 1936 and 1937, the market made a huge rounded top in response to the Fed's raising of margin requirements and member bank reserve requirements. The latter change was especially important; now the central reserve city banks and the reserve city banks were required to hold *twice as many reserves as before*. For example, after May 1, 1937, central reserve city banks were required to hold reserves of 26 percent deposits, whereas before (that is, prior to August 16, 1936) they had been required to hold only 13 percent. And reserve city banks had to hold 20 percent, compared with the previous requirement of 10 percent. The multiplier effect of reserves caused this situation to create a condition of very tight money. Over the following year, the market dropped by slightly more than 50 percent.

Two easy money signals occurred in late 1937, but they failed to slow the market's downward momentum. However, on April 16, 1938, the Fed lowered bank reserve requirements back to the levels it had established on March 1, 1937. *This released high-powered reserve dollars that helped the market to rise 47 percent over the next seven months.*

There were no TMT signals during the relatively quiet period from 1939 to 1941 (Figs. 3–5b and 3–5c). T-bill yields were negligible; government bonds yielded around 2 percent; and the stock market moved sideways. In 1941 the market declined, reflecting the growing concern over the spread of World War II.

A curious incident occurred in the T-bill market late in 1941. The yield on T-bills rose almost 500 percent in only two months—from an average of 0.05 percent in October 1941 to 0.24 percent in November 1941, the highest rate in four years. And yet the yield on government bonds remained at only 1.9 percent. It was as if the T-bill market sensed the growing probability that the United States would enter the war. Because bank reserve requirements were raised on November 1, 1941, and because of the uncertainties created by the war, the wavering stock market fell to its lowest level since 1933.

Starting in August 1942, the Fed made its contributions to the war effort: it made money easier by lowering reserve requirements three times, and it reduced the discount rate from 1 to 0.50 percent.[15] In response, the stock market rose 150 percent between May 1942 and June 1946.

Japan capitulated on August 15, 1945; the formal surrender was signed on September 2, but the Fed made no overt moves to tighten money. However, it did attempt to constrain the stock market by increasing margin requirements in three steps, from 40 percent on February 5, 1945 to 100 percent on January 21, 1946. *The Fed's ulterior motive in requiring 100 percent margin was to make it impossible for investors to exercise any leverage in purchasing stock, thus imposing the ultimate tight money signal on the stock market.* Then, on April 25, 1946, the Fed raised the discount rate from 0.50 to 1 percent. Together, these actions created such tight money that the market dropped almost 25 percent over the following seven months.

In 1947, the Fed reduced margin requirements from 100 percent to 75 percent (Fig. 3–5c), which apparently had no immediate effect. The market trended sideways for the rest of the year.

In 1948, there were five tight money signals. Except for preventing the market from rising, these signals had almost no effect. Why not? Perhaps because the changes involved were so small. For example, the prime rate was increased from 1.50 to 1.75 percent; the discount rate was increased from 1 to 1.50 percent. The market trended sideways for a full two years—through 1947 and 1948.

In 1949 there was a bull market, caused by several events. Margin requirements were lowered from 75 percent to 50 percent on March 3, 1949. It now took only one dollar to buy two dollars' worth of stock. *Reserve requirements were reduced a total of nine times*—a very strong signal that money was easy. These events set in motion a bull market that lasted for 3.5 years, from 1949 to 1953, during which time the market rose by 85 percent.

In 1950, only one tight money signal occurred: in August, the discount rate was increased from 1.50 to 1.75 percent. But this signal by itself wasn't enough to alter the course of the bull market. Even the Korean War, which began when U.S. military forces were ordered to South Korea on June 27, 1950, wasn't able to stop the bull market.

In January and February 1951, there were five tight money signals. The margin requirement was raised from 50 to 75 percent. Bank reserve requirements were raised in four relatively small increments. For central reserve city banks they were increased from 22 to 24 percent—a total of 9 percent. These relatively weak tight money signals failed to reverse the direction of the market; they merely made it rise more slowly. However, two more important tight money signals occurred in November 1952 and January 1953: free reserves dropped below a negative $500 million, and the discount rate was raised to 2 percent. Subsequently, the stock market declined by 10 percent.

In 1953, *three easy money signals halted the short-term decline and set the stage for the three-year bull market that followed.* The margin requirement was reduced from 75 to 50 percent. Free reserves dropped below a negative $500 million for about two months. And bank reserve requirements were reduced.

During 1954, a series of easy money signals pushed the market upward by 50 percent (Fig. 3-5c). The discount rate was lowered in two steps, from 2 to 1.50 percent. The prime rate dropped from 3.25 to 3 percent. Reserve requirements were lowered in four steps to the lowest levels since 1936.

In 1955, the Fed started to tighten money in many small increments. It raised margin requirements in two steps, from 50 to 70 percent. It raised the discount rate in four steps, from 1.5 to 2.5 percent. It raised the prime rate from 3 to 3.5 percent. All this slowed the market's rise and set the stage for a sideways market, which occurred in 1956 and 1957.

In 1956, several more tight money signals kept the market from rising. The discount rate was increased in two steps, from 2.5 to 3 percent. Free reserves dropped once below a negative $500 million, then later retreated.

In 1957, Regulation Q was raised from 2.5 to 3 percent. This made holding money in time deposits more attractive than holding it in stocks. Free reserves twice dropped below a negative $500 million, indicating tight money, and twice retreated. The final tight money signal occurred in August, when the discount rate was increased from 3 to 3.5 percent. During the next two months, the market dropped over 15 percent.

At the bottom of the 1957–58 market, 12 easy money signals clearly forecasted higher prices to come. The first easy money signal came in November 1957, when the discount rate was cut from 3.5 to 3 percent. Two more cuts brought the discount rate down to 1.75 percent. Margin requirements were lowered from 70 to 50 percent, and the prime rate was lowered from 4.5 to 4 percent. Reserve requirements were lowered in six steps. During 1958, the stock market rose over 35 percent. In August, the Fed began to check this rise by: (1) increasing margin requirements in two steps, from 50 to 90 percent; (2) increasing the discount rate in two steps, from 1.75 to 2.50 percent; and (3) increasing the prime rate from 3.5 to 4 percent.

In 1959, the market went sideways. There was only one easy money signal to offset the tight money signals of 1958 and the five new tight money signals of 1959. As a result, a ceiling was put on the market.

In January 1960, the market responded to the previous year's tight money signals by dropping approximately 5 percent. 1960 saw seven easy money signals and only one tight money signal. This situation prepared the way for a rise of almost 25 percent in 1961 (Fig. 3-5d).

On January 1, 1962, Regulation Q was changed to allow for three rate increases. Interest rates paid on savings and time deposits held for more than one year were increased from 3 to 4 percent. Rates on savings deposits held for less than one year were increased from 3 percent to 3.5 percent. These increases constituted 1962's only tight money signal. During the following six months, the market dropped over 20 percent. On July 10, margin requirements were lowered from 70 to 50 percent, creating a rise and subsequent drop in the market. Reserve requirements were lowered by 20 percent, from 5 to 4 percent on time deposits. The market's reaction? It rose vigorously into 1963.

In the second half of 1963, three tight money signals slowed the market's rise. These signals held the next year's market to a 10 percent gain. In 1964, two more tight money signals again held the next year's market to a 10 percent gain. No dramatic tight money signals occurred between 1963 and December 1965.

On December 6, 1965, three tight money signals occurred—all on the same day! The discount rate was increased from 4 to 4.5 percent; the prime rate rose from 4.5 to 5 percent; and Regulation Q was changed to allow a 5.5 percent interest on time deposits held less than one year. This last change made holding money in savings and time deposits more attractive than holding it in common stocks, and helped set the stage for the market's drop of 20 percent in 1966.

We've already analyzed the period 1966 through 1980 earlier in this chapter, using a series of weekly charts (Fig. 3-2a to 3-2h). Figures 3-5d and 3-5e are included here to provide continuity in the series of monthly charts. The Value Line Composite Index, initiated in 1961, has been superimposed on Figures 3-5d through 3-5e to illustrate the effect of TMT signals on the typical stock. And with these figures, our history of TMT signals for the period 1914 to 1981 is complete.

Findings

TMT signals apparently failed during several periods: The first seven months of 1928, late 1929, and all of 1930. Furthermore, during most of the 1950s and early 1960s, the increase in interest rates occurred when the stock market was making significant advances: In 1950 through 1952, in early 1955 through 1956, in late 1958 to 1960, and in 1963 through 1965. But these are the exceptions that prove the rule: TMT signals are superior forecasting tools.

A TMT signal can be weak, moderate, or strong. Its impact on the stock market depends on its direction, magnitude, and level. Just because a particular TMT signal may have failed doesn't mean that all TMT signals are inaccurate.

Let's take a simple analogy: A small airplane has a stall speed of 60 miles per hour. Therefore, if the wind speed crossing its wings is 55 miles per hour, the plane won't fly. But this doesn't mean that the plane won't fly at all, merely that a wind speed of 55 miles per hour isn't fast enough to permit the plane to fly. Once the wind speed reaches 65 miles per hour, the plane will fly—the wind speed now exceeds the plane's stall speed. We can apply the same general principle to TMT signals—at some point, these signals do have an effect on the stock market. Unlike the airplane, however, TMT signals have too many variables to allow us to determine the precise point at which they become effective.

As the historical view reveals, a signal's strength or weakness partially determines its effect on the market. Other determinants include level and direction. For example, the market should be more responsive to tight money signals if the relative level of the market is high and if it has been rising for several years. This is what happened at the end of 1952, in 1957, and in 1965. Conversely, a market that has declined should be more responsive to easy money signals, as was the case in 1949, 1953 through 1954, 1958, and 1962.

A rising stock market can gather so much momentum that it can't be stopped until all net investable funds are committed. This might have happened in 1951, 1955, and 1958, when groups of tight money signals failed to blunt rising markets. Or a collapsing market can continue its downward spiral unabated, until buyers finally bring the overabundance of margin calls and involuntary sellouts into balance. The stock market crash of 1929–32 is one—albeit extreme—example of this opposite trend.

Often a single TMT signal is enough to make the market react, especially when this signal represents a major change. In 1916, for example, a decrease of one full point in the discount rate temporarily lifted the market when the discount rate was reduced from 4 to 3 precent. The same thing happened in 1929–30, when the discount rate was reduced from 6 to 5 percent. In both cases the market seemed to react to this signal alone. On the other hand, the market was driven down by increases of one full point or more in the discount rate on three separate occasions. In 1920, the discount rate was raised from 4.75 to 6 percent, and later from 6 to 7 percent. In 1929, it was raised from 5 to 6 percent. And in 1931, it was raised from 1.5 to 2.5 percent and later from 2.5 to 3.5 percent. However, the market failed to decline further in 1933, when the discount rate was raised from 2.5 to 3.5 percent. In this case, the effect of an otherwise strong tight money signal was offset by an extremely low market.

Although TMT signals have not always forecast the market's direction, they generally have accurately forecast major intermediate and long-term trends. Groups of easy money signals have correctly forecast bull markets starting in 1915, 1921, 1924, 1942, 1949, 1953–54, 1958, 1960, 1962, 1967, 1970, 1974–75, and 1980. (See Appendix E.) The only notable exception occurred in late 1929 and in 1930, when eight easy money signals failed to halt the decline that had begun in 1929. Groups of tight money signals correctly forecast bear markets starting in 1929-30, 1937, 1965-66, 1968-69, and 1972-73. (See Appendix D.) The only notable exception occurred in 1928, when four tight money signals were followed by a 50 percent rise in the stock market. Groups of tight money signals did forecast bear markets incorrectly including the years of 1948, 1950–51, 1955–56, 1958, 1963, and 1967–68. However, some of these signals were relatively weak. For example, in 1948 the discount rate was increased in two steps, from 1 to 1.5 percent. These tight money signals were weak because they represented small increments, and the discount rate was still well below other risk-free short-term rates. The same thing occurred in 1950, when the discount rate was raised from 1.50 to 1.75 percent. Because the increment of 0.25 percent was small and the level itself was well below the 2.50 percent rate paid by banks on savings deposits, these signals had little effect on the stock market

The historical evidence suggests that *TMT signals forecast bull markets more accurately than they do bear markets.* Groups of easy money signals correctly forecast bull markets 13 out of 14 times. Groups of tight money signals correctly forecast bear markets five times out of six, not counting six other periods when tight money signals were weak.

The foregoing charts show the correlation between the Fed's actions and the stock market's reaction for 1914 to 1981—67 years. Now it's time to look at corporate bonds. Because they constitute an alternative investment, their reaction to tight and easy money signals must be determined. In the next chapter, we will examine the correlation between TMT signals and the bond market.

NOTES

1. Earlier changes in TMT signals are recorded in U.S. Federal Reserve Board, Division of Administrative Services, *Federal Reserve Bulletin* (published monthly). These bulletins are obtainable at business libraries or from the Division of Administrative Services, Board of Governors of the Federal Reserve System, Washington, D.C. 20551
2. The moving average technique used to trace the Federal funds rate is described in Chapter 1.
3. Subscriptions may be obtained by writing to Federal Reserve Bank of St. Louis, P.O. Box 442, St. Louis, Mo. 63166.
4. Paul Meek, *Open Market Operations.* New York: Federal Reserve Bank of New York, 1973, pp. 13–14.
5. Ibid., p. 14.

6. Ibid.
7. Ibid.
8. Ibid.
9. Ibid.
10. Changes in the prime rate are made by banks, not by the Federal Reserve.
11. David R. Sargent, *Stock Market Profits and Higher Income for You.* New York: Simon & Schuster, 1976, p. 265.
12. Had the Fed driven the market up, Gerald Ford might have won the election. The election results were very close, and a rising stock market generally creates public optimism and votes for the incumbent president, especially from the nation's then 25 million stockholders.
13. On April 6, 1917, the United States declared war on Germany. On November 11, 1918, the armistice ended World War I.
14. Some theories on the causes of the Great Depression are discussed in Chapter 6.
15. The discount rate of 0.50 percent was charged on advances secured by U.S. government securities maturing or callable in one year or less.

4

THE BOND MARKET'S REACTION
TO TMT SIGNALS

How TMT signals affect the stock market is the main concern of this book. However, since corporate bonds can be an important alternative or coinvestment, we need to see how this market is affected by TMT signals. We will look at a chart for the period 1966 to 1977, on which TMT sig.1als are plotted against the Standard and Poor's Corporate Bond Index (Fig. 4-1). This comparison will help us determine whether TMT signals are effective in predicting the trend in corporate bond interest rates.

THE CORPORATE BOND MARKET

The bond market was in a major decline during 1966–75. While this period may not represent the bond market perfectly, it does represent a particular historical period accurately—the segment that, because of similar economic problems (especially persistent inflation), probably will reoccur in the next ten years.

The findings shown below suggest that TMT signals do affect the bond market, and in much the same way as they affect the stock market. However, bear in mind that TMT signals represent changes in short-term money rates, while the bond market represents long-term rates. Short-term rates tend to lead long-term rates. Both rates tend to trend in the same direction, although at very different speeds. Short-term rates are sensitive and highly volatile; long-term rates are nonvolatile and slow to change. This is why you can use TMT signals to forecast long-term interest rates.

Figure 4-1 suggests the following observations: Just prior to 1966, there were four tight money signals. These, combined with the four tight money signals that occurred later in 1966, set the stage for the 1966 decline in the AAA Corporate Bond Index, from 90 to 85. Seven easy money signals followed in early 1967. These brought about a rise in the bond market, followed by a decline once the easy money signals were

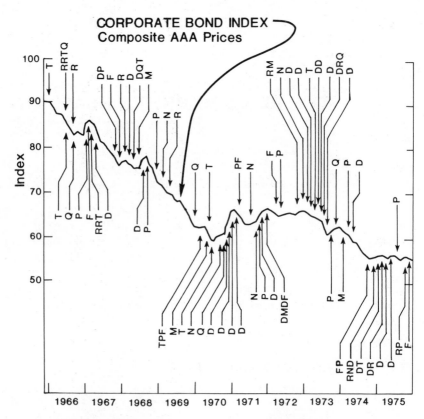

CORPORATE BOND INDEX
Composite AAA Prices

D	Discount Rate			Q	Regulation Q			
F	Federal Funds Trend			R	Reserve Requirements			
M	Margin Requirement			T	Treasury Bill vs.			
N	Net Borrowed Reserves				Government Bond Rate			
P	Prime Rate							

FIGURE 4-1.   Corporate bond prices versus tight and easy money signals.
[*SOURCES:*   D   F   M   P   Q   R   T: U.S. Federal Reserve Board, Division of
Administrative Services, Publications Services, *Annual Statistical Digest 1971-
1975,* October 1976, pp. 35; 122–25; 39; 117; 39; 38; 121; and U.S. Federal
Reserve Board, Division of Administrative Services, Publications Services, *Banking
and Monetary Statistics 1941–1970,* September 1976, pp. 667; 691–92; 799;
707; 673; 608; 693–96; 726–27. N: National Bureau of Economic Research,
Computer Services, 261 Madison Avenue, New York. Corporate Bond Index:
Standard & Poor's Corp., *Security Price Index Record 1976,* Orange, Conn.:

completed. Late in 1967, two tight money signals occurred near the bottom of the bond market, indicating a failure on the part of TMT signals to forecast the bond market for that year. In 1967, the bond market dropped from 85 to 77.

In 1968, a net of six tight money signals correctly forecast a declining bond market, which dropped from 77 to 72. In 1969, two more tight money signals encouraged a steep drop in the Corporate Bond Index, from 72 to 62.

In 1970 there were seven net easy money signals, which correctly forecast a rising bond market, from 62 to 66. In 1971, there were seven net easy money signals, but these had little effect on the bond market, which rose from 66 to 67.

In 1972, the bond market continued sideways, even though it absorbed six tight money signals. A net of ten tight money signals followed in 1973, bringing the bond market down from 66 to 62. Early in 1974, there was one tight money signal, and the Corporate Bond Index dropped from 62 to 56, continuing the decline that it began early in 1973. Later in 1974 and in 1975, there were 13 net easy money signals. During this period, the bond market trended sideways while the stock market soared upward.

TMT signals seem to affect the bond market much as they affect the stock market, but easy money signals seem to have a stronger effect on the stock market than on the bond market. For example, in 1967 six easy money signals boosted the stock market but failed to give more than a temporary boost to the bond market. Again, between late 1974 and early 1975, easy money signals drove up the bond market less than the stock market.

To move the AAA bond market, there must be large groups of TMT signals. Groups of ten or more net tight money signals moved the bond market down in 1965–67, 1968–69, and 1972–74. Groups of ten or more net easy money signals moved the market up in 1970–71 and 1974–76. Such groups seem to give accurate forecasts of future bond prices. As for the short term, the bond market seems to move coincidentally, or up, with easy money signals, and down with tight money signals.

THE BOND MARKET VERSUS
THE STOCK MARKET

As you can see in Figure 4-2, which plots the Corporate Bond Index against the S&P 500 Stock Index, there is a small correlation between the bond market and stock market: Both trend in the same direction at the same time, but at much different speeds. This correlation parallels the correlation between short-term and long-term rates just described. There-

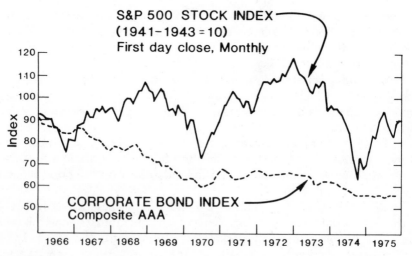

FIGURE 4–2.   Corporate bond index versus stock market index. [*SOURCES:* S&P 500 Stock Index: Standard & Poor's Corp., *Security Price Index Record 1976,* Orange, Conn.: Standard & Poor's Corp., 1976, pp. 187–94. Corporate Bond Index: Ibid., p 212.] NOTE: Bond prices are a conversion of yield indexes, based on a 4 percent coupon, 20-year maturity.

fore, the bond market is much more stable than the stock market. Of course, large sums of money *can* be lost in bonds. Investors who bought long-term bonds in 1965 had huge paper losses in 1975. *During this ten-year period, the Corporate Bond Index dropped 36 percent, from 91 to 58,* while the S&P 500 Stock Index dropped only about 2 percent.

Figure 4-3 illustrates the relationship between corporate bond yields and stock market yields. Between 1965 and 1975, bond prices dropped so low that corporate bond yields increased by 83 percent, from 4.7 to 8.6 percent. However, stock dividends increased by only 37 percent, from 3.0 to 4.1 percent, during this same period. Why? Largely because stock prices were falling, although the effect of the fall was partially offset by increasing dividend payments. Peaks and valleys in bond and stock yields were closely correlated prior to 1974. Stock market yields peaked in September 1974, but it was in August 1975 that bond yields peaked. This degree of lag merely reflects a strong stock market and a sideways bond market. If both markets had been equally strong, they would have fluctuated by approximately the same percentage. Some stock market analysts who forecast a weak market for 1975 were thrown off course by this chain of events. They believed that a strong corporate bond market was required to sustain a strong stock market, but, in fact, the rising stock market led the bond market by about one year. What can we learn from

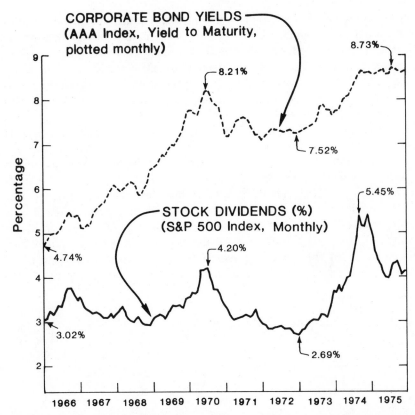

FIGURE 4-3. Corporate bond yields versus stock dividend yields.
[*SOURCE:* Standard & Poor's Corp., *Security Price Index Record 1976*, Orange, Conn.: Standard & Poor's Corp., 1976, pp. 133, 215.]

this? That the long-term bond market probably should not be used as a primary forecaster of stock market trends.

FIXED-INCOME MANAGEMENT

Managers of fixed-income portfolios usually monitor Federal Reserve policy very closely, as well as the various indexes that lead inflation rates (for example, producer price indexes). All these data help them to forecast money market and bond market trends. In order to make the most out of fixed-income investments, they shift money between short– and long-term debt media. For instance, when interest rates are rising, they shift new money or money from long-bond maturities into short-term debt media (for example, U.S. Treasury bills, certificates of deposit, or short-term corporate and government bonds). This prevents a loss of capital in long-term bonds due to rising interest rates and declining bond prices. When the managers feel that interest rates have peaked and short-term rates are declining, they shift the money from short-term to long-term bonds. In the face of declining interest rates and rising bond prices, this gives the investor a good chance to realize both capital gains and a high, locked-in, current yield.

TMT signals are correlated with changes in the corporate bond market, as well as with changes in the stock market (Fig. 4-1, 4-2, and 4-3). You can use TMT signals to achieve the aforementioned goals: Just switch from long-term bonds into short-term debt media as groups of tight money signals occur, and from short-term debt media into long-term bonds as groups of easy money signals occur. In Chapter 5 you will find out more about the Federal Reserve System and explore some of its reasons for creating tight or easy money.

5

WHY THE FED CREATES TIGHT OR EASY MONEY

WHAT IS THE FED?

The Federal Reserve System consists of 12 central banks that work through 6000 member banks. It is managed by a board of seven governors, who are appointed by the president to 14-year terms. As of July 30, 1976, the board consisted of four economists with doctorates, a commercial banker, a mortgage banker, and a businessman.[1] This Board of Governors has the power to create tight or easy money.

The Fed has some control over each of the eight TMT signals. Directly, it controls the discount rate, Regulation Q, bank reserve requirements, and stock margin requirements. Indirectly, it controls U.S. Treasury bill rates, Federal funds rates, and free bank reserves. Each commercial bank sets it own prime rate; however, even this is indirectly influenced by the Fed. Because it is the Fed that controls TMT signals, let's explore its functions and rationale behind its decisions.

The beginning of the Fed dates back to December 23, 1913, when President Woodrow Wilson signed the Federal Reserve Act. The function of the Fed was—and is—to promote a healthy economy by influencing U.S. monetary and credit conditions. What is a healthy economy? According to most economists, it is marked by a high but sustainable rate of growth, high employment, reasonable price stability, and balance in its international accounts.

To get an idea of the Fed's functions, let's look at the economic policies of the U.S. government. These policies may be divided into three categories: (1) fiscal policies, which are concerned with federal government taxes, expenditures, savings, and investment; (2) structural or income policies, which attempt to change the relationships between supply and demand and which include price and wage controls, antitrust policies, import policies, tax policies, and farm policies; and (3) monetary policies, which alter bank reserves and other financial relationships. Monetary policy is the Fed's special responsibility; this is what enables it to create tight or easy money.

119

The Fed's functions as of 1975 are summarized as follows:

> These are the men who create the money we all spend. Each month at their meetings they pore over charts, study economic indicators, receive special reports and argue among themselves whether or not to make more money. In effect, they determine whether you will be able to buy a car, can afford to take a vacation or buy a new home. Their decisions can affect the security of your job.
>
> One man dominates the meetings. He is Dr. Arthur Burns, Chairman of the Federal Reserve Board. Burns steers the discussion and usually it is his view that prevails.
>
> Listening closely is another man—Alan R. Holmes. It is his job to implement the decisions of the committee. By the next day Holmes is back in New York and closeted with his staff on the eighth floor of the New York Federal Reserve Bank building in Wall Street. There, in the deepest secrecy, they plot their strategy for the next week.
>
> During the early part of 1975 Holmes' mission was single-minded—to pump money into the stagnant market places. And how he does it is really quite simple.
>
> If the Open Market Committee want to create more money, then Holmes conjures it up out of thin air . . . .
>
> Holmes buys government securities from one of the two dozen big banks or dealers licensed to trade in them. In effect, he gives the dealer a check, drawn against the Federal Reserve account. The dealer deposits this check with his bank and when the bank presents it to the Fed for collection, the Fed merely punches a few computer buttons and tells the bank that it has credited its reserve with the due amount.
>
> So the bank has more reserves and thus can lend more money. Its borrowers find in turn that they can lend more, too. The sum the Fed has conjured out of thin air begins to circulate round the economic system.
>
> If Holmes writes out a lot of checks in one week, more money begins to circulate. Since the banks can make more loans, money becomes cheaper to borrow and hence business conditions pick up; loans for houses, car, business activities are easier to obtain.
>
> But how can the Fed write that check? Under law it has what amounts to an open-ended bank account. It can create money whenever it wants.[2]

The process the Fed uses to create money is illustrated in Figure 5-1.

The lengthy excerpt quoted above suggests how the Fed's role is perceived by those outside the system. Predictably, however, the members of the Federal Reserve Board have a different view if its functions. Arthur F. Burns, former chairman of the Board of Governors of the Federal Reserve System from 1970 to 1978, and mentioned in the previous quotation, portrays the Fed's role this way:

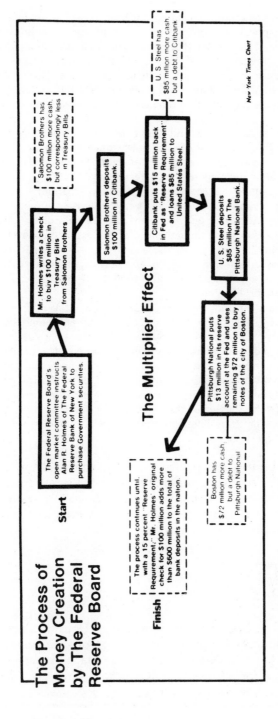

FIGURE 5-1. How the United States creates more money. [SOURCE: © 1976 by The New York Times Company. Reprinted by permission.]

Industrial nations, including our own, nowadays rely heavily on monetary policy to promote expansion of production and employment, to limit any decline that may occur in over-all economic activity, or to blunt the forces of inflation. There are two major reasons for the emphasis on monetary policy. In the first place, manipulation of governmental expenditures has proved to be a rather clumsy device for dealing with rapidly changing economic developments. Secondly, the process of reaching a consensus on needed tax changes usually turns out to be complex and time consuming. Experience has thus taught us that alterations of fiscal policy, once undertaken, frequently have a large part of their economic effect too late to be of much value in moderating fluctuations in business activity.

Even when the economy is booming, legislatures are rarely willing to increase tax rates or to restrain the rising curve of governmental expenditures. Such reluctance also limits the discretionary use of fiscal measures to counter the forces of recession that develop from time to time in a free enterprise economy. Once reduced, tax rates cannot easily be increased again, and new expenditure programs to stimulate a lagging economy all too often are the source of a new inflationary problem later on.

Fortunately, monetary policy is relatively free of these shortcomings. Flexibility is the great virtue of instruments of monetary and credit policy. Changes in the course of monetary policy can be made promptly and—if need be—frequently. Under our scheme of governmental organization, the Federal Reserve can make the hard decisions that might be avoided by decision-makers subject to the day-to-day pressures of political life. And experience indicates that the effects of substantial changes in the supply of money and credit are rather speedily transmitted through financial markets to the workshops of the economy ....[3]

In short, Burns seems to view the Fed as the regulator of the nation's economy: The Fed places public interest first; it is fast and flexible in its regulatory functions; it is independent of political pressures; and it is financed by its own operations. But, as the following discussion suggests, not all experts view the Fed in so rosy a light.

THE FEDERAL OPEN MARKET COMMITTEE (FOMC)

The Federal Open Market Committee (FOMC) is a powerful group within the Fed that determines the direction of U.S. Treasury bill rates. Even though the committee's decisions are made in secret and are kept from the public for 30 days, FOMC's actions often are reflected in the money markets immediately, and in the stock market later on.

The promotion of a healthy economy is the goal of most FOMC directives. For example:

> It is the policy of the Federal Open Market Committee to foster financial conditions consistent with sustainable real economic growth and increased employment, abatement of inflationary pressures, and attainment of reasonable equilibrium in the country's balance of payments.[4]

But there are frequent exceptions. Here's one: In February 1966, the FOMC directive was changed to instruct the manager of the Open Market Account to operate *"with a view toward a gradual reduction in reserve availability"*[5]—in other words, to create tighter money. *Within eight months, the stock market had dropped by 20 percent.* And another exception is illustrated in Table 5-1. The 1973 FOMC Targets indicated that money should definitely be tightened. The Federal Funds Rate Target was increased from 6.375 percent in January to over 10 percent in July. This brought about the first leg down of a bear market—a decline of 15 percent in six months.

A newspaper article described another example of money tightening: When monetary policy strategists, encouraged by periodic nudges, decide to allow interest rates to rise, the response is often pronounced. To illustrate, the article cited the following example: On June 16, 1975, 90-day T-bills sold at an average rate of 4.76 percent. On August 18, 1975, they sold at an average rate of 6.452 percent—an increase of over 35 percent in only two months. During this same period, the Dow Jones Industrial Index dropped 10 percent in six weeks—from 880 in late June to 790 in mid-August.[6]

PROBLEMS FACED BY THE FED

The Fed's goals don't appeal to every segment of the population equally. What's good policy for one group may be disastrous for another. Not all industries are equally affected by tight money policies, for instance. Those with a product (for example, food) whose demand is relatively fixed can thrive under tight money conditions. Others, however, may face bankruptcy when tight money policies lower the demand for their product (for example, houses). These inequities—and the public's response to them—can constitute a problem for the Fed.

Another of the Fed's basic problems, according to former board member Sherman Maisel, is how to operate while "knowing that it knows not."[7] Movements in money and interest rates come about when monetary instruments interact with other forces in the economy. But informa-

TABLE 5-1. 1973 FOMC targets for the open-market account manager.

Date of Meeting	Stated Intentions with Respect to Growth in Monetary Aggregates	Consistent "Tolerance" or Target Range in Two-Month Per-Annum Growth Rate in RPD Suggested by Staff Analysis	FOMC Decision on "RPD* Tolerance Range"	FFR Target Identified in Subsequent FOMC Policy Record
Jan. 16	"Slower ... over the months ahead than occurred in the second half of last year."	9 to 11%	4.5 to 10.5%	6⅜%
Feb. 13	"Slower ... over the months ahead than occurred on average in the past 6 months."	0.5 to 2.5%	−2.5 to 2.5%	7%+
Interim Telephone meeting (*ITM*) on March 1: Conferred about too-rapid growth in *RPD* and agreed to let the *FFR* rise to limit *RPD* growth.				
Mar. 19–20 Unchanged		14 to 16%	12 to 16%	7%
ITM on Apr. 11: Conferred about weaker-than-expected growth in *RPD* and aggregates, but declined to change policy guides so near the date of the next formal meeting.				
Apr. 17	"Moderate ... over the months ahead."	"relatively rapid rate of growth"	10 to 12%	7¾%
May 15	"Slower ... over the months immediately ahead than occurred on average in the past 6 months."	"relatively rapid growth"	9 to 11%	8 to 8½%
ITMs on May 24 and June 8: Conferred about too-rapid growth in *RPD* and aggregates, deciding to let the *FFR* rise if necessary to limit *RPD* growth.				

Date	Policy directive			
June 18–19	"Somewhat slower . . . over the months immediately ahead than appears indicated for the first half of the year."	9.5 to 11.5%	8 to 11.5%	9¾%
ITM on July 6: Conferred about too rapid growth in *RPD* and aggregates, deciding to let *FFR* rise if necessary.				
July 17	Same as June except for the deletion of "somewhat."	11.5 to 13.5%	11.5 to 13.5%	10½%
Aug. 21	"Slower . . . over the months immediately ahead than has occurred on average thus far this year."	13 to 15%	11 to 13%	10¾%
Sept. 18	"Moderate . . . over the months ahead."	15 to 17%	15 to 18%	10¾% to 10%
ITMs on Oct. 2 and 10: Conferred about slower than desired growth in *RPD* and aggregates and decided to pursue easier "money market conditions."				
Oct. 16	Unchanged	2 to 4%	2 to 5%	10%+
Nov. 19–20	Unchanged	–3 to –1%	–3 to –1%	10⅛%
ITM on Nov. 30: Conferred about too-rapid growth in aggregates, but decided, "to maintain current money market conditions for the time being."				
Dec. 17–18	"Some easing in . . . money market conditions, provided that the monetary aggregates do not appear to be growing excessively."	"moderate growth"	8¼ to 11%	9¾%
ITM on Jan. 11: Conferred about the possibility of *RPD* growth near upper tolerance limit and excessive growth in aggregates, but decided "to maintain the prevailing money market conditions for the time being."				

---

*RPD is Reserves Available to Support Private Nonbank Deposits and *FFR* is Federal funds rate.

[SOURCE: Reproduced from Edward J. Kane, "All for the Best: The Federal Reserve Board's 60th Annual Report," *American Economic Review* 64, December 1974: p. 838.]

tion about the economy, and about financial markets and their future trends, tends to be vague, contradictory, and sometimes inaccurate. Also, it's difficult to precisely define the effects of monetary variables in terms of time and scope. All this suggests that the Fed's decisions are largely based on impressionistic judgments, inadequate data, and unknown relationships.[8]

The Fed is secretive about its actions. Perhaps this is because it fears public criticism and political attack, and because its members believe that political pressures will lead to more inflation.[9] Whatever its motive, the Fed keeps its secrets by giving information summaries that are short and delayed, and by using deliberately vague language to describe its goals and operations. Some experts believe that this secretiveness weakens the Fed's ability to improve its own performance.[10]

But even if the Fed could overcome these problems, it still faces another that is more fundamental: Monetary policy can halt inflation only to a certain extent. Some of its limitations are inherent in the functioning of the economy itself. Thus, for example, lower consumer prices usually are balanced by higher unemployment, while lower unemployment comes with higher inflation. And since some consumer price increases originate on the cost side, or in certain industries, they cannot be controlled by any general policy. Finally, some sectors of the economy are hit disproportionately hard, regardless of how monetary policy is administered.

Why else is monetary policy often ineffective? According to Maisel, stringent money policy can cause a liquidity crisis, followed by a depression. Also, it is difficult to determine just what is the most effective combination of fiscal, monetary, and incomes policies, and errors in this field tend to produce inflationary results. In the past, monetary policy has been overemphasized at the expense of fiscal and incomes policy. As a result, other, perhaps more effective, forms of governmental action have not been used.[11] Maisel describes a time (February 1970) when the majority of FOMC "wanted a more serious recession" to correct inflationary tendencies, *even though the economy was already in a recession.*[12]

Some critics have argued that the Fed's actions can be compared to a bad thermostat: These actions cause the desired levels of monetary variables to be overshot and undershot.[13]

MAISEL'S LAW

Logically, the Fed should propose reforms to avert future problems. But, according to Maisel, it almost never does. On the contrary, "Maisel's Law" states that *"reform will be undertaken only after a crisis has occurred* [emphasis added]."[14] Maisel criticizes the Fed for its efforts to maintain the status quo at all costs, citing as an example the state of fixed foreign exchange rates in 1965, his first year in office. Foreign exchange rates during this period had become a drag on the economy, but the Fed acted only when the balance of payments rose to crisis proportions. It took a crisis to bring about substantial change.[15]

Maisel lists five unresolved international problems that faced the Fed in 1965: (1) the relationship of gold to other international reserves; (2) the lack of confidence in currencies; (3) the degree of rigidity or flexibility in exchange rates; (4) the control of speculative capital movements; and (5) the way in which internal policies should be altered in response to international imbalances.[16] Eight years later, when he published his study, almost none of these problems had been resolved.

If it is true that the Fed cannot implement reforms until after a crisis has occurred, then we can expect the crises to continue. This means that the stock market will continue to fluctuate, sometime violently. The lesson? Be careful, and take this probability into account.

THE FED'S CRITICS

As you can imagine, the Fed has many critics. Some of their arguments are based on fact, others on opinion, and still others on ignorance. Here are a few of the most frequently made criticisms.

The Fed neither requires nor seeks the approval of anyone—neither the president, nor the Congress, nor the people. This is true. The Fed is a completely autonomous agency. It was designed that way, to keep it from being affected by political pressures. But according to some critics, the Fed has, in fact, been motivated politically, tending to take easy money actions in the two years before elections.[17]

The Fed has never been subjected to an independent audit in 68 years. This is true as of January 1981.

The Fed creates booms and busts scientifically. It is true that the Fed's actions can bring about a boom or bust (though not always intentionally) in an effort to correct a short-term problem of excessive unemployment or inflation.

Officers of the Federal Reserve are engaged in a conflict of interest. These officers own more then $100 million in stocks. At the same time, they make decisions in secret that affect the prices of those stocks. This view is held by Gary Allen, contributing editor of *American Opinion*.[18]

Experts in the field have joined in, as well. Milton Friedman, the noted economist, says:

> Erratic swings in monetary growth are not a new phenomenon. They have been the major defect in Federal Reserve performance over the

whole of its 62-year history. Unduly rapid growth fueled the great inflations of World Wars I and II and the more recent double-digit inflation of 1974. Unduly slow growth or actual decline produced or deepened the sharp contractions of 1920–21, 1929–33, and 1937–38, as well as the milder recessions of the whole period.[19]

Gary Allen, an outspoken critic of the Fed, writes that when the cost of living rises sharply, the mass media usually blames the rise on greedy business people and selfish unions instead of the real culprits—the Fed and Congress. These two, according to Allen, could—but don't—stop inflation cold tomorrow morning by restricting the supply of new money. Consequently, the vast majority of the American people are confused about the causes of inflation and frustrated by their leaders' apparent inability to stop it.[20]

One economist calls the current situation "the economics of addiction." That is, to get the economy moving, the Fed inflates the money supply. But this works only temporarily; soon, the economy needs another injection of inflationary money. The vicious circle repeats itself until the economy is hooked, much like the dependency of a heroin addict. Each time, it needs a larger dosage to prevent withdrawal symptoms (recession). The presses that print the money run faster and faster. And if the presses were stopped, a recession or depression would follow.[21].

One of the Fed's strongest critics is economist Edward J. Kane, who criticizes the Fed's 1973 *Annual Report* on the following grounds:

- *The report doesn't discuss conflicts between short- and long-run policy.*
- The report doesn't mention unwise past policies of any official body that might have contributed to current inflation (This criticism tends to support the arguments of those who believe that the Fed is politically motivated and therefore that it cannot be completely objective.)
- The report notes that fiscal policy "turned somewhat more restrictive in 1973."

This last point is a gross understatement. These "somewhat more restrictive" policies contributed to the greatest loss of stock market dollars in history, far exceeding the dollar losses of 1929–32![22]

In short, the Fed has many critics with wide-ranging criticisms. Many of their criticisms seem justifiable. But in fairness, let us add that the Fed has at least one distinguished supporter: Paul Samuelson, the first American Nobel Prize laureate in economics. He has praised the Fed's policy during the 1960s as being not only admirable in its own right, but also superior to that of the 1950s, in terms of both technical proficiency and social goals.[23]

There is no doubt that the Federal Reserve System has a very powerful influence on the economy. It is hard to predict what the Fed may do to correct economic imbalances in the future. However, in Chapter 6, we will use two case histories to explore the logic of the Fed's actions.

NOTES

1. Membership of the Board of Governors of the Federal Reserve for the period 1913 through 1980 is shown in Appendix F.
2. Alexander Cockburn, and James Ridgeway, "Where Our Money Comes From," *Parade*, October 26, 1975, as cited in Gary Allen, "Federal Reserve: The Trillion-Dollar Conspiracy," *American Opinion*, February 1976, pp 76–77.
3. Arthur F. Burns, "The Independence of the Federal Reserve System," *Federal Reserve Bulletin* 62 (June 1976): 493.
4. Sherman J.Maisel, *Managing the Dollar,* New York: WW Norton, 1973, p. 64.
5. Ibid., p. 83.
6. "Wall Street Checking New Thesis," *San Francisco Chronicle,* August 25, 1975, p. 48.
7. Maisel, *Managing the Dollar,* p. 302.
8. Ibid.
9. Ibid., p. 117.
10. Ibid., pp. 305, 311.
11. Ibid., p. 15.
12. Ibid., p. 250.
13. Ibid., p. 295.
14. Ibid., p. 195.
15. Ibid.
16. Ibid., p. 227.
17. Ibid., p. 288
18. Gary Allen, "Federal Reserve: The Trillion-Dollar Conspiracy," *American Opinion,* February 1976, p. 79.
19. Milton Friedman, "How to Hit the Money Target," *Newsweek,* December 8, 1975, p. 85
20. Allen, "Federal Reserve," p. 85.
21. Gary North, as cited in Allen, "Federal Reserve," p. 87
22. Edward J. Kane, "All for the Best: The Federal Reserve Board's 60th Annual Report," *American Economic Review* 64 (December 1974):835–50.
23. Maisel, *Managing the Dollar,* p.23.

6

HISTORY CAN HELP YOU
FORECAST TIGHT MONEY

Although we may find it difficult to forecast how and when the Fed will act to make money tighter, we can get some excellent clues from history. In this chapter, we will look at two case histories that occurred in periods of violent economic swings. The first covers the period 1972–75; the second, the period 1928–33.

CASE HISTORY, 1972–75

Late 1972

In late 1972, unemployment was approximately 5 percent and declining slightly (Fig. 6-1). Real GNP was growing faster than usual—between 5 and 8 percent, compared to a historical 4 percent (Fig. 6-2). Auto sales were up at around 10 million units (Fig. 6-3). Industrial production and the leading indicators were rising (Fig. 6-4); so was the stock market (Fig. 6-5). In light of all these factors, the economy seemed to be booming.

In December 1972, the wholesale price index jumped to a high of 6 percent annualized (Fig. 6-6)—a jump that would be reflected the following year in the Consumer Price Index. By January 1973, persistent inflation had outpaced average weekly earnings (Fig. 6-7), resulting in declining real, spendable earnings. Money had to be tightened if inflation was to be controlled. In December 1972, rising interest rates revealed that the Fed had decided to tighten money. The result was a rise in borrowing costs (Fig. 6-8).

In November 1972, the Fed took the first action to tighten money: It raised bank reserve requirements and margin requirements. In December 1972, it decreased free bank reserves to a negative $500+ million. In January 1973, it raised the discount rate. In April 1973, 90-day U.S. T-

130

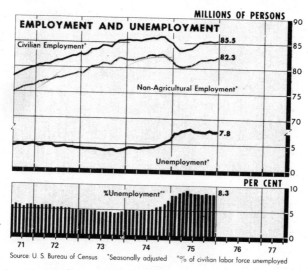

FIGURE 6-1.   Employment and unemployment. [*SOURCE:* Reproduced from "The Federal Budget," *Barometer of Business.* Chicago: Harris Bank, February 1976, pp. 2–3.]

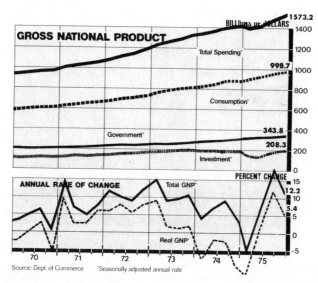

FIGURE 6–2.   Gross national product. [*SOURCE:* Reproduced from "The Federal Budget," *Barometer of Business.* Chicago: Harris Bank, February 1976, pp. 2–3.]

FIGURE 6-3. Automobile sales. [*SOURCE:* Reproduced from "The Federal Budget," *Barometer of Business.* Chicago: Harris Bank, February 1976, pp. 2–3.]

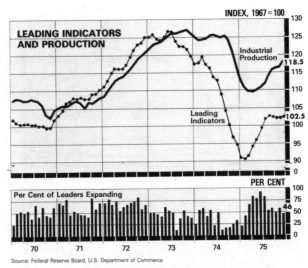

FIGURE 6-4. Leading indicators and production. [*SOURCE:* Reproduced from "The Federal Budget," *Barometer of Business.* Chicago: Harris Bank, February 1976, pp. 2–3.]

FIGURE 6–5. **Stock prices.** [*SOURCE:* Reproduced from "The Federal Budget," *Barometer of Business.* Chicago: Harris Bank, February 1976, pp. 2–3.]

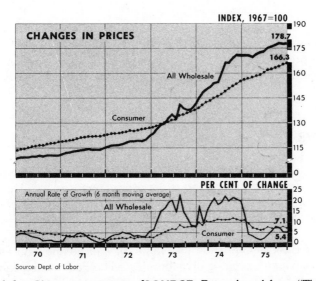

FIGURE 6-6. **Changes in prices.** [*SOURCE:* Reproduced from "The Federal Budget," *Barometer of Business.* Chicago: Harris Bank, February 1976, pp. 2–3.]

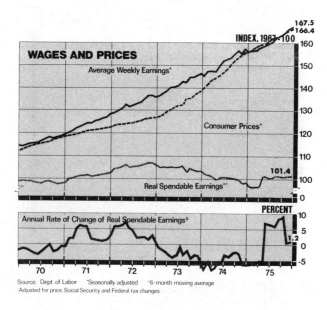

FIGURE 6-7.   Wages and prices. [*SOURCE:* Reproduced from "The Federal Budget," *Barometer of Business.* Chicago: Harris Bank, February 1976, pp. 2–3.]

bill rates rose above long-term government bond rates (Fig. 6-8). Combined, these signals indicated that money was extremely tight. *Investors who interpreted and acted on the signals were able to sell out near the top of the market. These people escaped the worst bear market since 1929.*

Late 1973

By late 1973, the economy was starting to decline. Unemployment was around 5 percent, and industrial production was flat. The GNP had turned down, auto sales were declining, and the stock market was heading down. At this point, what was needed was easier money. But the Fed decided to keep money tight.

Why? Basically, inflation was rampant and getting worse (Fig. 6-6), and wages weren't keeping up with prices. The Fed faced a very unusual situation: the combination of rising unemployment and rising inflation. Apparently, the Fed believed that inflation had to be slowed first; unemployment could be dealt with later.

Late 1974

By late 1974, the economic scene had degenerated even more. Unemployment was at 8 percent and rising sharply (Fig. 6-1). The GNP, auto sales, leading indicators and production, housing and stock prices were all declining dangerously (Figs. 6-2, 6-3, 6-4, 6-9, and 6-5, respectively). In fall 1974, short-term interest rates reached the highest peak in history (Fig. 6-8), which cut consumer and business spending sharply. Bankruptcies and insolvencies increased, particularly in industries such as construction and real estate, and in real estate investment trusts (REITS), all of which depend on orderly money market conditions.[1]

However, one important change occurred at this time: It looked like inflation (as measured by the wholesale and consumer price indexes) had peaked out (Fig. 6-6). Now it seemed that the Fed could make money easy without increasing inflation—and a good thing, too, because by this time the economy was on the brink of a major depression. Accordingly, the Fed lowered interest rates, and money grew easier. *The first easy money signal for buying stocks appeared as early as October 1974.*

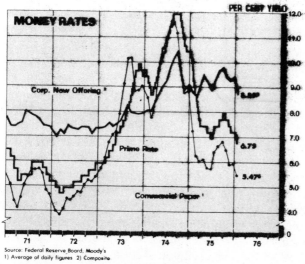

FIGURE 6-8. **Money rates.** [*SOURCE:* Reproduced from "Cautious Consumers Save," *Barometer of Business.* Chicago: Harris Bank, March 1976, pp. 2-3.]

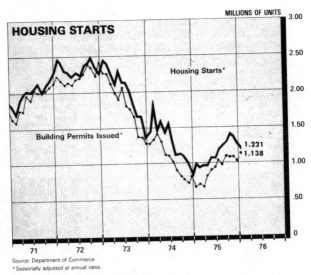

MILLIONS OF UNITS

FIGURE 6-9. Housing starts. [*Source:* Reproduced from "Cautious Consumers Save," *Barometer of Business.* Chicago: Harris Bank, March 1976, pp. 2–3.]

HOW TO FORECAST CHANGES IN
TIGHT AND EASY MONEY

This case history may lead you to think that forecasting the need for tight or easy money is a simple matter. But in practice, the Fed must consider hundreds of factors before making its decision, and this decision is always based on an uncertain future. Furthermore, it's hard to time the effects of a decision to ease or tighten money. For example, short-term interest rates reached their highest point in summer 1974. However, the stock market reached its lowest point in winter of the same year.

Timing will always pose problems, but as an investor you should be alert to conditions that signal a need to change from tight to easy money—or vice versa. For example, if inflation is rising, unemployment is low, and business is booming, tighter money is needed. Under these circumstances, the next move in the stock market is likely to be down. If you are prudent, you will sell you securities, perhaps relying on broken trend lines or support levels to time your sales.

The wisdom of hindsight always makes it easier to reconstruct why the Fed acted as it did in the past than to forecast what it will do in the future. This is why you generally will profit by acting on TMT signals when they occur, rather than attempting to forecast the Fed's future moves. The only exception to this rule is if you have a sizable portfolio. In this case you would need a longer lead time to become properly invested.

CASE HISTORY, 1929–32

The Great Depression is a prime example of how the stock market reacts to tight money. In 1922, the *New York Times* Industrial Stock Index was 108. *Seven years later, it had surged to 381—up 350 percent—reflecting an increase of 62 percent in the money supply over the previous eight years.* In an attempt to control the booming economic machine it had created, the Fed then timidly tried to tighten the superabundant credit supply by raising the discount rate three times in 1928 and once in 1929. It did nothing to change bank reserve requirements during this period. Unfortunately, however, the Fed acted too little and too late.[2] Fig 6-10 shows the status of the stock market in 1929, when the S&P 500 Stock Index peaked at 315. A little over two-and-a-half years later, this index was down to 44, a drop of 86 percent. The value of the listed shares on September 1, 1928 was $89,668,276,854. Three months later, as of December 1, it was $63,589,338,823—a loss of over $26 billion in only three months. According to the *Commercial and Financial Chronicle,* the total loss during the same period—including the curb (now the American Stock Exchange) and over-the-counter securities —was about $40 billion.[3]

Problems with TMT Signals, 1928–32

TMT signals have had a relatively good record, with one notable exception: the period 1928–32. In one respect, the tight money signals that occurred early in 1928, warning of the terrible decline to come in the U.S. stock market, were correct. However, the warning came a year and a half early. As "Sell" signals, they correlated less with the U.S. stock market than with the London and Berlin stock markets, both of which peaked in 1928 (Fig. 6-10).

The first tight money signal occurred in January 1928, when U.S. T-bill rates rose above long-term government bond rates. The market went sideways for three months, then it rose about 80 percent before peaking 18 months later.

The next tight money signal occurred in February 1928, when the Fed increased the discount rate from 3.5 to 4 percent. Over the next 18 months, it increased this rate to 4.5 percent, to 5 percent, and finally to 6 percent on August 9, 1929. *This last 20 percent rise in the discount rate constituted the coupe de grâce for the stock market* (Fig. 3–5b).[4]

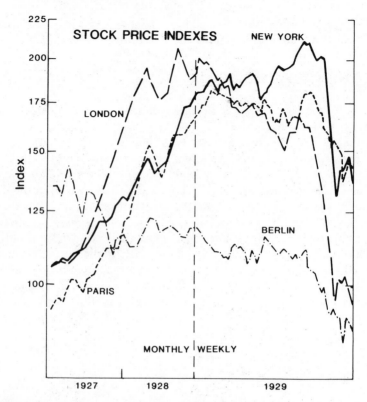

FIGURE 6-10.   Stock price indexes. [*SOURCE:* Adapted from, Irving Fisher, *"The Stock Market Crash—and After."* New York: Macmillan, 1930, p.33.

As Chapter 2 explained, the TMT signals I studied for the depression years were the discount rate, the U.S. Treasury bill rate versus the long-term government bond rate, and bank reserve requirements. I found that the Fed made no changes in bank reserve requirements from 1917 to 1936. The prime rate may, in fact, have signaled warnings, but we can't tell—accurate information on the prime rate is available only from 1933. Regulation Q, which sets the maximum rate of interest banks can pay on time deposits, was established in that same year. I studied free-reserve figures from 1946. Federal funds information was available only from July 1954.

In short, tight money signals occurred in the first part of 1928, but they were early and ineffective. Margin requirements were needed to curb speculation, but the Fed had no power to set them. Nor would it gain this power until 1934.

The Causes of
the Great Depression

Ever since it happened, people have been asking, "What caused the stock market crash of 1929–32?" Opinions vary. Some critics have blamed top government officials for describing business conditions via "unduly optimistic statements," which worked the country into a "fever of speculation." One critic blamed the then-chairman of the Democratic National Committee, John L. Raskob, for the collapse, since he had urged people to buy stocks. Other critics pointed fingers at stock gamblers, and at brokers and speculators who sold short. One critic blamed "this nation-wide gambling house which is called the New York Stock Exchange." A banker attributed the crash to the blocking of a congressional tariff bill. One prominent businessman criticizes the Fed for not lowering the rediscount rate (now called the discount rate) to 3 percent; another blamed it for not raising this rate drastically. Bankers were blamed for sending the populace into debt; trusts were blamed for dumping stocks on the market. Roger W. Babson, a noted financial analyst, was blamed for saying that a crash would come "sooner or later."[5]

On April 18, 1929, the National City Bank of New York released a special circular that said, "If the rate of credit increase rises above the rate of business growth, we have a condition of inflation which manifests itself in rising prices in some departments of the business structure, over-confidence, excessive speculation, and an eventual crash." One statistic noted in this report was the extraordinary growth of brokers' loans, from $1.6 billion at the end of 1927 to $3.3 billion at the end of 1928—an increase of 106 percent in one year.[6] By 1929, brokers' loans had reached over $8 billion, while call money rates exceeded 15 percent.

One of the most illuminating studies on the causes of the Great Depression, *Did Monetary Forces Cause the Great Depression?*,[7] lists a series of problems that preceded and coincided with the crash. To begin with, there was on oversupply of housing at then-current prices. Financial markets were tight, and personal income dropped, which resulted in lower spending. At this point, investors and corporations became eager to reduce their borrowings. Before 1929, leverage was more acceptable than cash in hand. But after 1929, it was the other way around. The weather also worsened the situation by causing a poor harvest in 1929; this, in turn, reduced agricultural income, affecting the 20 percent of the U.S. labor force employed in agriculture. In October of that year, the stock market collapsed. This combination of adverse events caused both consumption and public confidence to drop severely, which, in turn, had a profoundly depressing effect on the economy. At the same time, Europe was experiencing a parallel depression of its own, making it impossible for the United States to seek help abroad.

In November 1929, the Fed made a rather feeble attempt to stem the tide: It lowered the discount rate in two steps from 6 to 4.5 percent. During the following year, it lowered the discount rate further—from 4.5 to 2.5 percent—in four steps. This drove the market up briefly in early 1930. After this, the Fed's actions apparently lost their effectiveness until mid-1932, when the stock market almost doubled in three months. Milton Friedman argues that by reducing the nation's money supply in the 1930s, the Fed caused a mere recession to turn into the Great Depression.[8]

According to scholars who follow business cycles, particularly cycles of 50 years or more, the coincident downward waves of the business cycle reinforced the powerful initial effect that the Great Depression had on the world's economies.[9] That is, everything went wrong at once and became worse as the downward momentum accelerated.[10]

If we look at case histories for the periods 1972 to 1975 and 1928 to 1933, we can find many clues about forecasting the occurrence of tight money, and of subsequent stock market declines.[11] However, the effect of tight money is not confined to the U.S. stock market. It is felt worldwide, like a giant wave that strikes different shores at different times, and with different degrees of force. Tight money has other effects, as well: It brings about disintermediation; it affects the degree of public optimism; and it correlates with election results and unemployment. In Chapter 7, we will analyze all these effects.

NOTES

1. Raymond Jallow, *1976 Forecast.* Los Angeles, Calif.: United California Bank, Planning and Research Division, 1975, p. 10.
2. Susan L. Brown et al., *The Incredible Bread Machine.* San Diego, Calif.: World Research, 1974, pp 33–39.
3. Irving Fisher, *The Stock Market Crash—and After.* New York: Macmillan, 1930, p.1.
4. Ibid., p.1.
5. Ibid., pp. xi–xii.
6. Ibid., pp. xiv, xv.
7. Peter Temin, *Did Monetary Forces Cause the Great Depression?* New York: Norton, 1976.
8. Milton Friedman, "Medal for a Monetarist," *Time,* October 25, 1976, p. 58.
9. George Garvy, "Kondratieff's Theory of Long Cycles," *Review of Economics and Statistics* 25 (November 1943):203–20; N.D. Kondratieff, "The Long

Waves in Economic Life," *Review of Economics and Statistics* 17 (November 1935):105–15; and Joseph A. Schumpeter, *Business Cycles,* 2 vols. New York: McGraw-Hill, 1939.

10. One seasoned market observer believes that it is misleading to speak of the crash of 1929–32. This observer points out that after the discount rate had been cut twice—from 6 to 5 percent and then to 4.5 percent—a strong four-month rally took place, ending in April 1930. Many stocks reached new bull market highs in 1930; conversely, dozens of important stocks were in downtrends during the bull market that preceded the depression. A few stocks bottomed out in 1929 and started major bull market trends of their own. John Magee, *The General Semantics of Wall Street.* Springfield Mass.: John Magee, 1958, p. 187.

11. Appendix G shows the long-range market perspective on this topic, and lists the major market averages for the period 1949–80. Appendix B lists the monthly stock price indexes for 67 years, from 1914 to 1981.

7

TIGHT AND EASY MONEY: BEYOND THE U.S. STOCK MARKET

It isn't only in the United States that tight and easy money affect the stock market. Tight or easy money interacts internationally, cutting across political, sociological, psychological, and economic barriers. It can disrupt money markets in a process called *disintermediation*. It can bring about discomfort in the economy. There is a strong correlation between election and stock market cycles, and another strong correlation between the Federal Funds rate and rate of unemployment. Now let's examine each of these effects.

INTERNATIONAL INTERACTION

The Federal Reserve has the power to determine both the level and the direction of interest rates in the United States. The fact that short-term interest rates are very roughly correlated in most industrial nations caused me to investigate just how much international power the U.S. Federal Reserve exerts. Figure 7-1 shows the relationship among short-term interest rates in the United States, Germany, and the United Kingdom for the period 1969–77. Table 7–1 lists T-bill rates for the period 1972–76 for the United States, Canada, Japan, Australia, the United Kingdom, Belgium, Germany, the Netherlands, Sweden, Brazil, the Philippines, Singapore, and South Africa. As Figure 7-1 and Table 7-1 both illustrate, international interest rates tend to move together in a very broad correlation when their movements are measured in terms of years, but in a more random manner when their movements are measured in terms of months. This means that the Fed's actions are broadly correlated with international interest rates. While the Fed may influence these international interest rates, its own power to set interest rates is somewhat restricted by the

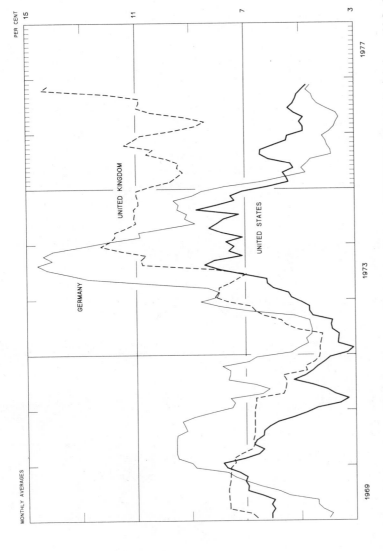

FIGURE 7-1. Short-term interest rates in selected countries. [SOURCE: Reproduced from U.S. Federal Reserve Board, Division of Administrative Services, Publications Services, *Monthly Chart Book,* 1976, p. 83.

TABLE 7-1. Treasury bill rates (international), 1972–76.

| | 1972 | 1973 | 1974 | | | | 1975 | | | | 1976 | | |
	Dec.	Dec.	Dec.	Aug.	Sept.	Oct.	Nov.	Dec.	Jan.	Feb.	Mar.		
United States	5.21	7.54	7.28	6.52	6.94	5.59	5.64	5.27	4.74	5.01	5.06
Canada	3.65	6.32	7.05	7.87	8.46	8.16	8.52	8.64	8.59	8.79	9.07
Japan	4.15	5.80	6.83	6.06	5.68	5.68	5.68	5.68	5.68	5.68	5.68
Australia	3.85	7.35	7.81	7.19	7.19	7.19	7.19	7.19	6.98	6.98	6.98
United Kingdom	8.48	12.82	11.44	10.66	11.79	11.74	11.30	10.78	9.52	8.80	8.60
Belgium	4.80	7.65	10.50	6.05	6.05	6.05	6.05	6.05	6.50	6.40	9.00
Germany	4.30	7.12	5.19	3.40	n.i.	n.i.	n.i.	n.i.	n.i.	n.i.	n.i.
Netherlands	4.25	10.00	7.50	2.75	3.75	4.50	4.75	5.00	4.50	2.50	2.50
Sweden	2.77	2.52	8.95	6.36	6.35	5.83	4.81	4.81	4.55	4.55	4.55
Brazil	15.36	14.75	18.35	17.37	18.73	20.59	24.16	25.10	25.51	26.32	n.a.
Philippines	12.29	9.66	10.31	11.84	10.88	9.46	9.51	9.62	9.77	9.64	9.41
Singapore	3.75	3.68	4.48	3.17	3.40	3.39	3.39	3.36	3.38	3.44	3.35
South Africa	4.42	3.21	6.16	6.51	6.75	6.96	6.96	7.05	7.12	7.29	7.52

Bond-Equivalent Yields, at or near End of Month

[SOURCE: *World Financial Markets*. New York: Morgan Guaranty Trust Co. of New York, April 1976, p. 15.]

interest rates in other industrialized countries. Certainly, a large difference between the interest rates in two or more countries cannot exist for long, all other things being equal.

Could the Federal Reserve slow down the U.S. economy without the cooperation of other industrial nations? Not likely. High interest rates in the United States probably would attract money from foreign nations, which would tend to force U.S. interest rates down and foreign interest rates up. One country may lower interest rates to stimulate its economy, but this attempt may be thwarted when another country raises interest rates to slow its economy. The funds needed to stimulate business in the country with low interest rates may flow instead to the country with high interest rates. Consequently, there is a great need for international cooperation in controlling interest rates to suit each country's particular requirements.

Does the Fed have the power to lead world interest rates? Will the proper level of interest rates for each industrial country eventually be determined by international consensus? I put these questions to William M. Burke, a senior economist at a Federal Reserve bank. He replied, "Indications are that there is a high degree of cooperation among nations regarding interest rates."[1] As international trade grows, this degree of economic cooperation should grow along with it.

Figure 7-2 shows stock prices for seven major nations for the period 1969–80. As you can see, the stock market tops and bottoms for Japan, West Germany, France, the United Kingdom, Italy, and Canada correlate only roughly with those of the United States, indicating that tight money occurs at different times in different countries. This matches the observation that international interest rates correlate with each other only very roughly. When the economies of two countries are tied together closely, their stock markets tend to be strongly correlated—for example, the United States and Canada. However, note that Canada's stock market made a very feeble recovery in 1975, compared to that of the United States (Fig. 7-2), probably because Canada's T-bill rates were rising while those of the United States were falling (Table 7-1). This merely confirms what I said before: *Rising interest rates in a particular country will put pressure on the stock market in that country.* Foreign investors in U.S. stocks face a double peril—they are exposed to the risk of (1) rising short-term interest rates in the United States; and (2) the falling foreign-exchange value of the dollar.

Because the U.S. dollar is so important in world trade, any changes the Fed makes in U.S. monetary policy are felt worldwide. However, the effectiveness of the Fed's actions in raising interest rates is limited by the international flow of funds. These funds tend to move to those countries that provide the greatest net return.

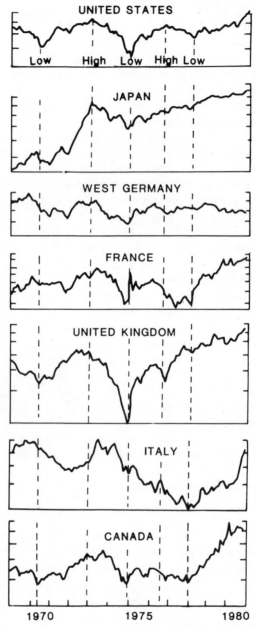

FIGURE 7-2.   International comparisons, stock prices, 1969–80. [*SOURCE:* Reproduced from U.S. Department of Commerce, *Business Conditions Digest,* December 1980, p. 59.]

DISINTERMEDIATION

Money tends to flow into investments where it can receive the greatest return, and out of investments where it receives a low return, assuming equal risk and maturity. This process is called *disintermediation*. In many cases, disintermediation is caused by tight money. For example, when interest rates paid by U.S. T-bills are higher than rates paid by savings and loan associations, depositors tend to withdraw funds from the latter and invest them in the former. Higher T-bill rates also attract money from the stock and bond markets, which creates lower prices for those securities.

Time deposits at financial institutions generally have a maximum interest rate ceiling set by law. When money is extremely tight, corporations often compete for money in the marketplace by offering commercial paper at higher yields than those offered by financial institutions. Since corporations have no interest rate ceilings, money from time deposits (which pay approximately 5 percent) tends to be removed and reinvested in commercial paper (which may pay 6 percent or more). When money becomes easy—that is, when the supply of funds becomes plentiful, and the demand for new funds lessens—yields decline so much that it is more attractive to put new funds into financial institutions. This is another example of disintermediation.

Disintermediation usually causes particularly serious problems for the housing construction industry. This is because savings and loan associations, mutual savings banks, and life insurance companies are the major sources of mortgage loans for housing in the United States. When disintermediation causes funds for these loans to shrink, severe housing shortages result.

Another example of disintermediation is shown in Figure 7-3. The volume of money invested in certificates of deposit (CDs) dropped by over $10 billion from January to March 1976. The 90-day CD rates dropped to 5 percent, which is below the 5.25 percent or more paid by an insured savings and loan account. We can conclude that part of these funds were moving out of CDs into higher yielding savings and loan deposits, or that the banks were offering fewer CDs due to the lower demand for business loans. These signs of easy money caused the rapid increase in stock prices that happened during this same period.

DISCOMFORT INDEX

One of the most important reasons for making changes in monetary policy is to keep inflation and unemployment under control. How much

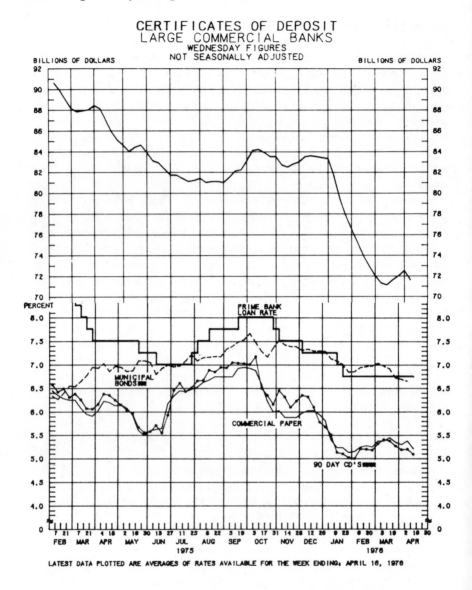

FIGURE 7-3.   **Certificates of deposit, 1975–76.** [*SOURCE:* Reproduced from *U.S. Financial Data.* St. Louis, Mo.: Federal Reserve Bank of St. Louis, week ending April 16 1976, released April 18, 1976, pp. 6, 10.]

this is achieved, in turn, affects the consumer's so-called "comfort" or "discomfort." Arthur Okun, former chairman of the Council of Economic Advisers, suggests a simple index for measuring the discomfort level in a given economy: Multiply the unemployment rate by the annual rate of change in consumer prices. The larger the product, the greater the discomfort.[2]

By looking at Figures 6-1 and 6-6, you will see that inflation peaked in fall 1974, and unemployment peaked in May 1975. This gave a discomfort index of 84 in fall 1974, but of only 54 in May 1975—a remarkable change for the better (Table 7-2). A more desirable discomfort index might be 10; this figure assumes an unemployment rate of 5 percent and an inflation rate of 2 percent.

Although the discomfort index is affected by tight or easy money, the index itself doesn't tell whether money is tight or easy. This is because unemployment is usually resolved with easier money, while inflation is usually resolved with tighter money. The chief value of the discomfort index is that it indicates how the U.S. population feels about the economy.

WHAT HAS THE STOCK MARKET TO DO WITH ELECTIONS?

A correlation between election results and stock market cycles has been observed by many market analysts. Figures 3–5a through 3–5e show election dates, along with the names of successful presidential candidates since 1914. Between 1914 and 1962, the presidential election cycle seems to have had little influence on stock market cycles. However, from

TABLE 7–2.   Discomfort index.

	Fall 1974	May 1975	December 1976	Desirable
Unemployment	7%	9%	8%	5%
Inflation	×12%	×6%	×6%	×2%
Discomfort Index	84	54	48	10

1962 to 1977 a strong pattern emerges. As Francis H. M. Kelly, research director at Blyth Eastman Dillion, says, "There is a great deal of orchestration that goes into the fine art of making the economy sing appropriate melodies to the score of quadrennial elections."[3]

What can we conclude from this? Perhaps that the Fed, in spite of its stated goals, has become much less independent in recent years and much more subject to political influence, particularly by the party in power. L. J. Santow, a Wall Street economist, says, "It's my own judgement that, yes, the Fed did act on political considerations in 1972. Its monetary policies were easier (more stimulative) than would have otherwise been the case. But, of course there's no proof."[4]

To test the correlation between the election and the stock market, we can use Table 7-3. It shows the results of buying stocks two years before a presidential election and selling stocks on that election and reveals that since 1962 this strategy has made it easy to outperform the stock market. This correlation could be a mere coincidence; or it could be based on business cycles or on the current need for tight or easy money; or it could be seen as a basis for doubting the political integrity of the nation's leaders.

This election strategy also can be reversed. Stocks can be sold short on election and bought back two years later (Table 7-4). The results of this strategy pretty well confirm that a strong election cycle has existed since 1962. A investor who sold stock short on each election and bought it back two years later would once again have outperformed the stock market. However, we don't mean to imply that it is valid to project future results on

TABLE 7–3.   Election/stock market cycles: first strategy.

Buy Stock Two Years Before Election		Sell Stock on Election		
Date*	Stock Market Index	Date	Stock Market Index	Gain (%)
1962	58	1964	85	+46
1966	81	1968	104	+28
1970	84	1972	115	+37
1974	71	1976	103	+45
1978	96	1980	129	+34
1982	?			

*Data based on November of each year.

TABLE 7–4. Election/stock market cycles: second strategy.

Sell Stock Short on Election		Buy Stock Back Two Years After Election		
Date	Stock Market Index	Date	Stock Market Index	Gain (%)
1964	85	1966	81	+ 5
1968	106	1970	84	+21
1972	115	1974	7·1	+38
1976	103	1978	96	+ 7
1980	129	1982	?	

*Data based on November of each year.

the basis of past performance. Stock market strategy is never that simple and it changes with the changing composition of the Fed.

The election cycle has paralleled the tight and easy money cycles since 1962. In 1964, 1968, and 1972, groups of tight money signals occurred within a relatively short period after the presidential election. In 1962, 1967, and 1970–71, groups of easy money signals have occurred one to two years before the presidential elections. This evidence supports the link between political cycles and TMT signals. This link could be weakened if the Fed were to become less sensitive to political influence, or reinforced if the Fed lost its present independence from political pressure.

WHAT HAS UNEMPLOYMENT TO DO WITH FEDERAL FUNDS?

The Fed's decisions are strongly influenced by the unemployment rate. This is apparent from the fact that there is a strong correlation between the Federal funds interest rate and the unemployment rate for the 20-year period 1955 to 1975. The Federal funds rate tended to be at its cyclical low point when the unemployment rate was at its high point. As Figure 7-4 illustrates, the *peaks in unemployment coincided with the low points in the Federal funds interest rates in 1958, 1961, and 1971.* The reverse was true in *1960, 1967, 1969, and 1973, when peaks in the Federal funds rate coincided with low points in unemployment.*[5]

Thus, a peak in unemployment indicates a probable turn in short-term interest rates. This conclusion is based upon cause (high unemployment) and effect (lower Federal funds interest rates). Of course, this

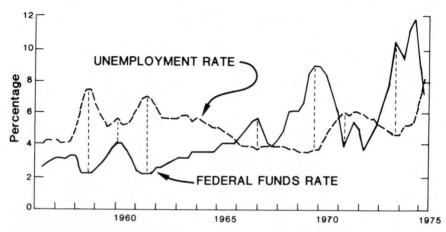

FIGURE 7-4. Federal funds rate versus unemployment rate. [*SOURCE:* Reproduced from Rod McKnew and Jan Wasilewsky, "Interest Rate Forecasting," *Weekly Monetary Summary.* San Francisco: Bank of America, February 14, 1975, p.1.]

simple correlation must be used wisely, in anticipation of exceptions and unforeseen events. For example, should the Fed consider double-digit inflation to be more important than rising unemployment, it might choose to raise the Federal funds rate in spite of the rising unemployment rate. (In fact, this happened in the first half of 1974.)

Whether directly or indirectly, the whole world is affected by tight and easy money. In this chapter we have examined the correlations between tight and easy money and various other factors—international interaction, disintermediation, the discomfort index, the election and stock market cycles, and the unemployment rate versus the Fed funds rate. In Chapter 8, we will summarize the observations and conclusions to be derived from this book.

NOTES

1. William M. Burke, Senior Economist and Director of Public Information, Federal Reserve Bank of San Francisco, interview held in San Francisco, March 8, 1976.
2. Sherman J. Maisel, *Managing the Dollar.* New York: Norton, 1973, p. 288.
3. Charles J. Elia, "Election Cycle Effect on Stock Market Linked to Politics of Short-Term Economic Remedies," *Wall Street Journal,* April 23, 1976, p. 29.

4. John Getz, "Fed's Role in Election Year," *San Francisco Chronicle,* September 23, 1976, p. 57.
5. Rod McKnew, and Jan Wasilewsky, "Interest Rate Forecasting," *Weekly Monetary Summary,* San Francisco: Bank of America, February 14, 1975, p.1.

8
OBSERVATIONS AND CONCLUSIONS

In this, the concluding chapter, we summarize the observations and conclusions to be drawn about Tight Money Timing.

MAJOR CONCLUSIONS

On the basis of the material presented in this book, we can draw three major conclusions:

- The TMT hypothesis is valid. Tight money occurring in a given time period is a major cause of a declining stock market. Easy money occurring in a given time period is a major cause of a rising stock market;
- For forecasting purposes, groups of easy money signals have historically been more reliable than groups of tight money signals; and
- TMT can be used in either of two ways: (1) to time purchases and sales of portfolio stock; or (2) to forecast the direction of the stock market.

SPECIFIC CONCLUSIONS

We can also make other, more specific observations and conclusions.

Forecasting and Timing

We can draw several conclusions about forecasting and timing. First, the stock market tends to decline or to slow its rise when one or any combination of the following tight money signals occurs:

- The discount rate is increased;

- The Federal funds rate changes from a downtrend to an uptrend;
- Initial margin requirements are raised;
- The banking system's free reserves exceed minus $500 million (e.g., minus $900 million);
- The prime rate is first raised after a decline;
- Regulation Q increases the maximum interest rates allowed on savings accounts;
- Bank reserve requirements are raised;
- Short-term interest rates exceed long-term interest rates, or the yield curve becomes inverted.

A knowledge of these data and of four-year political cycles provides valuable clues that will help you determine when to sell securities. *When money becomes tight, most stocks should be sold out of portfolios immediately or timed for near-term sale, because most common stocks can be expected to decline under tight money conditions.*

Second, TMT signals, while not concurrent, do tend to occur together within a matter of weeks or months at major market turns. For example, the 1972–73 market top was preceded by the following TMT signals: Reserve requirements were raised; margin requirements were raised, the prime rate was raised; the discount rate was raised; and net borrowed reserves exceeded $500 million. All these signals occurred within a two-month period. Money was tight, and the market, as measured by the S&P 500 Index, subsequently declined by almost 50 percent.

Third, the stock market tends to rise when one or any combination of the following easy money signals occurs:

- The discount rate is lowered;
- The Federal funds rate changes from an uptrend to a downtrend;
- Initial margin requirements are lowered;
- The banking system's free reserves decline below minus $500 million (e.g., minus $100 million);
- The prime rate is first lowered after an increase;
- Regulation Q decreases the maximum interest rates allowed on savings accounts;
- Bank reserve requirements are lowered;
- Short-term interest rates drop below long-term interest rates, or the yield curve returns to normal after having been inverted.

As money becomes easy, there is a better chance of making successful investments in common stocks, because most common stocks can be expected to rise under easy money conditions.

Fourth, *TMT signals provide a sound basis for forecasting stock market trends.* Each new signal may confirm a given forecast or call it into question. Thus, for example, if current and previous signals all indicate that money is growing easier, this confirms a forecast of a rising stock market. When a previous signal is reversed—for example, when a tight money signal occurs after a series of easy money signals—the previous forecast must be reviewed to determine the aberrant TMT signal's importance, direction, magnitude, and level.

Fifth, an investor must monitor all eight of the TMT signals in order to be aware of changing trends in monetary tightness. For example, if you monitored only the three TMT signals used in the three-step-and-stumble rule, you would have completely missed the change in Regulation Q that forecast the 1962 decline. Significant correlations can be made for a single TMT signal (for example, the discount rate), but if you monitor all eight signals you will greatly increase your chances of forecasting major moves in the stock market correctly.

Sixth, in a rising stock market, profitable performance depends on the selection of the right stocks and industry groups. However, accurate stock market forecasting is basic to profitable performance. According to economist Benjamin F. King, the direction of the market determines 31 percent of the movement of stocks. [1]

Forecasting Interest Rates

The record of forecasts of interest rates has been poor, in terms of direction and magnitude. Chester D. Goss, president of CIT Corp. and CIT Leasing Corp., had said, "The inability of trained people to forecast future money costs is one of the most intriguing things I encounter. These costs are vital to us. We trade in money."[2] This suggests that *TMT signals should be taken seriously, regardless of what other experts have forecast.* Markets have a way of proving the majority wrong and the minority right. Of course, you still must use good judgment in making decisions based on TMT analysis.

The Impact of TMT Signals

We can draw two conclusions regarding the impact of TMT signals on the stock market. First, this impact is hard to weigh and measure. How do you compare a 0.25 percent change in the prime rate with a change in the reserve requirements? Perhaps the most important use of Tight Money Timing is that it signals a change in monetary tightness, even though a single signal may not indicate the extent of this change.

However, an abnormally large change in one signal may be extremely important. For example, on August 9, 1929, the discount rate increased 20 percent—from 5 to 6 percent. On January 1, 1962, the maximum savings rate increased by one-third—from 3 to 4 percent. Both these signals preceded bear markets.

Second, the findings of this research on the impact of TMT signals are consistent with the theoretical findings of Friedmanite economists Robert E. Lucas, Jr., of the University of Chicago, and Thomas J. Sargent and Neil Wallace, both of the University of Minnesota:

> The first [of these economists' findings] is that any [government] policy move that is widely expected will have no impact at the time it is taken, since it has been discounted by thé public, much as the price of a stock already reflects all known information about the future earnings of a company. And second is the corollary that only policy moves that people do not expect will cause changes in current behavior, just as the only thing that moves a stock's price is some new information that has not been previously anticipated.[3]

Tight Money Timing is concerned with changes in monetary tightness that are usually unexpected and therefore haven't been discounted by the market. (Refer to Figs. 3–2a through 3–2h and 3–5a through 3–5e.)

Expert Opinions

Various experts use various approaches to tight money. And these approaches have different drawbacks. Forecasters who depend on specific rules to interpret tight money may miss important changes in the stock market. For example, because the three-step-and-stumble rule does not include bank reserve requirements or Regulation Q as signals, it missed the major stock market decline of over 50 percent in 1937, which occurred after the bank reserve requirements had been raised three times. It also missed the Regulation Q signal that occurred on January 1, 1962, and which was followed by a major market decline of over 25 percent. The latter is an example of how one strong signal may prove to be more accurate than three weaker ones.

Monetary factors can be combined to construct an index. This involves weighting the factors in question, a process that is arbitrary at best. Each new market will probably require index tuning (adjusting) because one factor was not properly weighted or was completely overlooked. For example, analysts now weight inflation heavily—but only *since* 1974, when it became a major problem. Because specific rules can miss important TMT signals, and because they cannot anticipate new variables, I did not develop mathematical models to support the TMT hypothesis.

TMT Definitions

We can make two observations regarding the definitions of tight money timing. First, while money managers generally agree that tight money makes the market go down and easy money makes the market go up, there aren't really any generally accepted definitions of tight or easy money. This book defines these terms relative to the timing and forecasting of the stock market.

Second, I define *tight money* as occurring at the point when short-term (T-bill) interest rates exceed long-term (government bond) rates, and when net borrowed reserves exceed $500 million.

Tighter money occurs at the point when there are increases in one or more of the following:[4]

- The discount rate;
- The Federal funds rate (if it moves and holds above its 10-week moving average, defined earlier);
- The prime rate;
- The margin requirements for securities;
- Negative free reserves;
- Regulation Q, savings account interest;
- Reserve requirements; and
- The T-bill rate.

The Federal Reserve System

We can draw several conclusions about the Federal Reserve System. First, *the Fed's actions are the single most important guide to stock market trends.*

Second, the Fed usually gives the stock market a low priority relative to other, more important areas in the economy (for example, inflation, employment, and housing). *It would be naive to assume that the Fed would deliberately act to help the stock market.* In fact, a change in the margin requirement is the only TMT signal that affects the market directly. A lower margin requirement allows investors and speculators to buy more stock, while a higher requirement allows them to buy less.

Third, Newton's second law of motion can be paraphrased as follows:

"For every Federal Reserve action there is (likely to be) a stock market reaction."[5]

Fourth, the Federal Reserve Board has more power to bring about tight or easy money than any other person or group in the United States. This, in turn, gives it an equivalent power to cause major changes in stock market trends. There is strong evidence in favor of the following assertions:

- The Fed's actions have a powerful influence on the stock and bond markets (a fact unknown to the average investor),
- The Fed's actions have influenced the stock market more greatly in recent years, and they will continue to have considerable influence in the future;
- *Investors will continue to be at the mercy of the Fed's decisions, unless they learn to turn these decisions to their own advantage.* To do so, they must understand the importance of tight money, learn to recognize it when it occurs, and be prepared to take appropriate action at the appropriate time; and
- *No institution or investor, no matter how big, can withstand the devastating effect of tight money on its portfolios.*[6]

GENERAL OBSERVATIONS

Finally, we can make a number of general observations and conclusions.

1. Money is made tighter in a series of actions that get more and more severe. The Fed can come close to shutting money off entirely by making it highly expensive and almost unavailable. The exact effect of tight money may never be known; however, it has an undeniably negative effect on the stock market.

2. TMT signals are not a recent phenomenon—they have been an extremely important force in the stock market since 1913 (during the total period covered in this book). In fact, tight and easy money have probably affected various stock and commodity markets for may thousands of years, through natural market forces.

3. Most TMT signals are leading indicators of the stock market.

4. Fourth, the effects of TMT signals tend to die out if they are not followed by other, similar, TMT signals.

5. The relationship between the growth in money supply and the stock market has been written about extensively. Some experts claim to have proved that growth in money supply can forecast the market.[7]

Others claim that it cannot.[8] As of this writing, the issue remains unresolved. I contend that at present there is no conclusive proof that money supply alone can be used to forecast the stock market.

6. Changes in tax policy have an important effect on the stock market. However, I have not included these changes as TMT signals—they are complex and can sometimes merely shift the tax burden from one group to another with little net effect on the tightness of money. Since such changes are usually discussed widely before they are implemented, stock market discounting occurs months before the actual change takes place.

7. The four-year, or election, cycle may accurately indicate tight or easy money, because it is more appropriate for the Fed to solve economic problems with tighter money in the two years after elections, and with easier money in the two years before elections. However, this hypothesis remains unproven.

8. All the forces of free markets are not allowed to operate in the contemporary U.S. economy. Labor union policy and minimum wage laws require that wages rise, rather than fluctuate with supply and demand as they would in a free market. Therefore, more pressure is placed on those markets that are free. For example, when wages rise and sales decline, corporate profits are squeezed. This brings about more volatile profits and losses, which in turn cause greater volatility in stock prices. Some experts believe that a totally free market would correct economic imbalances much faster than added government regulation would.[9]

9. Money tends to flow into those investments that give the best total yield, all other factors being equal. The direction in which investment money would be expected to flow is shown in Table 8-1.

10. A higher stock market sometimes tends to bring about lower interest rates, because it is much easier for companies to raise capital by issuing additional stock (thereby reducing their need to borrow) than by borrowing. This decrease in corporate borrowing needs reduces the pressure on interest rates. However, high stock markets

TABLE 8–1.   Flow of investment money.

Date	Savings Account Yields	Direction of Flow	T-Bill Yields
1974	5%	⟶	9%
1975	5%	?	5%
1976	5%	⟵	4%

can also bring about events that lead to tighter money. These events include excessive optimism, too-rapid business expansion, excessive demand for raw materials, stockpiling, and rising labor costs.

11.   The relative value of foreign currency to the U.S. dollar may be an important tight money variable in the future, as the following episode illustrates. In April and May 1978, foreign investors saw the Fed's actions to increase interest rates as generating a strong, sustained rally in the flagging U.S. dollar. Consequently, U.S. stocks were bought by foreign investors; as a result, the market rose. If these higher interest rates ultimately fail to strengthen the U.S. dollar, the result probably will be the foreign selling of U.S. stocks. This may well produce the classical effect of depressing the stock market. This phenomenon is too recent and too brief to be viewed in proper perspective right now, but it may prove worthy of future study.

Thus, you can see why tight and easy money signals are the basis of major changes in stock market trends. As an investor, you can use your knowledge to:

- Recognize tight and easy money signals;
- Draw the appropriate conclusions; and
- Take action to buy in the early stages of a rising market, and to sell in the early stages of a market top.

Best wishes! And may this book contribute to your health, wealth, and happiness (but not necessarily in that order).

NOTES

1. Benjamin F. King, "The Latent Statistical Structure of Security Price Changes," Ph.D. dissertation, University of Chicago, 1964, pp. 203–204.
2. Bill Doyle, "Eye the Economy," *Oakland Tribune*, January 21, 1977, p. F35.
3. "How Expectations Defeat Economic Policy," *Business Week,* November 8, 1976, p. 74.
4. "Tighter" money is the term used in this book to distinguish a certain directional condition in the money market. For example, if the discount rate is raised from 1 to 1.5 percent, this would indicate a move to "tighter" money, but could not be defined as creating a state of "tight" money.
5. Newton's second law: "The sum of the forces acting on a body is equal to the product of the mass of the body and the acceleration produced by the forces, with motion in the direction of the resultant of the forces."
6. In light of these conclusions, it is wise to bear in mind the warning of one

senior banker-economist: "If you watch the Fed under a microscope every week, you're likely to see a good deal more than is really there." Lindley H. Clark, Jr., "Calming the Fears," *Wall Street Journal,* March 8, 1976, p. 15.

7. Kenneth E. Homa, and Dwight M. Jaffee, "The Supply of Money and Common Stock Prices," *Journal of Finance* 26, December 1971: 1045-66; Michael W. Keran, "Expectations, Money, and the Stock Market," *Review,* St. Louis, Mo.: Federal Reserve Bank of St. Louis, January 1971, pp. 16–31; reprint ed., Reprint Series No. 63, St. Louis, Mo.: Federal Reserve Bank of St. Louis, n.d.; and Beryl W. Sprinkel, *Money and Stock Prices,* Homewood, Ill.: Irwin, 1964.

8. Robert D. Auerbach, "Money and Stock Prices," *Monthly Review,* Kansas City, Mo.: Federal Reserve Bank of Kansas City, September–October 1976, pp. 3–11; and Richard V. L. Cooper, "Efficient Capital Markets and the Quantity Theory of Money," *Journal of Finance,* June 1974: 887–908, as cited in *Monthly Review,* Kansas City, Mo.: Federal Reserve Bank of Kansas City, September–October 1976, p. 7.

9. Marshall Dimock, *Free Enterprise and the Administrative State,* University, Ala.: University of Alabama Press, 1951; Louis Kelso, and Mortimer J. Adler, *The Capitalist Manifesto,* New York: Random House, 1958; and National Association of Manufacturers, Economic Principles Commission, *The American Individual Enterprise System,* New York: McGraw-Hill, 1946.

APPENDIX A—DEFINITION OF INTEREST

I define interest as the rent paid by the borrower to the lender of money. Various factors determine interest rates. In theory these rates are determined by the marketplace, but in practice there are several factors— six of which are described briefly below—that create different rates for dissimilar loans.

1. "Pure" interest: Variations in pure interest are brought about by the demand for, and supply of, loanable funds, and by the actions of the Federal Reserve as outlined in this book.

2. Inflation Premium: A lender who expects prices to rise at 4 percent per year must demand repayment of at least $1.04 a year for every dollar lent, merely to retain his or her purchasing power. To retain after-tax purchasing power, the repayment figure would have to be even higher. For example, assuming a 6 percent annual inflation rate, the principal invested in a 30-year, $1000 bond in 1965 would be worth only $156 in buying power in 1995.

3. Clerical Expense: Small loans usually require the borrower to pay a very high interest rate to cover administrative costs.

4. Risk: Bills and bonds backed by the government are considered to be the safest. Therefore, they offer lower rates of interest than corporate bonds, which must offer a higher rate to offset the greater risk that the borrower may go bankrupt.

5. Tax Status of the Interest: Municipal bonds offer lower interest rates than corporate bonds, because their income is exempt from federal, and often from state, income taxes.

6. Maturity: Short-term bonds are assumed to be less risky than long-term bonds. The longer the loan commitment, the greater the chance that the lender will lose other good investment opportunities, and the greater the possibility of default. Therefore, long-term bonds usually offer higher yields than short-term bonds.

APPENDIX B. MONTHLY STOCK PRICE INDEX, YIELDS, AND FREE RESERVES.

	1	2	3	4	5
	Stock Price	Short-Term Rates		Long-Term	Free
Month	Index	Federal	Three-month	Government	Reserves
	(1941-1943=10)	Funds	U.S. T-Bills	Bonds	(Million $)
		(Percent)	(Percent)	(Percent)	
1914 Jan	8.37	(Starts	(Starts	(Starts	(Starts
Feb	8.48	Oct. 1960)	Jan. 1920)	Jan. 1919)	Jan. 1946)
Mar	8.32				
Apr	8.12				
May	8.17				
Jun	8.13				
Jul	7.68				
Aug					
Sep	N.Y.S.E.				
Oct	Closed				
Nov					
Dec	7.35				
1915 Jan	7.48				
Feb	7.38				
Mar	7.57				
Apr	8.14				
May	7.95				
Jun	8.04				
Jul	8.01				
Aug	8.35				
Sep	8.66				
Oct	9.14				
Nov	9.46				
Dec	9.48				
1916 Jan	9.33				
Feb	9.30				
Mar	9.17				
Apr	9.07				
May	9.27				
Jun	9.36				
Jul	9.23				
Aug	9.30				
Sep	9.68				
Oct	9.98				
Nov	10.21				
Dec	9.80				

APPENDIX B (Continued)

	1	2	3	4	5
Month	Stock Price Index (1941-1943=10)	Short-Term Rates		Long-Term Government Bonds (Percent)	Free Reserves (Million $)
		Federal Funds (Percent)	Three-month U.S. T-Bills (Percent)		
1917 Jan	9.57				
Feb	9.03				
Mar	9.31				
Apr	9.17				
May	8.86				
Jun	9.04				
Jul	8.79				
Aug	8.53				
Sep	8.12				
Oct	7.68				
Nov	7.04				
Dec	6.80				
1918 Jan	7.21				
Feb	7.43				
Mar	7.28				
Apr	7.21				
May	7.44				
Jun	7.45				
Jul	7.51				
Aug	7.58				
Sep	7.54				
Oct	7.86				
Nov	8.06				
Dec	7.90				
1919 Jan	7.85			4.63	
Feb	7.88			4.70	
Mar	8.12			4.73	
Apr	8.39			4.72	
May	8.97			4.67	
Jun	9.21			4.69	
Jul	9.51			4.72	
Aug	8.87			4.78	
Sep	9.01			4.73	
Oct	9.47			4.71	
Nov	9.19			4.81	
Dec	8.92			4.90	

APPENDIX B (Continued)

		1	2	3	4	5
		Stock Price	Short-Term Rates		Long-Term	Free
Month		Index	Federal	Three-month	Government	Reserves
		(1941-1943=10)	Funds	U.S. T-Bills	Bonds	(Million $)
			(Percent)	(Percent)	(Percent)	
1920	Jan	8.83		4.50	4.93	
	Feb	8.10		4.50	5.05	
	Mar	8.67		4.75	5.09	
	Apr	8.60		5.25	5.28	
	May	8.06		5.50	5.58	
	Jun	7.92		5.75	5.54	
	Jul	7.91		5.81	5.57	
	Aug	7.60		5.83	5.67	
	Sep	7.87		5.81	5.43	
	Oct	7.88		5.75	5.08	
	Nov	7.48		5.75	5.21	
	Dec	6.81		5.88	5.40	
1921	Jan	7.11		5.67	5.23	
	Feb	7.06		5.30	5.28	
	Mar	6.88		5.38	5.27	
	Apr	6.91		5.20	5.24	
	May	7.12		5.16	5.25	
	Jun	6.55		4.99	5.27	
	Jul	6.53		4.60	5.26	
	Aug	6.45		4.75	5.22	
	Sep	6.61		4.75	5.12	
	Oct	6.70		4.21	4.83	
	Nov	7.06		4.03	4.64	
	Dec	7.31		3.90	4.47	
1922	Jan	7.30		3.90	4.45	
	Feb	7.46		3.81	4.50	
	Mar	7.74		3.55	4.41	
	Apr	8.21		3.21	4.28	
	May	8.53		3.25	4.26	
	Jun	8.45		3.25	4.24	
	Jul	8.51		3.20	4.14	
	Aug	8.83		3.13	4.12	
	Sep	9.06		3.34	4.19	
	Oct	9.26		3.71	4.30	
	Nov	8.80		3.66	4.33	
	Dec	8.78		3.65	4.32	

APPENDIX B (Continued)

	1	2	3	4	5
Month	Stock Price Index (1941-1943=10)	Short-Term Rates Federal Funds (Percent)	Three-month U.S. T-Bills (Percent)	Long-Term Government Bonds (Percent)	Free Reserves (Million $)
1923 Jan	8.90		3.66	4.32	
Feb	9.28		3.65	4.33	
Mar	9.43		4.12	4.38	
Apr	9.10		4.13	4.39	
May	8.67		3.95	4.37	
Jun	8.34		3.84	4.34	
Jul	8.06		3.91	4.34	
Aug	8.10		3.86	4.35	
Sep	8.15		4.01	4.36	
Oct	8.03		4.22	4.40	
Nov	8.27		3.94	4.37	
Dec	8.55		3.88	4.35	
1924 Jan	8.83		3.76	4.30	
Feb	8.87		3.54	4.28	
Mar	8.70		3.57	4.28	
Apr	8.50		3.38	4.23	
May	8.47		2.99	4.15	
Jun	8.63		2.44	3.98	
Jul	9.03		1.92	3.94	
Aug	9.34		1.90	3.91	
Sep	9.25		2.14	3.92	
Oct	9.13		2.41	3.87	
Nov	9.64		2.58	3.90	
Dec	10.16		2.57	3.96	
1925 Jan	10.58		2.61	3.96	
Feb	10.67		2.62	3.95	
Mar	10.39		2.78	3.96	
Apr	10.28		2.78	3.93	
May	10.61		2.73	3.87	
Jun	10.80		2.86	3.79	
Jul	11.10		3.06	3.79	
Aug	11.25		3.01	3.85	
Sep	11.51		3.17	3.85	
Oct	11.89		3.53	3.82	
Nov	12.26		3.65	3.79	
Dec	12.46		3.51	3.80	

APPENDIX B (Continued)

Month		1 Stock Price Index (1941-1943=10)	2 Short-Term Rates Federal Funds (Percent)	3 Short-Term Rates Three-month U.S. T-Bills (Percent)	4 Long-Term Government Bonds (Percent)	5 Free Reserves (Million $)
1926	Jan	12.65		3.49	3.77	
	Feb	12.67		3.18	3.71	
	Mar	11.81		3.14	3.71	
	Apr	11.48		3.08	3.70	
	May	11.56		3.17	3.67	
	Jun	12.11		2.93	3.67	
	Jul	12.62		3.11	3.68	
	Aug	13.12		3.27	3.70	
	Sep	13.32		3.42	3.70	
	Oct	13.02		3.58	3.68	
	Nov	13.19		3.35	3.62	
	Dec	13.49		3.07	3.56	
1927	Jan	13.40		3.23	3.51	
	Feb	13.66		3.29	3.48	
	Mar	13.87		3.20	3.37	
	Apr	14.21		3.39	3.35	
	May	14.70		3.33	3.31	
	Jun	14.89		3.07	3.34	
	Jul	15.22		2.96	3.36	
	Aug	16.03		2.70	3.32	
	Sep	16.94		2.68	3.30	
	Oct	16.68		3.08	3.29	
	Nov	17.06		3.04	3.23	
	Dec	17.46		3.17	3.17	
1928	Jan	17.53		3.31	3.18	
	Feb	17.32		3.33	3.19	
	Mar	18.25		3.27	3.17	
	Apr	19.40		3.62	3.20	
	May	20.00		3.90	3.24	
	Jun	19.02		3.92	3.29	
	Jul	19.16		4.12	3.42	
	Aug	19.78		4.36	3.48	
	Sep	21.17		4.57	3.46	
	Oct	21.60		4.70	3.47	
	Nov	23.06		4.26	3.38	
	Dec	23.15		4.26	3.45	

APPENDIX B (Continued)

Month	1 Stock Price Index (1941-1943=10)	2 Short-Term Rates Federal Funds (Percent)	3 Three-month U.S. T-Bills (Percent)	4 Long-Term Government Bonds (Percent)	5 Free Reserves (Million $)
1929 Jan	24.86		4.66	3.52	
Feb	24.99		4.39	3.62	
Mar	25.43		4.60	3.74	
Apr	25.28		4.80	3.64	
May	25.66		5.09	3.64	
Jun	26.15		4.80	3.69	
Jul	28.48		4.55	3.64	
Aug	30.10		4.70	3.71	
Sep	31.30		4.58	3.70	
Oct	27.99		4.37	3.61	
Nov	20.58		3.47	3.35	
Dec	21.40		3.03	3.36	
1930 Jan	21.71		3.39	3.43	
Feb	23.07		3.36	3.41	
Mar	23.94		2.95	3.29	
Apr	25.46		3.00	3.37	
May	23.94		2.41	3.31	
Jun	21.52		1.89	3.25	
Jul	21.06		1.83	3.25	
Aug	20.79		1.53	3.26	
Sep	20.78		1.77	3.24	
Oct	17.74		1.74	3.21	
Nov	16.62		1.40	3.19	
Dec	15.51		1.48	3.22	
1931 Jan	15.98		.95	3.20	
Feb	17.20		1.21	3.30	
Mar	17.53		1.47	3.27	
Apr	15.86		1.31	3.26	
May	14.33		1.01	3.16	
Jun	13.87		.63	3.13	
Jul	14.33		.49	3.15	
Aug	13.90		.60	3.18	
Sep	11.83		1.22	3.25	
Oct	10.25		2.47	3.63	
Nov	10.39		2.23	3.63	
Dec	8.44		3.25	3.93	

APPENDIX B (Continued)

		1	2	3	4	5
Month		Stock Price Index (1941-1943=10)	Short-Term Rates Federal Funds (Percent)	Three-month U.S. T-Bills (Percent)	Long-Term Government Bonds (Percent)	Free Reserves (Million $)
1932	Jan	8.30		2.68	4.26	
	Feb	8.23		2.66	4.11	
	Mar	8.26		2.08	3.92	
	Apr	6.28		.77	3.68	
	May	5.51		.43	3.76	
	Jun	4.77		.41	3.76	
	Jul	5.01		.42	3.58	
	Aug	7.53		.44	3.45	
	Sep	8.26		.23	3.42	
	Oct	7.12		.18	3.43	
	Nov	7.05		.18	3.45	
	Dec	6.82		.09	3.35	
1933	Jan	7.09		.21	3.22	
	Feb	6.25		.49	3.31	
	Mar	6.23		2.29	3.42	
	Apr	6.89		.57	3.42	
	May	8.87		.42	3.30	
	Jun	10.39		.27	3.21	
	Jul	11.23		.37	3.20	
	Aug	10.67		.21	3.21	
	Sep	10.58		.10	3.19	
	Oct	9.55		.16	3.22	
	Nov	9.78		.42	3.46	
	Dec	9.97		.70	3.53	
1934	Jan	10.54		.67	3.50	
	Feb	11.32		.63	3.32	
	Mar	10.74		.27	3.20	
	Apr	10.92		.18	3.11	
	May	9.81		.14	3.02	
	Jun	9.94		.07	2.98	
	Jul	9.47		.07	2.92	
	Aug	9.10		.20	3.03	
	Sep	8.88		.27	3.20	
	Oct	8.95		.21	3.10	
	Nov	9.20		.22	3.07	
	Dec	9.26		.14	3.01	

APPENDIX B (Continued)

		1	2	3	4	5
Month		Stock Price Index (1941-1943=10)	Short-Term Rates		Long-Term Government Bonds (Percent)	Free Reserves (Million $)
			Federal Funds (Percent)	Three-month U.S. T-Bills (Percent)		
1935	Jan	9.26		.14	2.88	
	Feb	8.98		.11	2.79	
	Mar	8.41		.15	2.77	
	Apr	9.04		.17	2.74	
	May	9.75		.15	2.72	
	Jun	10.12		.13	2.72	
	Jul	10.65		.07	2.69	
	Aug	11.37		.10	2.76	
	Sep	11.61		.21	2.85	
	Oct	11.92		.19	2.85	
	Nov	13.04		.14	2.83	
	Dec	13.04		.09	2.83	
1936	Jan	13.76		.10	2.80	
	Feb	14.55		.08	2.77	
	Mar	14.86		.11	2.71	
	Apr	14.88		.10	2.68	
	May	14.09		.18	2.66	
	Jun	14.69		.23	2.66	
	Jul	15.56		.14	2.65	
	Aug	15.87		.18	2.61	
	Sep	16.05		.16	2.60	
	Oct	16.89		.13	2.62	
	Nov	17.36		.10	2.53	
	Dec	17.06		.21	2.51	
1937	Jan	17.59		.36	2.47	
	Feb	18.11		.38	2.46	
	Mar	18.09		.58	2.60	
	Apr	17.01		.70	2.80	
	May	16.25		.65	2.76	
	Jun	15.64		.56	2.76	
	Jul	16.57		.49	2.72	
	Aug	16.74		.52	2.72	
	Sep	14.37		.53	2.77	
	Oct	12.28		.34	2.76	
	Nov	11.20		.15	2.71	
	Dec	11.02		.10	2.67	

APPENDIX B (Continued)

	1	2	3	4	5
Month	Stock Price Index (1941-1943=10)	Short-Term Rates		Long-Term Government Bonds (Percent)	Free Reserves (Million $)
		Federal Funds (Percent)	Three-month U.S. T-Bills (Percent)		
1938 Jan	11.31		.10	2.65	
Feb	11.04		.08	2.64	
Mar	10.31		.07	2.64	
Apr	9.89		.08	2.62	
May	9.98		.03	2.51	
Jun	10.21		.02	2.52	
Jul	12.24		.05	2.52	
Aug	12.31		.05	2.51	
Sep	11.75		.10	2.58	
Oct	13.06		.02	2.48	
Nov	13.07		.02	2.50	
Dec	12.69		.01	2.49	
1939 Jan	12.50		.002	2.47	
Feb	12.40		.004	2.44	
Mar	12.39		.005	2.34	
Apr	10.83		.02	2.30	
May	11.23		.01	2.17	
Jun	11.43		.01	2.13	
Jul	11.71		.02	2.16	
Aug	11.54		.06	2.21	
Sep	12.77		.10	2.65	
Oct	12.90		.03	2.60	
Nov	12.67		.02	2.46	
Dec	12.37		.01	2.35	
1940 Jan	12.30		*	2.30	
Feb	12.22		.004	2.32	
Mar	12.15		*	2.25	
Apr	12.27		.003	2.25	
May	10.58		.04	2.38	
Jun	9.67		.07	2.39	
Jul	9.99		.01	2.28	
Aug	10.20		.02	2.25	
Sep	10.63		.02	2.18	
Oct	10.73		*	2.10	
Nov	10.98		.003	1.97	
Dec	10.53		*	1.89	

*Negative yield.

APPENDIX B (Continued)

	1	2	3	4	5
Month	Stock Price Index (1941-1943=10)	Short-Term Rates Federal Funds (Percent)	Three-month U.S. T-Bills (Percent)	Long-Term Government Bonds (Percent)	Free Reserves (Million $)
1941 Jan	10.55		*	1.99	
Feb	9.89		.03	2.10	
Mar	9.95		.09	2.01	
Apr	9.64		.09	1.96	
May	9.43		.08	1.92	
Jun	9.76		.09	1.91	
Jul	10.26		.10	1.90	
Aug	10.21		.11	1.94	
Sep	10.24		.06	1.94	
Oct	9.83		.05	1.88	
Nov	9.37		.24	1.85	
Dec	8.76		.30	1.96	
1942 Jan	8.93		.21	2.48	
Feb	8.65		.25	2.48	
Mar	8.18		.21	2.46	
Apr	7.84		.30	2.44	
May	7.93		.36	2.45	
Jun	8.33		.36	2.43	
Jul	8.64		.37	2.46	
Aug	8.59		.37	2.47	
Sep	8.68		.37	2.46	
Oct	9.32		.37	2.45	
Nov	9.47		.37	2.47	
Dec	9.52		.36	2.49	
1943 Jan	10.09		.37	2.46	
Feb	10.69		.37	2.46	
Mar	11.07		.37	2.48	
Apr	11.44		.37	2.48	
May	11.89		.37	2.46	
Jun	12.10		.37	2.45	
Jul	12.35		.37	2.45	
Aug	11.74		.38	2.46	
Sep	11.99		.38	2.48	
Oct	11.88		.38	2.48	
Nov	11.33		.38	2.48	
Dec	11.48		.38	2.49	

*Negative yield.

APPENDIX B (Continued)

		1	2	3	4	5
		Stock Price	Short-Term Rates		Long-Term	Free
Month		Index	Federal	Three-month	Government	Reserves
		(1941-1943=10)	Funds	U.S. T-Bills	Bonds	(Million $)
			(Percent)	(Percent)	(Percent)	
1944	Jan	11.85		.37	2.49	
	Feb	11.77		.38	2.49	
	Mar	12.10		.38	2.48	
	Apr	11.89		.38	2.48	
	May	12.10		.38	2.49	
	Jun	12.67		.38	2.49	
	Jul	13.00		.38	2.49	
	Aug	12.81		.38	2.48	
	Sep	12.60		.38	2.47	
	Oct	12.91		.38	2.48	
	Nov	12.82		.38	2.48	
	Dec	13.10		.38	2.48	
1945	Jan	13.49		.38	2.44	
	Feb	13.94		.38	2.38	
	Mar	13.93		.38	2.40	
	Apr	14.28		.38	2.39	
	May	14.82		.38	2.39	
	Jun	15.09		.38	2.35	
	Jul	14.78		.38	2.34	
	Aug	14.83		.38	2.36	
	Sep	15.84		.38	2.37	
	Oct	16.50		.38	2.35	
	Nov	17.04		.38	2.33	
	Dec	17.33		.38	2.33	
1946	Jan	18.02		.38	2.21	1126
	Feb	18.07		.38	2.12	807
	Mar	17.53		.38	2.09	505
	Apr	18.66		.38	2.08	631
	May	18.70		.38	2.19	806
	Jun	18.58		.38	2.16	816
	Jul	18.05		.38	2.18	807
	Aug	17.70		.38	2.23	765
	Sep	15.09		.38	2.28	736
	Oct	14.75		.38	2.26	756
	Nov	14.69		.38	2.25	643
	Dec	15.13		.38	2.24	743

APPENDIX B (Continued)

Month		1 Stock Price Index (1941-1943=10)	2 Federal Funds (Percent)	3 Three-month U.S. T-Bills (Percent)	4 Long-Term Government Bonds (Percent)	5 Free Reserves (Million $)
			Short-Term Rates			
1947	Jan	15.21		.38	2.21	744
	Feb	15.80		.38	2.21	602
	Mar	15.16		.38	2.19	698
	Apr	14.60		.38	2.19	707
	May	14.34		.38	2.19	677
	Jun	14.84		.38	2.22	650
	Jul	15.77		.64	2.25	689
	Aug	15.46		.74	2.24	673
	Sep	15.06		.79	2.24	798
	Oct	15.45		.84	2.27	783
	Nov	15.27		.92	2.36	576
	Dec	15.03		.95	2.39	762
1948	Jan	14.83		.97	2.45	938
	Feb	14.10		.99	2.45	560
	Mar	14.30		1.00	2.44	552
	Apr	15.40		1.00	2.44	700
	May	16.15		1.00	2.42	599
	Jun	16.82		1.00	2.41	752
	Jul	16.42		1.00	2.41	722
	Aug	15.94		1.03	2.45	750
	Sep	15.76		1.09	2.45	756
	Oct	16.19		1.12	2.45	706
	Nov	15.29		1.14	2.44	655
	Dec	15.19		1.15	2.44	663
1949	Jan	15.36		1.16	2.42	669
	Feb	14.77		1.16	2.39	600
	Mar	14.91		1.16	2.38	546
	Apr	14.89		1.16	2.38	608
	May	14.78		1.15	2.38	601
	Jun	13.97		1.16	2.38	658
	Jul	14.76		.98	2.27	910
	Aug	15.29		1.02	2.24	861
	Sep	15.49		1.06	2.22	847
	Oct	15.89		1.04	2.22	816
	Nov	16.11		1.06	2.20	677
	Dec	16.54		1.10	2.19	685

APPENDIX B (Continued)

Month		1 Stock Price Index (1941-1943=10)	Short-Term Rates		4 Long-Term Government Bonds (Percent)	5 Free Reserves (Million $)
			2 Federal Funds (Percent)	3 Three-month U.S. T-Bills (Percent)		
1950	Jan	16.88		1.09	2.20	900
	Feb	17.21		1.13	2.24	614
	Mar	17.35		1.14	2.27	655
	Apr	17.84		1.16	2.30	593
	May	18.44		1.17	2.31	624
	Jun	18.74		1.17	2.33	700
	Jul	17.38		1.17	2.34	623
	Aug	18.43		1.21	2.33	483
	Sep	19.08		1.32	2.36	669
	Oct	19.87		1.33	2.38	775
	Nov	19.83		1.36	2.38	586
	Dec	19.75		1.37	2.39	885
1951	Jan	21.21		1.39	2.39	613
	Feb	22.00		1.39	2.40	298
	Mar	21.63		1.42	2.47	471
	Apr	21.92		1.52	2.56	672
	May	21.93		1.58	2.63	152
	Jun	21.55		1.50	2.65	664
	Jul	21.93		1.59	2.63	562
	Aug	22.89		1.64	2.57	412
	Sep	23.48		1.65	2.56	383
	Oct	23.36		1.61	2.61	821
	Nov	22.71		1.61	2.66	389
	Dec	23.41		1.73	2.70	169
1952	Jan	24.19		1.69	2.74	723
	Feb	23.75		1.57	2.71	330
	Mar	23.81		1.66	2.70	578
	Apr	23.74		1.62	2.64	283
	May	23.73		1.71	2.57	65
	Jun	24.38		1.70	2.61	130
	Jul	25.08		1.82	2.61	-468
	Aug	25.18		1.88	2.70	-383
	Sep	24.78		1.79	2.71	95
	Oct	24.26		1.78	2.74	-400
	Nov	25.03		1.86	2.71	-875
	Dec	26.04		2.13	2.75	-870

APPENDIX B (Continued)

		1	2	3	4	5
Month		Stock Price Index (1941-1943=10)	Short-Term Rates Federal Funds (Percent)	Three-month U.S. T-Bills (Percent)	Long-Term Government Bonds (Percent)	Free Reserves (Million $)
1953	Jan	26.18		2.04	2.80	-640
	Feb	25.86		2.02	2.83	-672
	Mar	25.99		2.08	2.89	-614
	Apr	24.71		2.18	2.97	-631
	May	24.84		2.20	3.12	-353
	Jun	23.95		2.23	3.13	365
	Jul	24.29		2.10	3.04	366
	Aug	24.39		2.09	3.05	-7
	Sep	23.27		1.88	3.01	250
	Oct	23.97		1.40	2.87	390
	Nov	24.50		1.43	2.86	198
	Dec	24.83		1.63	2.79	252
1954	Jan	25.46		1.21	2.69	836
	Feb	26.02		.98	2.62	339
	Mar	26.57		1.05	2.53	503
	Apr	27.63		1.01	2.48	626
	May	28.73		.78	2.54	561
	Jun	28.96		.65	2.55	711
	Jul	30.13		.71	2.47	770
	Aug	30.73		.89	2.48	725
	Sep	31.45		1.01	2.52	708
	Oct	32.18		.99	2.54	638
	Nov	33.44		.95	2.57	650
	Dec	34.97		1.17	2.59	457
1955	Jan	35.60		1.26	2.68	369
	Feb	36.79		1.18	2.77	270
	Mar	36.50		1.34	2.78	122
	Apr	37.76		1.62	2.82	95
	May	37.60		1.49	2.81	212
	Jun	39.78		1.43	2.82	168
	Jul	42.69		1.62	2.91	92
	Aug	42.43		1.88	2.95	-189
	Sep	44.34		2.09	2.92	-286
	Oct	42.11		2.26	2.87	-359
	Nov	44.95		2.23	2.89	-492
	Dec	45.37		2.56	2.91	-245

APPENDIX B (Continued)

	1	2	3	4	5
	Stock Price	Short-Term Rates		Long-Term	Free
Month	Index	Federal	Three-month	Government	Reserves
	(1941-1943=10)	Funds	U.S. T-Bills	Bonds	(Million $)
		(Percent)	(Percent)	(Percent)	
1956 Jan	44.15		2.46	2.88	-255
Feb	44.43		2.37	2.85	-267
Mar	47.49		2.31	2.93	-409
Apr	48.05		2.61	3.07	-533
May	46.54		2.65	2.97	-504
Jun	46.27		2.53	2.93	-195
Jul	48.78		2.33	3.00	-139
Aug	48.49		2.61	3.17	-339
Sep	46.84		2.85	3.21	-214
Oct	46.24		2.96	3.20	-195
Nov	45.76		3.00	3.00	-154
Dec	46.44		3.23	3.40	-36
1957 Jan	45.43		3.21	3.34	116
Feb	43.47		3.17	3.22	-126
Mar	44.03		3.14	3.26	-316
Apr	45.05		3.11	3.32	-504
May	46.78		3.04	3.40	-444
Jun	47.55		3.32	3.58	-508
Jul	48.51		3.17	3.60	-383
Aug	45.84		3.40	3.63	-471
Sep	43.98		· 3.58	3.66	-466
Oct	41.24		3.59	3.73	-344
Nov	40.?5		3.34	3.57	-293
Dec	40.33		3.10	3.30	-133
1958 Jan	41.12		2.60	3.24	122
Feb	41.26		1.56	3.26	324
Mar	42.11		1.35	3.25	495
Apr	42.34		1.13	3.12	492
May	43.70		1.05	3.14	547
Jun	44.75		.88	3.19	484
Jul	45.98		.96	3.36	547
Aug	47.70		1.69	3.60	382
Sep	48.96		2.48	3.75	95
Oct	50.95		2.79	3.76	96
Nov	52.50		2.76	3.70	20
Dec	53.49		2.81	3.80	-41

APPENDIX B (Continued)

		1	2	3	4	5
Month		Stock Price Index (1941-1943=10)	Short-Term Rates Federal Funds (Percent)	Three-month U.S. T-Bills (Percent)	Long-Term Government Bonds (Percent)	Free Reserves (Million $)
1959	Jan	55.62		2.84	3.90	-59
	Feb	54.77		2.71	3.92	-48
	Mar	56.16		2.85	3.92	-140
	Apr	57.10		2.96	4.01	-259
	May	57.96		2.85	4.08	-319
	Jun	57.46		3.25	4.09	-513
	Jul	59.74		3.24	4.11	-556
	Aug	59.40		3.36	4.10	-536
	Sep	57.05		4.00	4.26	-493
	Oct	57.00		4.12	4.11	-459
	Nov	57.23		4.21	4.12	-433
	Dec	59.06		4.57	4.27	-424
1960	Jan	58.03		4.44	4.37	-375
	Feb	55.78		3.95	4.22	-365
	Mar	55.02		3.44	4.08	-219
	Apr	55.73		3.24	4.17	-194
	May	55.22		3.39	4.16	-33
	Jun	57.26		2.64	3.99	37
	Jul	55.84		2.40	3.86	120
	Aug	56.51		2.29	3.79	247
	Sep	54.81		2.49	3.82	414
	Oct	53.73	2.86	2.43	3.91	480
	Nov	55.47	2.86	2.38	3.93	614
	Dec	56.80	1.64	2.27	3.88	669
1961	Jan	59.72	2.50	2.30	3.89	696
	Feb	62.17	1.36	2.41	3.81	517
	Mar	64.12	2.50	2.42	3.78	486
	Apr	65.83	1.79	2.33	3.80	551
	May	66.50	.57	2.29	3.73	453
	Jun	65.62	2.50	2.36	3.88	549
	Jul	65.44	1.04	2.27	3.90	530
	Aug	67.79	1.64	2.40	4.00	537
	Sep	67.26	1.32	2.30	4.02	547
	Oct	68.00	1.64	2.35	3.98	442
	Nov	71.08	2.14	2.46	3.98	517
	Dec	71.74	2.25	2.62	4.06	419

APPENDIX B (Continued)

	1	2	3	4	5
Month	Stock Price Index (1941-1943=10)	Short-Term Rates Federal Funds (Percent)	Three-month U.S. T-Bills (Percent)	Long-Term Government Bonds (Percent)	Free Reserves (Million $)
1962 Jan	69.07	2.61	2.75	4.08	555
Feb	70.22	2.04	2.75	4.09	434
Mar	70.29	2.68	2.72	4.01	382
Apr	68.05	2.71	2.74	3.89	441
May	62.99	2.75	2.69	3.88	440
Jun	55.63	2.46	2.72	3.90	391
Jul	56.97	2.82	2.95	4.02	440
Aug	58.52	2.75	2.84	3.97	439
Sep	58.00	2.96	2.79	3.94	375
Oct	56.17	2.89	2.75	3.89	419
Nov	60.04	2.95	2.80	3.87	473
Dec	62.64	2.79	2.86	3.87	268
1963 Jan	65.06	2.90	2.91	3.88	375
Feb	65.92	3.00	2.92	3.92	301
Mar	65.67	3.00	2.90	3.93	269
Apr	68.76	2.75	2.91	3.97	313
May	70.14	2.95	2.92	3.97	247
Jun	70.11	3.00	3.00	4.00	138
Jul	69.07	3.00	3.14	4.01	161
Aug	70.98	3.50	3.32	3.99	133
Sep	72.85	3.50	3.38	4.04	91
Oct	73.03	3.50	3.45	4.07	94
Nov	72.62	3.50	3.52	4.10	33
Dec	74.17	3.32	3.52	4.14	209
1964 Jan	76.45	3.43	3.53	4.15	175
Feb	77.39	3.50	3.53	4.14	89
Mar	78.80	3.29	3.55	4.18	99
Apr	79.94	3.50	3.48	4.20	167
May	80.72	3.50	3.48	4.16	82
Jun	80.24	3.50	3.48	4.13	120
Jul	83.22	3.50	3.48	4.13	135
Aug	82.00	3.50	3.51	4.14	83
Sep	83.41	3.50	3.53	4.16	89
Oct	84.85	3.36	3.58	4.16	106
Nov	85.44	3.50	3.62	4.12	-34
Dec	83.96	3.71	3.86	4.14	168

APPENDIX B (Continued)

	1	2	3	4	5
Month	Stock Price Index (1941-1943=10)	Short-Term Rates		Long-Term Government Bonds (Percent)	Free Reserves (Million $)
		Federal Funds (Percent)	Three-month U.S. T-Bills (Percent)		
1965 Jan	86.12	4.00	3.83	4.14	106
Feb	86.75	4.00	3.93	4.16	36
Mar	86.83	4.00	3.94	4.15	-75
Apr	87.97	4.11	3.93	4.15	-105
May	89.28	4.13	3.90	4.14	-180
Jun	85.04	4.11	3.81	4.14	-182
Jul	84.91	4.13	3.83	4.15	-174
Aug	86.49	4.11	3.84	4.19	-134
Sep	89.38	4.05	3.91	4.25	-144
Oct	91.39	4.09	4.03	4.27	-146
Nov	92.15	4.13	4.08	4.34	-83
Dec	91.73	4.13	4.36	4.43	-2
1966 Jan	93.32	4.61	4.60	4.43	-44
Feb	92.69	4.54	4.67	4.61	-107
Mar	88.88	4.63	4.63	4.63	-246
Apr	91.60	4.75	4.61	4.55	-268
May	86.78	4.73	4.64	4.57	-352
Jun	86.06	4.95	4.54	4.63	-352
Jul	85.84	5.36	4.86	4.74	-362
Aug	80.65	5.63	4.93	4.80	-390
Sep	77.81	5.89	5.36	4.79	-368
Oct	77.13	5.86	5.39	4.70	-431
Nov	80.99	5.86	5.34	4.74	-222
Dec	81.33	5.36	5.01	4.65	-165
1967 Jan	84.45	5.14	4.76	4.40	-16
Feb	87.36	4.21	4.55	4.47	-4
Mar	89.42	4.68	4.29	4.45	236
Apr	90.96	4.55	3.85	4.51	175
May	92.59	4.00	3.64	4.76	269
Jun	91.43	3.93	3.48	4.86	297
Jul	93.01	3.73	4.31	4.86	272
Aug	94.49	3.75	4.28	4.95	298
Sep	95.81	4.02	4.45	4.99	268
Oct	95.66	3.96	4.59	5.18	160
Nov	92.66	3.89	4.76	5.44	270
Dec	95.30	4.36	5.01	5.36	107

APPENDIX B (Continued)

		1	2	3	4	5
Month		Stock Price Index (1941-1943=10)	Short-Term Rates		Long-Term Government Bonds (Percent)	Free Reserves (Million $)
			Federal Funds (Percent)	Three-month U.S. T-Bills (Percent)		
1968	Jan	95.04	4.54	5.08	5.18	144
	Feb	90.75	4.73	4.97	5.16	38
	Mar	89.09	4.82	5.14	5.39	-315
	Apr	95.67	5.52	5.37	5.28	-413
	May	97.87	6.14	5.62	5.40	-326
	Jun	100.5	5.93	5.54	5.23	-341
	Jul	100.3	5.73	5.38	5.09	-226
	Aug	98.11	6.11	5.10	5.04	-190
	Sep	101.3	5.80	5.20	5.09	-132
	Oct	103.8	5.93	5.33	5.24	-167
	Nov	105.4	6.05	5.49	5.36	-245
	Dec	106.5	5.71	5.92	5.65	-310
1969	Jan	102.0	5.95	6.18	5.74	-480
	Feb	101.5	6.32	6.16	5.86	-596
	Mar	99.30	6.75	6.08	6.05	-701
	Apr	101.3	6.66	6.15	5.84	-844
	May	104.6	8.23	6.08	5.85	-1102
	Jun	99.14	9.20	6.49	6.06	-1064
	Jul	94.71	9.00	7.00	6.07	-1074
	Aug	94.18	9.57	7.01	6.02	-946
	Sep	94.51	9.57	7.13	6.32	-831
	Oct	95.52	9.11	7.04	6.27	-992
	Nov	96.21	9.07	7.19	6.51	-988
	Dec	91.11	8.91	7.72	6.81	-829
1970	Jan	90.31	8.45	7.91	6.86	-799
	Feb	87.16	9.21	7.16	6.44	-819
	Mar	88.65	8.32	6.71	6.39	-781
	Apr	85.95	7.93	6.48	6.53	-704
	May	76.06	8.46	7.04	6.94	-795
	Jun	75.59	7.84	6.74	6.99	-701
	Jul	75.72	7.23	6.47	6.57	-1217
	Aug	77.92	6.93	6.41	6.75	-682
	Sep	82.58	6.46	6.24	6.63	-335
	Oct	84.37	6.36	5.93	6.59	-208
	Nov	84.28	6.07	5.29	6.24	-305
	Dec	90.05	5.50	4.86	5.97	-49

APPENDIX B (Continued)

	1	2	3	4	5
Month	Stock Price Index (1941-1943=10)	Short-Term Rates Federal Funds (Percent)	Three-month U.S. T-Bills (Percent)	Long-Term Government Bonds (Percent)	Free Reserves (Million $)
1971 Jan	93.49	4.82	4.49	5.91	-91
Feb	97.11	4.09	3.77	5.84	-127
Mar	99.60	3.41	3.32	5.71	-120
Apr	103.0	4.02	3.78	5.75	-8
May	101.6	4.14	4.14	5.96	-18
Jun	99.72	4.82	4.70	5.94	-322
Jul	99.00	5.07	5.41	5.91	-658
Aug	97.24	5.57	5.08	5.78	-606
Sep	99.40	5.59	4.67	5.56	-295
Oct	97.29	5.43	4.49	5.46	-153
Nov	92.78	5.16	4.19	5.44	-144
Dec	99.17	4.68	4.02	5.62	58
1972 Jan	103.3	4.05	3.40	5.62	153
Feb	105.2	3.23	3.18	5.67	91
Mar	107.7	3.18	3.72	5.66	134
Apr	108.8	4.09	3.72	5.74	27
May	107.7	4.25	3.65	5.64	-15
Jun	108.0	4.38	3.87	5.59	110
Jul	107.2	4.49	4.06	5.57	-55
Aug	111.0	4.56	4.01	5.54	-183
Sep	109.4	4.90	4.65	5.70	-352
Oct	109.6	5.15	4.72	5.69	-327
Nov	115.1	5.06	4.77	5.50	-292
Dec	117.5	5.03	5.06	5.63	-830
1973 Jan	118.4	5.61	5.31	5.94	-815
Feb	114.2	6.35	5.56	6.14	-1396
Mar	112.4	6.75	6.05	6.20	-1571
Apr	110.3	7.18	6.29	6.11	-1572
May	107.2	7.43	6.35	6.22	-1727
Jun	104.8	7.95	7.19	6.32	-1729
Jul	105.8	10.21	8.02	6.53	-1659
Aug	103.8	10.57	8.67	6.81	-1901
Sep	105.6	10.79	8.48	6.42	-1616
Oct	109.8	10.72	7.16	6.26	-1242
Nov	102.0	9.90	7.87	6.31	-1217
Dec	94.78	10.09	7.36	6.35	-1036

APPENDIX B (Continued)

Month		1 Stock Price Index (1941-1943=10)	2 Short-Term Rates Federal Funds (Percent)	3 Three-month U.S. T-Bills (Percent)	4 Long-Term Government Bonds (Percent)	5 Free Reserves (Million $)
1974	Jan	96.11	9.87	7.76	6.56	-808
	Feb	93.45	9.47	7.06	6.54	-997
	Mar	97.44	8.81	7.99	6.81	-1176
	Apr	92.46	9.93	8.23	7.04	-1556
	May	89.67	11.17	8.43	7.07	-2386
	Jun	89.79	11.54	8.15	7.03	-2869
	Jul	79.31	13.55	7.75	7.18	-3131
	Aug	76.03	12.29	8.74	7.33	-3183
	Sep	68.12	11.64	8.36	7.30	-3096
	Oct	69.44	11.04	7.24	7.22	-1702
	Nov	71.74	9.72	7.59	6.93	-1027
	Dec	67.07	9.02	7.18	6.78	-364
1975	Jan	72.56	7.35	6.49	6.68	-454
	Feb	80.10	6.99	5.58	6.61	85
	Mar	83.78	6.15	5.54	6.73	160
	Apr	84.72	5.59	5.69	7.03	10
	May	90.10	5.71	5.32	6.99	-51
	Jun	92.40	5.55	5.19	6.86	277
	Jul	92.49	6.10	6.16	6.89	-293
	Aug	85.71	6.14	6.46	7.06	6
	Sep	84.67	6.24	6.38	7.29	-197
	Oct	88.57	5.82	6.08	7.29	-35
	Nov	90.07	5.22	5.47	7.21	229
	Dec	88.70	5.20	5.50	7.17	135
1976	Jan	96.86	4.87	4.96	6.94	130
	Feb	100.6	4.77	4.85	6.92	-62
	Mar	101.1	4.84	5.05	6.87	378
	Apr	101.9	4.82	4.88	6.73	45
	May	101.2	5.29	5.19	6.99	261
	Jun	101.8	5.48	5.44	6.92	-3
	Jul	104.2	5.31	5.28	6.85	-53
	Aug	103.3	5.29	5.15	6.79	193
	Sep	105.5	5.25	5.08	6.70	212
	Oct	101.9	5.03	4.93	6.65	123
	Nov	101.2	4.95	4.81	6.62	280
	Dec	104.7	4.65	4.36	6.39	110

APPENDIX B (Continued)

Month		1 Stock Price Index (1941-1943=10)	Short-Term Rates		4 Long-Term Government Bonds (Percent)	5 Free Reserves (Million $)
			2 Federal Funds (Percent)	3 Three-month U.S. T-Bills (Percent)		
1977	Jan	103.8	4.61	4.60	6.68	433
	Feb	101.0	4.68	4.66	7.15	-114
	Mar	100.6	4.69	4.61	7.20	38
	Apr	99.05	4.73	4.54	7.14	-62
	May	98.76	5.35	4.94	7.17	72
	Jun	99.29	5.39	5.00	6.99	-149
	Jul	100.2	5.42	5.15	6.97	12
	Aug	97.75	5.90	5.50	7.00	-872
	Sep	96.23	6.14	5.77	6.94	-443
	Oct	93.74	6.47	6.19	7.08	-980
	Nov	94.28	6.51	6.16	7.14	-705
	Dec	93.82	6.56	6.06	7.23	-384
1978	Jan	90.25	6.70	6.45	7.50	-176
	Feb	88.98	6.78	6.46	7.60	-272
	Mar	88.82	6.79	6.32	7.63	-38
	Apr	92.71	6.89	6.31	7.74	-475
	May	97.41	7.36	6.43	7.87	-975
	Jun	97.66	7.60	6.71	7.94	-974
	Jul	97.19	7.81	7.07	8.09	-1146
	Aug	103.9	8.04	7.04	7.87	-885
	Sep	103.9	8.45	7.84	7.82	-993
	Oct	100.6	8.96	8.13	8.07	-1049
	Nov	94.71	9.76	8.79	8.16	-417
	Dec	96.11	10.03	9.12	8.36	-749
1979	Jan	99.71	10.07	9.35	8.43	-692
	Feb	98.23	10.06	9.27	8.43	-764
	Mar	100.1	10.09	9.46	8.45	-742
	Apr	102.1	10.01	9.49	8.44	-899
	May	99.73	10.24	9.59	8.55	-1490
	Jun	101.7	10.29	9.05	8.32	-1119
	Jul	102.7	10.47	9.26	8.35	-989
	Aug	107.4	10.94	9.45	8.42	-904
	Sep	108.6	11.43	10.18	8.68	-1339
	Oct	104.5	13.77	11.47	9.44	-1750
	Nov	103.7	13.18	11.87	9.80	-1751
	Dec	107.8	13.78	12.07	9.59	-1079

APPENDIX B (Continued)

	1	2	3	4	5
Month	Stock Price Index (1941-1943=10)	Short-Term Rates Federal Funds (Percent)	Three-month U.S. T-Bills (Percent)	Long-Term Government Bonds (Percent)	Free Reserves (Million $)
1980 Jan	110.8	13.82	12.04	10.03	-999
Feb	115.3	14.13	12.81	11.55	-1465
Mar	104.7	17.19	15.53	11.87	-2383
Apr	103.0	17.61	14.00	10.83	-2352
May	107.7	10.98	9.15	9.82	-888
Jun	114.6	9.47	7.00	9.40	-169
Jul	119.8	9.03	8.13	9.83	-111
Aug	123.5	9.61	9.26	10.53	-357
Sep	126.5	10.87	10.32	10.94	-1055
Oct	130.2	12.81	11.58	11.20	-1018
Nov	135.7	15.85	13.89	11.83	-1201
Dec	133.5	18.90	15.66	11.89	-1587

Sources below refer to column numbers of Appendix B:

(1) Stock Price Indexes are compiled from Standard & Poor's Corp., Security Price Index Record (Orange, Conn.: Standard & Poor's Corp., 1980), p. 126. From January 1918 to date, these indexes are a monthly average of the Standard & Poor's Stock Price Indexes. The Indexes for earlier years have been converted to the 1941-1943 base from the Cowles Commission Stock Price Indexes.

(2) Federal funds; (3) Three-month U.S. Treasury bills; and (4) Long-term government bond rates are compiled from U.S. Federal Reserve Board, Division of Administrative Services, Publications Services, Banking and Monetary Statistics 1914-1941 (November 1943); U.S. Federal Reserve Board, Division of Administrative Services, Publications Services, Banking and Monetary Statistics 1941-1970 (September 1976); U.S. Federal Reserve Board, Division of Administrative Services, Publications Services, Annual Statistical Digest 1971-1975 (October 1976); and from monthly Federal Reserve Bulletins, vols. 61-67, nos. 1, 4, 7, and 10 for each year.

(5) Free reserves are compiled from National Bureau of Economic Research, Computer Service, New York. Information for years 1977-1980 is computed from monthly Federal Reserve Bulletins, vols. 63-67, nos. 1, 4, 7, and 10 for each year.

APPENDIX C. DISCOUNT RATE AND PRIME RATE CHANGES.

Rate in Effect			Discount Rate* (Percent)	Prime Rate† (Percent)
1914	Nov	16	6.0	
	Dec	18	5.5	
		23	5.0	
1915	Feb	3	4.5	
		18	4.0	
1916	Sept	26	3.0	
1917	Dec	21	3.5	
1918	Apr	6	4.0	
1919	Nov	3	4.75	
1920	Jan	23	6.0	
	Jun	1	7.0	
1921	May	5	6.5	
	Jun	16	6.0	
	Jul	21	5.5	
	Sept	22	5.0	
	Nov	3	4.5	
1922	Jun	22	4.0	
1923	Feb	23	4.5	
1924	May	1	4.0	
	Jun	12	3.5	
	Aug	8	3.0	
1925	Feb	27	3.5	
1926	Jan	8	4.0	
	Apr	23	3.5	
	Aug	13	4.0	
1927	Aug	5	3.5	
1928	Feb	3	4.0	
	May	18	4.5	
	Jul	13	5.0	
1929				5.5-6.0
	Aug	9	6.0	
	Nov	1	5.0	
		15	4.5	
1930				3.5-6.0
	Feb	7	4.0	
	Mar	14	3.5	
	May	2	3.0	
	Jun	20	2.5	
	Dec	24	2.0	
1931				2.75-5.0
	May	8	1.5	
	Oct	9	2.5	
		16	3.5	
1932				3.25-4.0
	Feb	26	3.0	
	Jun	24	2.5	
1933				1.5-4.0
	Mar	3	3.5	
	Apr	7	3.0	
	May	26	2.5	
	Oct	20	2.0	
1934				1.5
	Feb	2	1.5	
1937	Aug	27	1.0	
1947	Dec			1.75
1948	Jan	12	1.25	
	Aug	13	1.5	
	Aug			2.0
1950	Aug	21	1.75	
	Sep	22		2.25
1951	Jan	8		2.5
	Oct	17		2.75
	Dec	19		3.0
1953	Jan	16	2.0	
	Apr	27		3.25
1954	Feb	5	1.75	
	Mar	17		3.0
	Apr	16	1.5	
1955	Apr	15	1.75	
	Aug	4		3.25
		5	2.0	
	Sep	9	2.25	
	Oct	14		3.5
	Nov	18	2.5	
1956	Apr	13	2.75	3.75
	Aug	21		4.0
		24	3.0	
1957	Aug	6		4.5
		23	3.5	
	Nov	15	3.0	
1958	Jan	22		4.0
		24	2.75	
	Mar	7	2.25	
	Apr	18	1.75	
		21		3.5
	Sep	11		4.0
		12	2.0	
	Nov	7	2.5	
1959	Mar	6	3.0	
	May	18		4.5
		29	3.5	

APPENDIX C (Continued)

Rate in Effect		Discount Rate* (Percent)	Prime Rate† (Percent)	Rate in Effect		Discount Rate* (Percent)	Prime Rate† (Percent)
1959 (continued)				1971 (continued)			
Sep	1		5.0	May	11		5.5
	11	4.0		Jul	6		5.5-6.0
1960 Jun	10	3.5			7		6.0
Aug	12	3.0			16	5.0	
	23		4.5	Oct	20		5.75
1963 Jul	17	3.5		Nov	4		5.5
1964 Nov	24	4.0			19	4.75	
1965 Dec	6	4.5	5.0	Dec	17	4.5	
1966 Mar	10		5.5		31		5.25
Jun	29		5.75	1972 Jan	24		5.0
Aug	16		6.0		31		4.75
1967 Jan	26-27		5.5-5.75	Apr	5		5.0
Mar	27		5.5	Jun	26		5.25
Apr	7	4.0		Aug	29		5.5
Nov	20	4.5	6.0	Oct	4		5.75
1968 Mar	22	5.0		Dec	27		6.0
Apr	19	5.5	6.5	1973 Jan	15	5.0	
Aug	30	5.25		Feb	26	5.5	
Sep	25		6.0-6.25		27		6.25
Nov	13		6.25	Mar	26		6.5
Dec	2		6.5	Apr	18		6.75
	18	5.5	6.75	May	4	5.75	
1969 Jan	7		7.0		7		7.0
Mar	17		7.5		11	6.0	
Apr	4	6.0			25		7.25
Jun	9		8.5	Jun	8		7.5
1970 Mar	25		8.0		11	6.5	
Sep	21		7.5		25		7.75
Nov	12		7.25	Jul	2	7.0	
	13	5.75			3		8.0
	23		7.0		9		8.25
Dec	4	5.5			18		8.5
	22		6.75		30		8.75
1971 Jan	6		6.5	Aug	6		9.0
	8	5.25			13		9.25
	15		6.25		14	7.5	
	18		6.0		22		9.5
	22	5.0			28		9.75
Feb	16		5.75	Sep	18		10.0
	19	4.75		Oct	24		9.75
Mar	11		5.25-5.5	1974 Jan	29		9.5
	19		5.25	Feb	11		9.25
Apr	23		5.25-5.5		19		9.0
					25		8.75

APPENDIX C (Continued)

Rate in Effect		Discount Rate* (Percent)	Prime Rate† (Percent)	Rate in Effect		Discount Rate* (Percent)	Prime Rate† (Percent)
1974 (continued)				1975 (continued)			
Mar	22		9.0	Oct	27		7.75
	29		9.25	Nov	5		7.5
Apr	3		9.5	Dec	2		7.25
	5		9.75	1976 Jan	12		7.0
	11		10.0		19	5.5	
	19		10.25		21		6.75
	25	8.0	10.5	Jun	1		7.0
May	2		10.75		7		7.25
	6		11.0	Aug	2		7.0
	10		11.25	Oct	4		6.75
	17		11.5	Nov	1		6.5
Jun	26		11.75		22	5.25	
Jul	5		12.0	Dec	13		6.25
Oct	7		11.75	1977 May	13		6.5
	21		11.5		31		6.75
	28		11.25	Aug	22		7.0
Nov	4		11.0		31	5.75	
	14		10.75	Sep	16		7.25
	25		10.5	Oct	7		7.5
Dec	9	7.75			24		7.75
1975 Jan	6	7.25			26	6.0	
	9		10.25	1978 Jan	9	6.5	
	15		10.0		10		8.0
	20		9.75	May	5		8.25
	28		9.5		11	7.0	
Feb	3		9.25		26		8.5
	5	6.75		Jun	16		8.75
	10		9.0		30		9.0
	18		8.75	Jul	3	7.25	
	24		8.5	Aug	21	7.75	
Mar	5		8.25		31		9.25
	10	6.25	8.0	Sep	15		9.5
	18		7.75		22	8.0	
	24		7.5		28		9.75
May	16	6.0		Oct	13		10.0
	20		7.25		16	8.5	
Jun	9		7.0		27		10.25
Jul	18		7.25	Nov	1	9.5	10.5
	28		7.5		6		10.75
Aug	12		7.75		17		11.00
Sep	15		8.0		24		11.5
				Dec	26		11.75

APPENDIX C (Continued)

Rate in Effect			Discount Rate* (Percent)	Prime Rate† (Percent)	Rate in Effect			Discount Rate* (Percent)	Prime Rate† (Percent)
1979	Jun	19		11.25	1980	(continued)			
	Jul	20	10.0			May	7		17.5
		27		11.75			16		16.5
	Aug	16		12.0			23		14.5
		17	10.5				30	12.0	14.0
		28		12.25		Jun	6		13.0
	Sep	7		12.75			13	11.0	12.0-12.5
		14		13.0			20		12.0
		19	11.0			Jul	7		11.5
		21		13.25			25		11.0
		28		13.5			28	10.0	
	Oct	8	12.0			Aug	22		11.25
		9		14.5			27		11.5
		23		15.0		Sep	8		12.0
	Nov	1		15.25			12		12.25
		9		15.5			19		12.5
		16		15.75			26	11.0	13.0
		30		15.5		Oct	1		13.5
	Dec	7		15.25			17		14.0
1980	Feb	15	13.0				29		14.5
		19		15.75		Nov	6		15.5
		22		16.25-16.5			17	12.0	16.25
		29		16.75			21		17.0
	Mar	4		17.25			26		17.75
		7		17.75		Dec	2		18.5
		14		18.5			5	13.0	19.0
		19		19.0			10		20.0
		28		19.5			16		21.0
	Apr	2		20.0			19		21.5
		18		19.5	1981	Jan	2		20.5
	May	1		18.5-19.0					
		2		18.5					

SOURCES:
    *The discount rates shown are for the Federal Reserve Bank of New York and compiled from U.S. Federal Reserve Board, Division of Administrative Services, Publications Services, Banking and Monetary Statistics 1914-1941 (November 1943), pp. 439-42; U.S. Federal Reserve Board, Division of Administrative Services, Publications Services, Banking and Monetary Statistics 1941-1970 (September 1976), p. 667; U.S. Federal Reserve Board, Division of Administrative Services, Publications Services, Annual Statistical Digest 1971-1975 (October 1976), p. 35; and Annual Statistical Digest 1974-178 (January 1980), p. 27.

    †The prime rate is the rate that banks charge their most credit-worthy business customers on short-term loans. Until recent years, movements in the rate tended to be infrequent and to lag changes in open market rates.
    In November 1971, however, several large banks decided to coordinate changes in their prime rate with movements in money market rates. Rates so established are referred to as "floating" rates. Not all banks followed this procedure; hence, two--and sometimes three--prime rates have been quoted simultaneously. For the period since the start of the floating rate, the table shows the date on which a new rate came to be the predominant one quoted, rather than the date when the first bank made a change in the rate.
    Effective April 16, 1973, the Committee on Interest and Dividends introduced a "two tier" approach to rates on business loans. This system allowed rates on large prime loans to move in concert with advances on smaller loans. For the duration of the Committee on Interest and Dividends, which was abolished on May 31, 1974, the prime rate shown in the table is that on "large" loans.
    The prime rates shown are compiled from U.S. Federal Reserve Board, Division of Administrative Services, Publications Services, Banking and Monetary Statistics 1941-1970 (September 1976), p. 707; U.S. Federal Reserve Board, Division of Administrative Services, Publications Services, Annual Statistical Digest 1971-1975 (October 1976), p. 117; and Annual Statistical Digest 1974-1978 (January 1980), p. 81.

APPENDIX D. BEAR MARKETS AND
TIGHT MONEY CLUES.

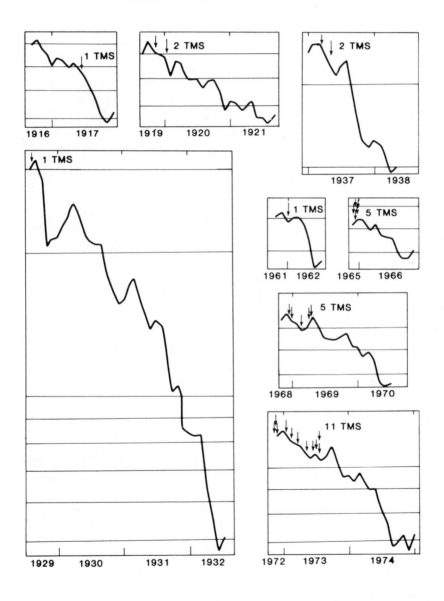

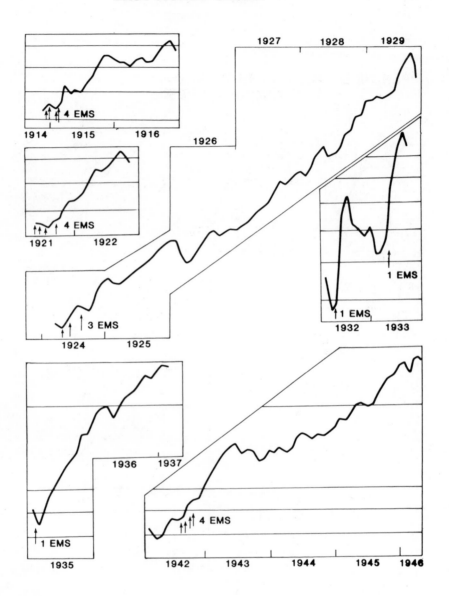

APPENDIX E (Continued)

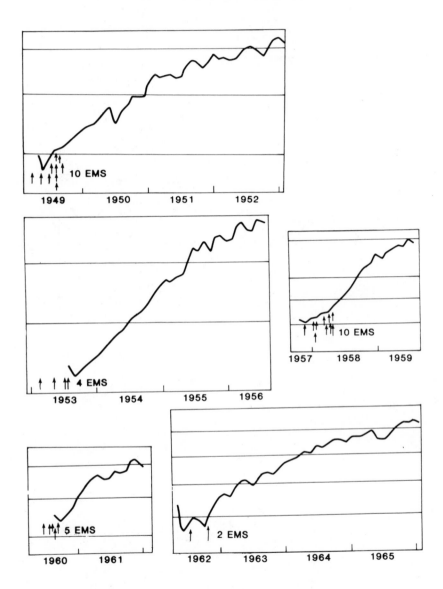

APPENDIX E (Continued)

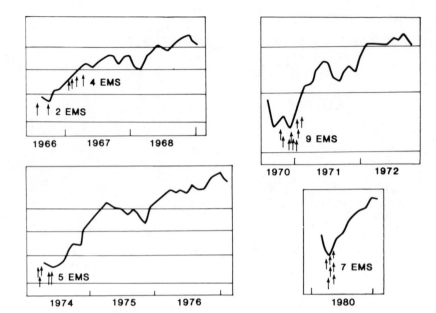

APPENDIX F. MEMBERSHIP OF THE BOARD OF GOVERNORS OF THE FEDERAL RESERVE SYSTEM, 1913–80.

APPOINTIVE MEMBERS

Name	Federal Reserve District	Date of initial oath of office	Other dates and information relating to membership[2]
Charles S. Hamlin	Boston	Aug. 10, 1914	Reappointed in 1916 and 1926. Served until Feb. 3, 1936.[3]
Paul M. Warburg	New York	do	Term expired Aug. 9, 1918.
Frederic A. Delano	Chicago	do	Resigned July 21, 1918.
W. P. G. Harding	Atlanta	do	Term expired Aug. 9, 1922.
Adolph C. Miller	San Francisco	do	Reappointed in 1924. Reappointed in 1934 from the Richmond District. Served until Feb. 3, 1936.[3]
Albert Strauss	New York	Oct. 26, 1918	Resigned Mar. 15, 1920.
Henry A. Moehlenpah	Chicago	Nov. 10, 1919	Term expired Aug. 9, 1920.
Edmund Platt	New York	June 8, 1920	Reappointed in 1928. Resigned Sept. 14, 1930.
David C. Wills	Cleveland	Sept. 29, 1920	Term expired Mar. 4, 1921.
John R. Mitchell	Minneapolis	May 12, 1921	Resigned May 12, 1923.
Milo D. Campbell	Chicago	Mar. 14, 1923	Died Mar. 22, 1923.
Daniel R. Crissinger	Cleveland	May 1, 1923	Resigned Sept. 15, 1927.
George R. James	St. Louis	May 14, 1923	Reappointed in 1931. Served until Feb. 3, 1936.[3]
Edward H. Cunningham	Chicago	do	Died Nov. 28, 1930.
Roy A. Young	Minneapolis	Oct. 4, 1927	Resigned Aug. 31, 1930.
Eugene Meyer	New York	Sept.16, 1930	Resigned May 10, 1933.
Wayland W. Magee	Kansas City	May 18, 1931	Term expired Jan. 24, 1933.
Eugene R. Black	Atlanta	May 19, 1933	Resigned Aug. 15, 1934.
M. S. Szymczak	Chicago	June 14, 1933	Reappointed in 1936 and 1948. Resigned May 31, 1961.
J. J. Thomas	Kansas City	do	Served until Feb. 10, 1936.[3]
Marriner S. Eccles	San Francisco	Nov. 15, 1934	Reappointed in 1936, 1940, and 1944. Resigned July 14, 1951.
Joseph A. Broderick	New York	Feb. 3, 1936	Resigned Sept. 30, 1937.
John K. McKee	Cleveland	do	Served until Apr. 4, 1946.[3]
Ronald Ransom	Atlanta	do	Reappointed in 1942. Died Dec. 2, 1947.
Ralph W. Morrison	Dallas	Feb. 10, 1936	Resigned July 9, 1936.
Chester C. Davis	Richmond	June 25, 1936	Reappointed in 1940. Resigned Apr. 15, 1941.
Ernest G. Draper	New York	Mar. 30, 1938	Served until Sept. 1, 1950.[3]
Rudolph M. Evans	Richmond	Mar. 14, 1942	Served until Aug. 13, 1954.[3]
James K. Vardaman, Jr.	St. Louis	Apr. 4, 1946	Resigned Nov. 30, 1958.
Lawrence Clayton	Boston	Feb. 14, 1947	Died Dec. 4, 1949.
Thomas B. McCabe	Philadelphia	Apr. 15, 1948	Resigned Mar. 31, 1951.
Edward L. Norton	Atlanta	Sept. 1, 1950	Resigned Jan. 31, 1952.
Oliver S. Powell	Minneapolis	do	Resigned June 30, 1952.
Wm. McC. Martin, Jr.	New York	Apr. 2, 1951	Reappointed in 1956. Term expired Jan. 31, 1970.
A. L. Mills, Jr.	San Francisco	Feb. 18, 1952	Reappointed in 1958. Resigned Feb. 28, 1965.
J. L. Robertson	Kansas City	do	Reappointed in 1964. Resigned Apr. 30, 1973.
C. Canby Balderston	Philadelphia	Aug. 12, 1954	Served through Feb. 28, 1966.
Paul E. Miller	Minneapolis	Aug. 13, 1954	Died Oct. 21, 1954.

195

APPENDIX F (Continued)

Name	Federal Reserve District	Date of initial oath of office	Other dates and information relating to membership[2]
Chas. N. Shepardson	Dallas	Mar. 17, 1955	Retired Apr. 30, 1967.
G. H. King. Jr.	Atlanta	Mar. 25, 1959	Reappointed in 1960. Resigned Sept. 18, 1963.
George W. Mitchell	Chicago	Aug. 31, 1961	Reappointed in 1962. Served until Feb. 13, 1976.[3]
J. Dewey Daane	Richmond	Nov. 29, 1963	Served until Mar. 8, 1974.[3]
Sherman J. Maisel	San Francisco	Apr. 30, 1965	Served through May 31, 1972.
Andrew F. Brimmer	Philadelphia	Mar. 9, 1966	Resigned Aug. 31, 1974.
William W. Sherrill	Dallas	May 1, 1967	Reappointed in 1968. Resigned Nov. 15, 1971.
Arthur F. Burns	New York	Jan. 31, 1970	Term began Feb. 1, 1970. Resigned Mar. 31, 1978.
John E. Sheehan	St. Louis	Jan. 4, 1972	Resigned June 1, 1975.
Jeffrey M. Bucher	San Francisco	June 5, 1972	Resigned Jan. 2, 1976.
Robert C. Holland	Kansas City	June 11, 1973	Resigned May 15, 1976.
Henry C. Wallich	Boston	Mar. 8, 1974	
Philip E. Coldwell	Dallas	Oct. 29, 1974	Served through Feb. 29, 1980.
Philip C. Jackson. Jr.	Atlanta	July 14, 1975	Resigned Nov. 17, 1978.
J. Charles Partee	Richmond	Jan. 5, 1976	
Stephen S. Gardner	Philadelphia	Feb. 13, 1976	Died Nov. 19, 1978.
David M. Lilly	Minneapolis	June 1, 1976	Resigned Feb. 24. 1978.
G. William Miller	San Francisco	Mar. 8, 1978	Resigned Aug. 6, 1979.
Nancy H. Teeters	Chicago	Sept. 18, 1978	
Emmett J. Rice	New York	June 20, 1979	
Frederick H. Schultz	Atlanta	July 27, 1979	
Paul A. Volcker	Philadelphia	Aug. 6, 1979	
Lyle E. Gramley	Kansas City	May 28, 1980	

Chairmen[4]

Charles S. Hamlin	Aug. 10, 1914–Aug. 9, 1916
W. P. G. Harding	Aug. 10, 1916–Aug. 9, 1922
Daniel R. Crissinger	May 1, 1923–Sept. 15, 1927
Roy A. Young	Oct. 4. 1927–Aug. 31, 1930
Eugene Meyer	Sept. 16, 1930–May 10, 1933
Eugene R. Black	May 19. 1933–Aug. 15, 1934
Marriner S. Eccles	Nov. 15, 1934–Jan. 31, 1948
Thomas B. McCabe	Apr. 15. 1948–Mar. 31, 1951
Wm. McC.Martin. Jr.	Apr. 2. 1951–Jan. 31, 1970
Arthur F. Burns	Feb. 1. 1970–Jan. 31, 1978
G. William Miller	Mar. 8. 1978–Aug. 6, 1979
Paul A. Volcker	Aug. 6, 1979–

Vice Chairmen[4]

Frederic A. Delano	Aug. 10, 1914–Aug. 9, 1916
Paul M. Warburg	Aug. 10, 1916–Aug. 9, 1918
Albert Strauss	Oct. 26, 1918–Mar. 15, 1920
Edmund Platt	July 23, 1920–Sept. 14, 1930
J. J. Thomas	Aug. 21, 1934–Feb. 10, 1936
Ronald Ransom	Aug. 6, 1936–Dec. 2, 1947
C. Canby Balderston	Mar. 11, 1955–Feb. 28, 1966
J. L. Robertson	Mar. 1, 1966–Apr. 30, 1973
George W. Mitchell	May 1, 1973–Feb. 13, 1976
Stephen S. Gardner	Feb. 13, 1976–Nov. 19, 1978
Frederick H. Schultz	July 27, 1979–

EX-OFFICIO MEMBERS[1]

Secretaries of the Treasury

W. G. McAdoo	Dec. 23. 1913–Dec. 15, 1918
Carter Glass	Dec. 16. 1918–Feb. 1, 1920
David F. Houston	Feb. 2, 1920–Mar. 3, 1921
Andrew W. Mellon	Mar. 4, 1921–Feb. 12, 1932
Ogden L. Mills	Feb. 12. 1932–Mar. 4, 1933
William H. Woodin	Mar. 4, 1933–Dec. 31, 1933
Henry Morgenthau, Jr.	Jan. 1. 1934–Feb. 1, 1936

Comptrollers of the Currency

John Skelton Williams	Feb. 2, 1914–Mar. 2, 1921
Daniel R. Crissinger	Mar. 17, 1921–Apr. 30, 1923
Henry M. Dawes	May 1, 1923–Dec. 17, 1924
Joseph W. McIntosh	Dec. 20. 1924–Nov. 20, 1928
J. W. Pole	Nov. 21, 1928–Sept. 20, 1932
J. F. T. O'Connor	May 11, 1933–Feb. 1, 1936

1. Under the provisions of the original Federal Reserve Act the Federal Reserve Board was composed of seven members, including five appointive members, the Secretary of the Treasury, who was ex-officio chairman of the Board, and the Comptroller of the Currency. The original term of office was ten years, and the five original appointive members had terms of two, four, six, eight, and ten years respectively. In 1922 the number of appointive members was increased to six, and in 1933 the term of office was increased to 12 years. The Banking Act of 1935, approved Aug. 23, 1935, changed the name of the Federal Reserve Board to the Board of Governors of the Federal Reserve System and provided that the Board should be composed of seven appointive members; that the Secretary of the Treasury and the Comptroller of the Currency should continue to serve as members until Feb. 1, 1936; that the appointive members in the office on the date of that act should continue to serve until Feb. 1, 1936, or until their successors were appointed and had qualified; and that thereafter the terms of members should be 14 years and that the designation of Chairman and Vice Chairman of the Board should be for a term of four years.

2. Date after words "Resigned" and "Retired" denotes final day of service.

3. Successor took office on this date.

4. Chairman and Vice Chairman were designated Governor and Vice Governor before Aug. 23, 1935.

Reproduced from U.S. Federal Reserve Board, Division of Administrative Services, *Federal Reserve Bulletin* 66 (June 1980): 490-91.

APPENDIX G. THE MAJOR MARKET AVERAGES, 1949–80.

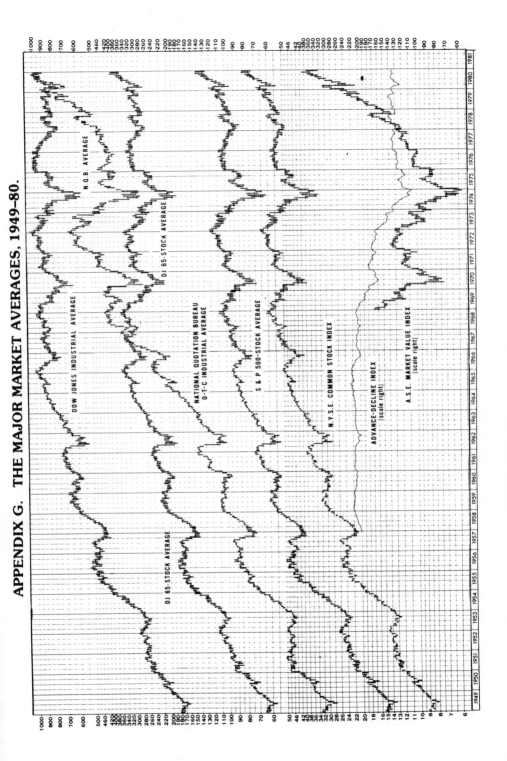

N.Q.B. AVERAGE

DOW JONES INDUSTRIAL AVERAGE

DJ 65-STOCK AVERAGE

NATIONAL QUOTATION BUREAU
O-T-C INDUSTRIAL AVERAGE

S & P 500-STOCK AVERAGE

N.Y.S.E. COMMON STOCK INDEX

ADVANCE-DECLINE INDEX
(scale right)

A.S.E. MARKET VALUE INDEX
(scale right)

DJ 65-STOCK AVERAGE

197

APPENDIX G (Continued)

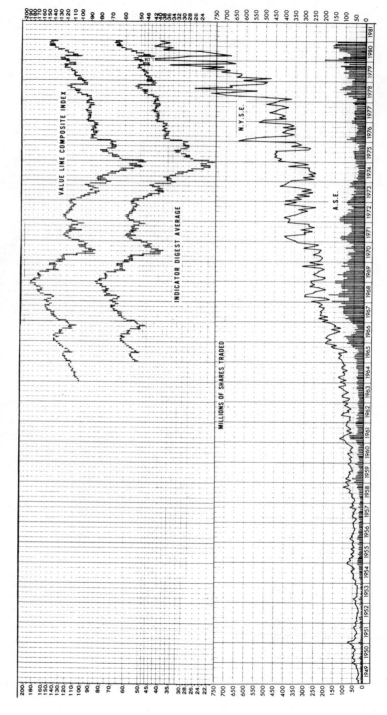

[SOURCE: Reproduced from *3-Trend Cycli-Graphs*, Securities Research Co., Boston, Mass., January 1980, p. 1.]

198

BIBLIOGRAPHY

Books

Allen, Frederick Lewis. *Only Yesterday.* 1931; reprint ed. New York: Harper & Row, 1959.

American Research Council. *Your Investments.* 16th ed. Rye, N.Y.: American Research Council, 1969.

Bernhard, Arnold & Co. *The Value Line Stock Market Averages, 1962 to 1974.* Part 4, vol. 30, no. 15. New York: Arnold Bernhard, 1975.

Bohan, James, and Farrell, Robert J. *Interest Rates and Stock Prices.* New York: Merrill Lynch, Pierce, Fenner & Smith, Securities Research Division, 1976.

Bolton, Arthur H. *Money and Investment Profits.* Homewood, Ill.: Dow Jones-Irwin, 1967.

Bretz, William G. *Juncture Recognition in the Stock Market.* New York: Vantage Press, 1972.

Brown, Susan L.; Keating, Karl; Mellinger, David; Post, Patrea; Smith, Stuart; and Tudor, Catriona. *The Incredible Bread Machine.* San Diego, Calif.: World Research, 1974.

CFA Readings in Financial Analysis. Homewood, Ill.: Irwin, 1966.

CFA Readings in Financial Analysis. 2d ed. Homewood, Ill.: Irwin, 1970.

CFA Research Foundation. *Personal Trust Investment Management.* Homewood, Ill.: Irwin, 1968.

_____. *Pension Fund Investment Management.* Homewood, Ill.: Irwin, 1970.

_____. *Investment Company Portfolio Management.* Homewood, Ill.: Irwin, 1971.

_____. *Property and Liability Insurance Investment Management.* Homewood, Ill.: Irwin, 1971.

Cohen, E. W., ed. *The Encyclopedia of Stock Market Techniques.* Larchmont, N.Y.: Investors Intelligence, 1970.

Cootner, Paul, ed. *The Random Character of Stock Market Prices.* Cambridge, Mass.: MIT Press, 1964.

Crane, Burton. *The Sophisticated Investor.* New York: Simon Schuster, 1959.

Dimock, Marshall. *Free Enterprise and the Administrative State.* University, Ala.: University of Alabama Press, 1951.

Engle Louis, *How to Buy Stocks.* New York: Bantam Books, 1972.

Fisher, Irving. *The Stock Market Crash—and After.* New York: Macmillan, 1930.

Fosback, Norman. G. *Stock Market Logic.* Ft. Lauderdale, Fla.: Institute for Economic Research, 1976.

Friedman, Milton and Rose. *Free to Choose.* New York: Avon, 1980.

Friedman, Milton. *Studies in the Quantity Theory of Money.* Chicago: University of Chicago Press, 1956.

Friedman, Milton, and Schwartz, Anna J. *A Monetary History of the United States, 1867–1960.* Princeton, N.J.: Princeton University Press, 1963.

George, Wilfred R. *The Profit Box System of Forecasting Stock Prices.* Homewood, Ill.: Dow Jones-Irwin, 1976.

Graham, Benjamin, and Dodd, David L. *Security Analysis.* 3d ed. New York: McGraw-Hill, 1951.

Greenwald, Douglas; Arnold, Henry C. F.; Brown, William J.; Koflowitz, Lewis G.; Mc Croskey, Jack L.; Mattersdorff, Guenter H.; and Meyers, Edward G. *The McGraw-Hill Dictionary of Modern Economics.* New York: McGraw-Hill, 1973.

Hazlitt, Henry. *What You Should Know about Inflation.* 2d ed. New York: Funk & Wagnalls, 1968.

Homer, Sidney. A History of Interest Rates. New Brunswick, N.J.: Rutgers University Press, 1963.

————, and Johannesen, Richard R. *The Price of Money.* New Brunswick, N.J.: Rutgers University Press, 1969.

Jallow, Raymond. *1976 Forecast.* Los Angeles, Calif.: United California Bank, Planning and Research Division, 1975.

Kelso, Louis, and Adler, Mortimer J. *The Capitalist Manifesto.* New York: Random House, 1958.

Keran, Michael W. "Expectations, Money, and the Stock Market." *Review,* Federal Reserve Bank of St. Louis, St. Louis, Mo., January 1971, pp. 16–31; reprint ed., Reprint Series No. 63, St. Louis, Mo.: Federal Reserve Bank of St. Louis, n.d.

Keynes, John M. *The General Theory of Employment, Interest, and Money.* New York: Harcourt, Brace & World, 1936.

Klein, Frederick C., and Prestbo, John A. *News and the Market.* Chicago: Regnery, 1974.

Leffler, George L. *The Stock Market.* 3d ed. New York: Ronald Press, 1963.

LeFurgey, J. O. *How to Make and Keep Profits in Today's Market.* San Francisco, Calif.: Market Trend Publications, 1962.

Levine, Sumner N. *The Financial Analyst's Handbook.* Vol. 1. Homewood, Ill.: Dow Jones-Irwin, 1975.

McKenna, Joseph P. *Aggregate Economic Analysis.* 4th ed. Hinsdale, Ill.: Dryden, 1972.

Mader, Chris, and Hagin, Robert. *The Dow Jones-Irwin Guide to Common Stocks.* Homewood, Ill.: Dow Jones-Irwin, 1976.

Magee, John. *The General Semantics of Wall Street.* Springfield, Mass.: John Magee, 1958.

Maisel, Sherman J. *Managing the Dollar.* New York: Norton, 1973.

Meek, Paul. *Open Market Operations.* New York: Federal Reserve Bank of New York, 1973.

Merrill, Arthur A. *Behavior of Prices on Wall Street.* Chappaqua, N.Y.: Analysis Press, 1966.

_____. *Indicator Accuracy.* Paper presented at the meeting of the Market Technicians Association and the New York Society of Security Analysts, New York, October 5, 1977. Chappaqua, N.Y.: Analysis Press, n.d.

Money and Credit—Their Influence on Jobs, Prices, and Growth. The Report of the Commission on Money and Credit. By Frazar Wilde, Chairman. Englewood Cliffs, N.J.: Prentice-Hall, 1961.

Murphy, Thomas T., ed. *The New York Stock Exchange Fact Book.* 21st ed. New York: New York Stock Exchange, 1976.

National Association of Manufacturers, Economic Principles Commission. *The American Individual Enterprise System.* New York: McGraw-Hill, 1946.

New York Stock Exchange. *Common Stock Indexes 1939–1975.* New York: New York Stock Exchange, Research Department, n.d.

Owens, Richard N., and Hardy, Charles O. *Interest Rates and Stock Speculation.* 2d. ed. Washington, D.C.: Brookings Institution, 1930.

Patinkin, Don. *Money, Interest and Prices: An Integration of Monetary and Value Theory.* 2d ed. New York: Harper & Row, 1965.

Sargent, David R. *Stock Market Profits and Higher Income for You.* New York: Simon & Schuster, 1976.

Schumpeter, Joseph A. *Business Cycles.* 2 vols. New York: McGraw-Hill, 1939.

Selden, G.C. *Psychology of the Stock Market.* 1912; reprint ed., Wells, Vt.: Fraser Publishing Co., 1965.

Sprinkel, Beryl W. *Money and Stock Prices.* Homewood, Ill.: Irwin, 1964.

_____. *Money and Markets: A Monetarist View.* Homewood, Ill.: Irwin, 1971.

_____, and Genetski, Robert J. *Winning with Money.* Homewood, Ill.: Dow Jones-Irwin, 1977.

Standard & Poor's Corp. *Daily Stock Price Record, New York Stock Exchange.* 68 vols. New York: Standard & Poor's, 1961 through 1976.

_____. *Security Price Index Record 1974.* Orange, Conn.: Standard & Poor's, 1974.

_____. *Security Price Index 1976.* Orange, Conn.: Standard & Poor's, 1976.

Teigen, Ronald L. "The Demand for and Supply of Money." In *Readings in Money, National Income and Stabilization Policy,* 3d ed., edited by W. L. Smith and Ronald L. Teigen, pp. 68–103. Homewood, Ill; Irwin, 1963.

Temin, Peter. *Did Monetary Forces Cause the Great Depression?* New York: Norton, 1976.

Tobin, James. "Commercial Banks as Creators of Money." In *Banking and Monetary Studies,* edited by Deane Carson, pp. 408–19. Homewood, Ill.: Irwin, 1963.

United States League of Savings Associations. *'74 Savings & Loan Fact Book.* Chicago: United States League of Savings Associations, 1974.

Weiss, J. Irving. *The Money Squeeze.* New York: Capital Advisors, 1969.

Woy, James B. *Investment Information: A Guide to Information Sources.* Detroit, Mich.: Gale Research, 1970.

Zerden, Sheldon. *Best Books on the Stock Market: An Analytical Bibliography.* New York: Bowker, 1972.

U.S. Government Documents

U.S. Bureau of Census. *Historical Statistics of the United States, Colonial Times to 1957,* 1960.

_____. *Statistical Abstract of the United States,* 1960.

U.S. Congress. Joint Economic Committee. *Economic Indicators, June 1976,* prepared by the Council of Economic Advisers. Washington, D.C.: Government Printing Office, 1976.

U.S. Department of Commerce. *Business Conditions Digest,* 1976.

U.S. Federal Reserve Board, Division of Administrative Services. *Federal Reserve Bulletin* (published monthly).

U.S. Federal Reserve Board, Division of Administrative Services, Publications Services. *Banking and Monetary Statistics 1914–1941,* November 1943.

_____. *Supplement to Banking and Monetary Statistics for the Period January 1941 to July 1964, 1966.*

_____. *The Federal Reserve System–Purposes and Functions.* 6th ed., 1974.

_____. *Historical Chart Book,* 1980 (published annually in September).

_____*Monthly Chart Book,* 1980 (published four times a year).

_____. *Banking and Monetary Statistics 1941–1970,* September 1976.

_____. *Annual Statistical Digest 1971–1975,* October 1976 and 1974–78 (1980).

U.S. Federal Reserve Board, Division of Research and Statistics. *Flow of Funds* (published quarterly).

U.S. Small Business Administration. *Report of the Small Business Administration Task Force on Venture and Equity Capital for Small Business,* January 1977.

U.S. Department of Treasury, Office of the Secretary, Superintendent of Documents. *Treasury Bulletin* (published monthly).

Periodicals

Allen, Gary. "Federal Reserve: The Trillion-Dollar Conspiracy." *American Opinion,* February 1976, p. 15.

Benston, George J. "Interest Rates Are a Random Walk Too." *Fortune,* August 1976, pp. 105–13.

Burns, Arthur F. "The Independence of the Federal Reserve System." *Federal Reserve Bulletin* 62 (June 1976): 493–98.

Cockburn, Alexander, and Ridgeway, James. "Where Our Money Comes From." *Parade,* October 26, 1975, as cited in Allen Gary. "Federal Reserve: The Trillion-Dollar Conspiracy." *American Opinion,* February 1976, pp. 76–77.

Cooper, Richard V. L. "Efficient Capital Markets and the Quantity Theory of Money." Journal of Finance (June 1974): 887–908, as cited in *Monthly Review,* Federal Reserve Bank of Kansas City, Kansas City, Mo., September–October 1976, p. 7.

Dorfman, Dan. "The Next Big Market Play: The View from B of A." *New West Magazine,* June 7, 1976, p. 14.

Ehrbar, A. F. "How the Money Supply Drives the Stock Market." *Fortune,* October 1975, pp. 105–109.

"A Fed Heavyweight Sizes up Monetary Policy." *Business Week,* August 11, 1975, pp. 52–53.

Friedman, Milton. "How to Hit the Money Target." *Newsweek,* December 8, 1975, p. 85.

_____. "Medal for a Monetarist." *Time,* October 25, 1976, p. 58.

Garvy, George. "Kondratieff's Theory of Long Cycles." *Review of Economics and Statistics* 25 (November 1943):203–20.

Granger, C. W. J., and Morgenstern, Oskar. "Spectral Analysis of New York Stock Market Prices." *Kyklos* 16 (1963):1–27.

Homa, Kenneth E., and Jaffee, Dwight M. "The Supply of Money and Common Stock Prices." *Journal of Finance* 26 (December 1971): 1045–66.

"How Expectations Defeat Economic Policy." *Business Week,* November 8, 1976, pp. 74–76.

"Investment Decisions." *Boardroom Reports,* February 29, 1976, pp. 5–6.

James, F. F. "Monthly Moving Averages—an Effective Investment Tool?" *Journal of Financial and Quantitative Analysis* 3 (September 1968): 315–26.

Kane, Edward J. "All for the Best: The Federal Reserve Board's 60th Annual Report." *American Economic Review* 64 (December 1974): 835–50.

Keran, Michael W. "Forecasting Stock Prices." *Journal of Portfolio Management* 1 (Winter 1975):52–60.

Kondratieff, N. D., "The Long Waves in Economic Life." *Review of Economics and Statistics* 17 (November 1935):105–15.

"Look Before You Leap—to Conclusions." *Forbes,* January 1, 1977, p. 207.

Merrill, Arthur A. "Delayed Reaction." *Barron's National Business and Financial Weekly,* December 13, 1965, p. 9.

Palmer, Michael. "Money Supply, Portfolio Adjustments and Stock Prices." *Financial Analysts Journal* 26 (July–August 1970): 19–22.

Quint, Barbara. "When to Bail Out of Your Stocks," *Money Magazine,* December 1976, pp. 36–38.

Rozeff, Michael. "The Money Supply and Common Stock Prices." *Journal of Financial Economics,* September 1974, pp. 245–302.

Rudolph, Allan. "The Money Supply and Common Stock Prices." *Financial Analysts Journal* 28 (March–April 1972): 19–25.

"Statistics Watching for Fun and Prophecy." *Money Magazine,* July 1976, pp. 50–58.

"Stimulus Becomes the Inevitable Policy." *Business Week,* December 6, 1976, pp. 18–20.

Weberman, Ben. "The Oracle Has Spoken." *Forbes,* January 15, 1977, p. 78.

Newspapers

"Basic Money Supply Fell $600 Million in Week Ended March 2, Fed Report Says." *Wall Street Journal,* March 11, 1977, p. 26.

Clark, Lindley H., Jr. "Calming the Fears." *Wall Street Journal,* March 8, 1976, p.1.

Doyle, Bill. "Eye the Economy." *Oakland Tribune,* January 21, 1977, p. F35.

Elia, Charles J. "Heard on the Street." *Wall Street Journal,* December 9, 1974, p. 35; December 10, 1974, p. 45.

_____. "Election Cycle Effect on Stock Market Linked to Politics of Short-Term Economic Remedies." *Wall Street Journal,* April 23, 1976, p. 29.

_____. "Moves in Treasury-Bill Yields, Discount Rate Correlated by Analyst to Major Market Swings." *Wall Street Journal,* May 26, 1976, p. 39.

_____. "Short-Term Rates Seen Rising as Recovery Resumes, Though Analysts' Timetables Differ." *Wall Street Journal,* October 13, 1976, p. 43.

_____. "Top Growth Stocks, Third Period Resurgence Seen as Sign of Adjustment to Economic Shifts." *Wall Street Journal,* October 27, 1976, p. 47.

"Fed's High Turnover Diminishes Expertise, Seems to Bolster Burns," *Wall Street Journal,* July 30, 1976, p. 1.

Getz, John. "Fed's Role in Election Year." *San Francisco Chronicle,* September 23, 1976, p. 57.

"How the U.S. Creates More Money." *San Francisco Chronicle,* June 7, 1976, p. 46.

Levine, Richard J. "Reserve's Resolves." *Wall Street Journal,* November 20, 1979, p. 1.

"Money Supply Surged in October 27 Week, Putting Growth Rate Near Maximum." *Wall Street Journal,* November 5, 1976, p. 22.

Quinn, Jane. "Harmful to Investor Health." *Oakland Tribune,* August 17, 1978, p. 49.

_____. "Bears, Bulls Make Their Points." *Oakland Tribune,* January 15, 1979, p. D33.

"Wall Street Checking New Thesis." *San Francisco Chronicle,* August 25, 1975, p. 48.

Rustin, Richard E. "Remaking of a Market." *Wall Street Journal,* October 25, 1979, p. 46.

Newsletters and Investment Services

Bank Credit Analyst. Montreal (published monthly.)

Barometer of Business. Chicago: Harris Bank (published monthly.)

Chartist. Long Beach, Calif. (published weekly).

Commentary. San Francisco: Federal Home Loan Bank of San Francisco (published monthly).

Commodity Chart Service. New York: Commodity Research Bureau (published weekly).

Daily Stock Price Record, New York Stock Exchange. New York: Standard & Poor's (published quarterly).

Findings and Forecasts. New York: Anemetrics (published bimonthly).

Lifetime Investment Concepts. San Jose, Calif.: (published monthly).

Market Comment. New York: White, Weld & Co. (published weekly).

Monthly Investment Strategy. New York: Bache, Halsey, Stuart & Co. (published bimonthly).

Monthly Review. Kansas City, Mo.: Federal Reserve Bank of Kansas City (published bimonthly).

Professional Tape Reader. New York: Radcap (published weekly).

Standard & Poor's Bond Guide. New York: Standard & Poor's Corp. (published monthly).

Standard & Poor's Stock Guide. New York: Standard & Poor's Corp. (published monthly).

3-Trend Cycli-Graphs. Boston, Mass.: Securities Research Co. (published monthly).

U. S. Financial Data. St. Louis, Mo.: Federal Reserve Bank of St. Louis (published weekly).

Weekly Monetary Summary. San Francisco, Calif.: Bank of America, Bank Investment Services Division (published weekly).

World Financial Markets. New York: Morgan Guaranty Trust Co. of New York (published monthly).

Other Sources

Burke, William M., Senior Economist and Director of Public Information, Federal Reserve Bank of San Francisco. San Francisco, Calif. Interview, March 8, 1976.

Caulfield, John P., Vice-President, Investment Department, Wells Fargo Bank. San Francisco, Calif. Interview, February 17, 1976.

Gordon, Monte, Director of Research, Dreyfus Corp., New York. Interview held by telephone, February 13, 1976 and December 29, 1980.

Greene, Warren, Vice-President, American Investors Fund, Greenwich Conn. Interview held by telephone, March 3, 1976, and in person July 31, 1981.

Hanan, Richard A. San Francisco, Calif. Interview, March 3, 1976.

Keran, Michael, Vice-President and Director of Research, Federal Reserve Bank of San Francisco. Meeting of the Technical Securities Analysts of San Francisco, San Francisco, Calif. Interview, March 18, 1976.

Maisel, Sherman J., Professor of Applied Economics and Finance, University of California, Berkeley. Berkeley, Calif. Interview, April 15, 1976.

PBS. "Wall Street Week," November 12, 1976.

Steinmetz, William Q., Business Consultant. Piedmont Calif. Interview, May 15, 1976.

Wahead, Joe, Economist, Wells Fargo Bank, San Francisco, Calif. Interview held by telephone, February 25, 1976.

Wong, Sue E., Professor of Investments, San Francisco State University, San Francisco, Calif. Interview, March 3, 1976.

Unpublished Materials

Bernard, Normand, Special Assistant to the Board of Governors of the Federal Reserve System. Letter to Wilfred R. George, August 16, 1976.

Doane, J. Dewey. "New Frontier for the Monetarists." Paper presented at the Northern New England School of Banking, Dartmouth College, Hanover, N. H., September 8, 1969.

George, Wilfred R. Letter to Dr. Arthur F. Burns, Chairman, Board of Governors of the Federal Reserve System, August 6, 1976.

Keran, Michael W. "Expectations and the Stock Market." Paper presented at the meeting of the Technical Securities Analysts of San Francisco, San Francisco, Calif., March 18, 1976.

King, Benjamin F. "The Latent Statistical Structure of Security Price Changes." Ph.D. dissertation, University of Chicago, 1964.

National Bureau of Economic Research, Computer Service 261 Madison Avenue, New York.

Stephénson & Co. Denver, Colo. Response to a survey conducted by Bache & Co., San Francisco, Calif., ca.1975.

INDEX

ABOUT THE AUTHOR

Wilfred R. George is Vice President-Investments in the San Francisco branch of a major investment firm. He is a director and past president of the Technical Securities Analysts Association of San Francisco and a member of the Market Technicians Association of New York and the Security Analysts of San Francisco. He teaches investments to M.B.A. candidates at Golden Gate University. He is trustee of the St. Andrew's Society of San Francisco and the British Benevolent Society of California and is listed in "Who's Who in Finance and Industry." He is an inventor and patent holder.

Dr. George's first book, *The Profit Box System of Forecasting Stock Prices*, was published in 1976 and later abridged and published in "The Encyclopedia of Stock Market Techniques" in 1980.

Dr. George holds a B.S. (engineering) from the University of Iowa, an M.B.A. from Harvard Business School, and a Ph.D. from Golden Gate University.

Tight Money Timing, the result of four years of research based on studies covering the sixty-seven year period from 1914 to 1981, sets criteria for forecasting major moves and times for caution in the stock market.